MONEY ROAD

Tools for the wild ride ahead

Garth Turner

Xurbia
BOOKS

Library and Archives Canada Cataloguing in Publication

Turner, Garth

   Money road : tools for the wild ride ahead / Garth Turner

Includes index.

ISBN 978-0-9813613-0-7

1. Finance, Personal—Canada. 2. Financial security. 3. Investments.
I. Title.

HG179.T866 2010   332.024'010971   C2009-907492-3

Notice to readers
This book is not subsidized by the Canadian taxpayer.
   The publisher, Xurbia Books, has neither applied for nor received government assistance.

Xurbia Books
Box 9
Caledon Village
Ontario Canada
L7K 3L3
www.xurbia.ca

Editor: Catherine Leek, Green Onion Publishing, Toronto, ON
   www.greenonionpublishing.com
Text design and formatting: Kim Monteforte, WeMakeBooks.ca, Toronto,
   ON, www.wemakebooks.ca
Cover design: Cindy Cake, WeMakeBooks.ca, Toronto, ON,
   www.wemakebooks.ca
Printing: Webcom Inc., Toronto, ON, www.webcomlink.com

Dedication

To people with the courage to learn and improve
their lives without waiting for happenstance.
To middle class families determined to stay that way.
To those who know wealth is not a goal or a right,
but an opportunity to give, share and enjoy.
To those who care for others in want,
and all creatures.
To Dorothy.

Contents

ROAD TRIP

We know this about the future, so you'd better buckle up

Half a dozen bored-looking cops stood over a line that snaked down one side of Bloor Street in mid-town Toronto. More of the burly guardians watched a competing line on the south side. But the presence of police, or even news cameras from Global and City-TV, did little to stop a skirmish that briefly had the air full of elbows and insults.

Less than a year after the world came to the brink of total financial collapse, with teetering banks, galloping layoffs and a looming neo-depression, realtors, speculators and frenzied young couples had slept on the pavement for a chance to buy an unbuilt condo. They fought over little numbers being handed out by the developer—precious cards of entry to the sales centre. Once inside, they'd snap up units starting at a bargain $300,000 in far less time than anyone would spend buying jeans. And in a development that had yet to release either floor plans or a price list.

Speculators seeking a silver bullet

A few days later and 4,500 kilometres away, more people slept on rain-soaked sidewalks to be the first into a Yaletown room where a plastic model of 'The Mark' condo soared from the top of a table. This time the entry price was a stunning $704 per square foot for a unit the size of a single-car garage—stiff even for Vancouver where the average detached family home had just topped $930,000. The line was rife with rumours that prices had been raised $50,000 overnight, a fact later reported as true. But that seemed okay. After all, prices would go up forever.

At the same time, 357,000 Canadians had just been put out of work. Many of them would still be jobless a year later. Tens of thousands, mostly Boomers in their 50s, would never work again. Of those still with a job, three-quarters were without pension plans. In fact, almost half of everybody with employment income in Canada has no retirement plan and no retirement savings. In the words of one laid-off Nortel employee, whose former company used bankruptcy to weasel out of pension commitments, "I am so utterly, relentlessly screwed."

We live in a conflicted time. Obviously things aren't going to work out well for a large number of us. Rank real estate speculation and financial despair don't usually crop up together. Days of extremes suggest serious confusion about where we're headed, and what to do about it. Some people grasp for the silver bullet—gold bullion, urban condos or leveraged ETFs—while millions of others hide under the covers. Meanwhile the country sinks into debt, our major trading partner's empire is crumbling and we're in the path of a tidal wave of house-rich and cash-poor, worried, retired people.

This is the road we're all on. It snakes off into a future that's almost certainly strewn with wrecks. But that doesn't mean you have to crash into them.

Here's what we know about the future

I think we know this about the next few years.

- With so many jobs exported to China, so few remaining factories, the US in big economic trouble and public finances a mess, there's no reason to think the economy will take off. The years ahead will be ones of slow growth yet with rising taxes and higher energy costs. Stagflation, it used to be called.

- Nine million Boomers start turning into seniors after 2011. This will officially be the beginning of Canada's retirement crisis since the majority are walking financial failures. By 2014 public pensions alone will cost another $45 billion. Health care will explode.

- A surge in houses for sale as the Boomers try to cash in will likely coincide with a return to normal interest rates and the end of our greatest-ever asset bubble. Real estate will be a dangerous place to have your wealth.

- Governments—in Ottawa, the provinces and everywhere—will scramble to meet the consequences of their actions. To keep a financial crisis from turning into a new version of the Dirty Thirties, they spent billions they didn't have and vastly over-mortgaged the future. Far less spending and painfully higher taxes are inevitable.

- Trillions of dollars will flow from houses into financial assets and from governments into bond markets. Bay Street and Wall Street will be rocked with volatility and opportunity.

If the future's anything like the past, you can also count on the unexpected, from terrorism to pandemics, wars to financial failures, peak oil to technological miracles. It looks like a decent bet the corporate pension system will break down, government support for social programs will be crowded out by debt and consumer spending will take a dive after 2015 as an incredible 40% of today's workers head for retirement.

These aren't wild predictions. All these future events are already in motion. You may not hear about a retirement crisis, tax surge, housing crunch or jobs deficit on the news now, but you will. And when the TV anchor is talking about it, chances are there'll be no time left to prepare.

But there's time now. Take it.

Why this is the time for contrarians

Whether you're 20 or 60, a wide array of options are available to prepare for what's down the road, to shield you from it, get around it and avoid the crashes most people will end up in. For example, there's no reason a young person who understands how to mitigate risk, use leverage or exploit tax shelters can't build a lot of wealth on even a modest income. No reason, either, someone nearing retirement can't slash their living costs, bail out of assets with no future or create a tax-free pension.

This book has dozens and dozens of strategies for driving straight through the mess ahead. None of them involve lining up in the cold to buy the wrong asset at the wrong price, at the wrong time. In fact, much of what you'll read is contrarian—actions based on the simple belief that what most people are doing is the polar opposite of what you should consider. The very fact that half the population has no savings or investments and fewer than a third put any money away for a retirement that could be three decades long shows the foolishness or inattention of those around you.

Greed and fear are still the accelerator and the brake of most people's financial lives. They lurch along, racing toward a perceived profit or skidding to avoid a failure or loss—almost never with a sense of the journey or a secure destination in mind. This behaviour, as I will show you, results in erratic, emotional prices, booms and busts and asset bubbles that inevitably burst—surprising everyone, when they were totally predictable. So by studying and understanding the forces behind markets, and realizing humans almost always act in exactly the same patterns, rational investors can do very well. Especially when they understand the economy, business cycles and the tricks the pros use to level risk and lever returns.

Money Road is about stocks, real estate, bonds, taxes, market analysis, derivatives, funds and shelters. Every tip and strategy can be used immediately to get you on course, or steer away from looming trouble. Much of this you will be able to do yourself. Some of it is best accomplished with the help of a financial advisor—especially one who doesn't have a conflict of interest selling you products, but rather is a fee-based professional who benefits when you do.

Hope and action in an upsetting time

The next five or ten years will be extremely upsetting and disappointing for most Canadians. They will learn the financial crisis of 2008-9 did not end in 2010 but simply continued to roll out in different forms.

It will seem at times like millions of people made bad decisions. When the housing market takes its tumble, for example, it will be amid denial and shock, especially in Vancouver and

Toronto. When legions of people stop working, or the work runs out, so many will regret never having learned how to invest, or the true nature of risk. When sales taxes rise and incomes stagnant, untold Canadians will wish they'd had a deductible mortgage or multiplied their money in a tax-free account.

When others are fighting on the sidewalk, the smart ones will be on the road.

Hop in.

One

ALERT

On the road ahead, bubbles and busts

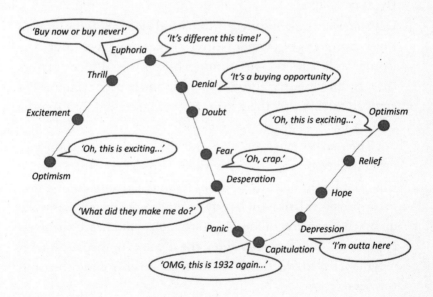

Our world has changed, forever

Vancouver

A dozen couples or more moved through the dreary 1956 bungalow, past the fake stone fireplace with press-on, mirrored tiles above and a crude wooden stag guarding the mantle. It was October 2009, showing day for a non-descript, tired suburban Vancouver property whose owners were asking north of $800,000. The agent holding court in the arborite kitchen neglected to mention a buried oil tank in the backyard.

But he did say offers would be accepted later that afternoon.

There were nine. The 'winning' bid was for almost $200,000 over asking. No conditions. Not even about the tank.

Ottawa

Days later, as the irritating autumn wind blew up off the Ottawa River, hundreds of former Nortel workers amassed under the iconic Peace Tower. Like countless others who'd spent careers labouring for forestry, automotive, pulp and paper or giant media companies, they were there to protest being screwed. Four-tenths of their pension was now a black hole.

The market crash of 2008 and the ensuing recession had lifted the veil on the actions of their corporate bosses. So while CEOs collected historic bonuses from collapsing companies, many pension plans went largely unfunded. When families woke up on the morning of January 14th, 2009, and heard the news Nortel was filing for bankruptcy, the shock of immediate unemployment rolled over them. The devastation of an empty pension was yet to come.

Winnipeg

I walked down Ellice Avenue, a mile or so from the airport and through the sliding glass doors of my hotel. At the end of the lobby, past the bar full of VLTs and clacking drinkers I could see the banners were already up for the seminar that night. I went and looked at the room full of chairs, pencils and notepaper neatly laid out on every seat, imagining the questions distraught investors would ask. Stock markets might have bounced back after a devastating crash when Wall Street investment banks collapsed and the world teetered on the edge of a neo-depression, but most people had already flamed out. They panicked when the headlines hit, looked at their diminshing mutual funds, and bailed.

I could hear the voices. "How can we trust anyone anymore?" It was so typical, everywhere.

He was sitting in the restaurant nursing an iced tea when I found him. After the hockey talk I asked what he expected tonight from the crowd. "Not much," he said. "You're just entertainment. They're all happy."

Tell me what you did, I said. "Two words," he responded, dragging noisily on his straw. "Seg funds."

Hours later, proof. Clients came up after the event to praise the guy. Most of them had locked into segregated funds with daily resets a couple of years earlier. So every day that markets crazily advanced, their gains were locked in and guaranteed. Every day markets fell, or were shredded in a financial freefall, they lost nothing.

"So tell me," a woman in a ski jacket and Capri pants asked. "Why wouldn't everybody do this?"

Toronto

The room was far too small for all the stuff in there. Two digital cameras, four banks of fluorescents, two technicians, a table, two chairs and us. We taped three segments to be broadcast in a few days on the *Globe and Mail*'s web site, as I played the role of a willing contrarian. After all, there weren't too many people willing to refute the prevailing logic that Canada was different—that while real asset values around the world had collapsed, this country could sustain an endless housing boom.

In the middle of a recession, incredibly, average home prices had raced ahead 21% in a year when inflation was negative. By the end of 2009, sales had advanced by 80% in Toronto, 100% in Vancouver and 74% across the nation. Multiple offers were the norm as lenders doled out endless billions to people making 5% downpayments and assuming 95% debt loads with mortgages that wouldn't be paid back for 35 years. Or, more likely, never.

I was of interest to the *Globe* reporter because of the heresy of my words. With rising unemployment, stagnant family incomes and rapidly rising debt, when the average detached house cost seven times the average Toronto income and ten times that in North Vancouver, how could this end well? The American real estate market collapsed under its own weight when the income-to-house ratio hit just five and a half.

"But we love publishing stories on this boom," he said when the session ended. "Reporters and editors have houses too."

And so did the camera guy. He was clearly juiced on my prediction of a coming market correction once interest rates started their inevitable climb and taxes rose to reflect the government spending orgy. Eight houses on his street had just sold, he said, most of them with multiple offers and all above asking. He'd been trying for weeks to convince his wife to cash out and bank the capital gain.

I asked how many years he'd owned the place. "All the way since January," he said. And now he stood to make more money, selling at the top of the curve to a greater fool, than he'd earn standing behind his camera for the next three years.

The interviewer, a *Globe* personal finance columnist, listened. He just shook his head.

■ ■ ■

So, we're all on this road—like it or not. It's measured in dollars and wealth, not kilometres or miles. Money means security and success, or despair and danger. Most of us are motivated by greed or fear, take little time to understand the consequences of our actions and are guided by the common wisdom. Lemming-like, we pay too much for things when they become popular and overvalued, eschew assets when they're cheap and trust nobody when it comes to advice.

A man I knew well for 30 years called every professional he ever met a 'phoney' and was convinced when it came to money he must make his own choices, despite my interventions. Cleaning up his estate after he died took little time. He left a house, no income, plus $50,000 in Canada Savings Bonds. And an astonished wife.

Eleven million now have no pensions

Eleven million Canadian families have no corporate pensions. That's 60% of the workforce. About four in ten of us have no retirement savings of any kind, either stashed in a bank account, an investment account, a tax-free savings account or an RRSP. Of those who do have assets tucked away, the average amount is less than $60,000, or enough to live about two years in retirement. Boomers, that big whack of people now hitting their sixties, are the worst, having lived their lives during expansionary, inflationary, go-go growth years, yet with little to show for it other than a possibly unsaleable suburban palace.

The public pension system provides a mere $17,000 a year to live on, so no salvation there. Meanwhile GenXers and GenYers are slogging through their early and middle adult lives staring at unaffordable house prices, stagflation, rising living costs and runaway government debt ensuring higher mortgage and income tax rates until they retire. Many of them furious at the Boomers for such a legacy. Not hard to see why.

So many bad turns possible on this road, and so many who have taken them already. It's hard to believe a majority of people won't end up as financial wrecks. Needlessly.

The first five years of the second decade will bring surprises, without a doubt. More market mayhem, more weather events, terrorism, medical advance, energy shocks, moments of hope and triumph, pandemics, climate change, political turmoil and reality TV. But they're also predictable.

■ ■ ■

Did we learn nothing from US house collapse?

And there will be more. Because the cost of money's going up.

Way up, since there is no alternative. Following the crash of 2008 and the recession that followed, central banks from Ottawa to Washington to London and Melbourne collapsed the cost of borrowing. As interest rates tumbled to the lowest point on record, the intent was clear—to make money so irresistibly cheap consumers would borrow their brains out, spend and kickstart recovery. And they did. At least in Canada.

Within just a year, the amount of mortgage debt in the country rocketed ahead 12%. Consumer debt—credit cards, lines of credit and car loans—soared by 9%. The country's accountants warned that household debt was getting completely out of whack. In fact, Canadian families soon had average debt equal to 140% of disposable income—rivalling those profligate Americans we love to feel superior to. While US households had actually paid off debt and increased their savings rate during the housing crash, we were doing exactly the opposite—saving nothing, borrowing massive amounts and buying houses at historic high levels.

You'd think we'd learn. Or, maybe the guys in charge would.

They rolled the dice on a new asset bubble

In dropping its key rate to just 0.25% and leaving it there for month after month, Bank of Canada governor and former Goldman Sachs investment banker Mark Carney knew what he was doing risked creating an asset bubble. After all, when US central banker Alan Greenspan used the same technique following Nine Eleven, crashing rates to forestall a recession, he ended up fuelling a housing boom so massive that when it ultimately popped, it brought down great swaths of the global economy with it.

Cheap mortgages and lenders keen to shovel loans out the door encouraged all kinds of people to 'get in' on the US housing bonanza. Families with lousy credit and no savings still qualified for loans enabling them to become homeowners. And to widen the pool of potential victims, lenders lowered standards with subprime mortgage products that featured low teaser rates guaranteed to be reset in the years ahead, plus reduced credit standards. As long as home values continued to advance, nobody cared—refinancing could always suck enough of that new equity out to pay down the home loan. Until, of course, the bubble burst. That happened when the average family, even with cheap money, could no longer afford the average home.

Meanwhile investment bankers had bundled millions of those flimsy mortgages together into 'securitized' investments and sold them to teachers' pension funds in Ohio, municipalities in Germany and untold private investors. You know the rest.

This time, in the wake of that disaster, they did it again. US Fed boss Ben Bernanke, with backing from Barack Obama, collapsed borrowing costs, as did Carney in Ottawa with the encouragement of Stephen Harper. Suddenly in Halifax, Toronto and Edmonton it became possible to borrow five-year variable-rate mortgage money at 2.25%. By the same token, returns on GICs crumbled, and the 2009 offering of Canada Savings Bonds paid the most pathetic return since they'd been created in 1946—less than one half of one per cent.

Bond prices jumped as bond yields eroded, richly rewarding fixed-income investors who had seen glimmers of this coming. Then with rates so low, money started to pour into the equity markets even though the economy was slagging, driving the TSX and the Dow just months after they'd been devastated. But this financial bubble on Bay and Wall Streets paled in comparison to the froth that spread over Main Street—the direct legacy of Carney's fateful decision to bring a subprime borrowing culture to Canada. Desperate men do desperate things.

By the end of 2009, after broadcasting that cheap money would be available for another year, Carney was starting to get it.

But not in time.

In North Vancouver a one-bedroom, one-bathroom cottage, unrenovated since it was built half a century ago, sold for the full asking price of $990,000. In Toronto, a semi-detached house in Koreatown, covered with insulbrick and fake stone, attracted 17 offers and sold for $62,000 over asking, at $541,000. In suburban Milton, Ontario, dozens of young couples camped out in freezing rain in front of a developer's sales trailer waiting for a 'new release' of homes on 30-foot lots. As they endured a night without sleep, to stagger in hours later and sign up for the greatest amount of debt in their lives, staff inside were raising prices by $5,000 a unit.

Back in Toronto, an attached home with a flat roof and no street presence but a double garage steel door sold for $440,000 after 13 days on the market. The owners had purchased it six months earlier for $290,000.

How mortgages have turned into rent

As a direct result of this flood of cheap money, real estate values jumped. As that happened, lenders—whose loan risk was wiped away by government-sponsored CMHC (Canada Mortgage and Housing Corporation) insurance—doled out mortgages to borrowers with the minimum of 5% down, and who could only afford payments based on 35-year amortizations. With that long a payback period, monthly payments in the early years were virtually all interest. It was just like rent, but with a lifetime worth of debt attached.

In other words, even a modest housing market correction, taking values down 10 to15%, would wipe away what little equity new buyers had, and drop the resale price of a home below the value of the mortgage placed upon it. This was exactly the 'negative equity' nightmare which, by the beginning of 2010, had trashed the financial lives of 16 million American families. Owing more than they owned, it was impossible to sell their homes without showing up on closing day with a cheque for tens or hundreds of thousands of dollars to pay the difference. As a result, they were trapped. Deceived, many believed, by central bankers who were more concerned with their legacy than their duty. More worried about having an economic correction on their watch than risking an asset bubble that would sucker the wealth out of millions of citizens.

By the end of 2009, Carney sounded the alarm. "We expect prudence from lenders. We expect, and we have confidence in, prudence from Canadians. We remind people that borrowing is for the period you are going to borrow, not just for the moment you take out the loan," he told reporters. Then, "Obviously, consumer borrowing cannot grow faster than the economy forever."

But he did not move to raise rates. A federal election was in the air.

The meaning, still, should have been obvious. Those borrowing at less than 3%, able to afford ever-more-costly homes based only on that interest rate, could be demolished if the price of money moved higher, to more normal values. In fact, the average five-year mortgage rate for the previous twenty years had been 8.25%.

For those putting down $500,000 for a 700-square-foot condo in Vancouver's Yaletown or spending $900,000 for an unrenovated, 70-year-old house on a thirty foot lot in Toronto's Leaside, a doubling or tripling in rates was unimaginable. But too few listened.

The central banker's message was simple: the cost of money is going to go up. Prepare now.

And on the money road, this is a guidepost. Higher rates. They invariably bring lower real estate prices. Plunging bond values. Soaring bond yields. Hijacked stock markets. Shocked homeowners. Volatility. And a cry of anguish from those who never saw it coming, because they never looked.

Soon, no more multiple offers and bidding wars between young couples freaked out that they must act rashly and dangerously, or never own a home. No more auction mentality forcing buyers to spend less time researching a new home than they would shopping for a pair of jeans. No more greedy vendors dumping their imperfect houses on the market, restricting viewings, then conducting a cattle call of offers.

All bubbles burst. But not before record numbers of us enter into record amounts of debt at rates that only rise on assets that only devalue. Like those mutual fund victims who caved and sold when markets crashed in the financial panic, they repeat a cycle of buying higher and selling lower. And when it's all so obvious.

Billions will vanish in real estate equity

- Billions of dollars are going to vanish in lost real estate equity and in capital losses on bonds.
- Billions of dollars are about to be made by those who understand this will happen. The victims and the winners will pass each other on the money road.
- This book will give you some guidance on real estate and borrowing strategies.
- It will show you how to make money in the bond market, taking advantage of changeable interest rates.
- It will give you guidelines for being a housing vulture when the time is right.
- And it will show you how to make money in real estate, whether the market is steamy or frigid.
- It will lead you to the markets with the most investment opportunity and least danger, and show you the options for guaranteed gains that most Canadians will never take, let alone even hear of.

■ ■ ■

Why your taxes are set to soar

The next years will be remembered for what they do to the country. The province you live in. Even your city. Maybe, especially your city. And then your taxes.

Just as debt has taken up residence in the spare bedrooms of the nation, so it's come to dominate public life. Almost every decision taken in the next five years by a Canadian politician will be dictated by one reality: governments are broke, or on the way there. They've been crushed by mismanagement, vanity, recessionary spending, inattention, incompetence, shifting demographics or a heady mix of them all.

In this new reality, we'll be paying more for less. At least, some of us will.

Faced with the loss of 20,000 students over the next few years and struggling with a $90 million capital deficit, the Toronto District School Board plans to shutter dozens of schools, massively inconveniencing parents in the nation's largest urban area.

Faced with a $60 million hole in its budget as fees from new development drop by half, even in an Olympic year, Vancouver city politicians warned services, and jobs, will have to be sliced, or property taxes will increase as much as 11%. Or both.

Faced with a stunning and record $24.7 billion budget deficit, Canada's richest province contemplated a financial crisis as 2010 dawned. Ontario saw its revenues from business taxes plunge by 50% as the recession ravaged manufacturing, exports and the car companies. The government warned of across-the-board spending hikes, at the same time as it (along with British Columbia) launched its HST—the Harmonized Sales Tax—sticker-shocking consumers as 13% is tacked on to the cost of everything from vet bills to plumbers and many new houses.

Faced with a record $4.7 billion deficit, Alberta made it clear that if revenues don't rebound and oil prices soar (and they will), the province will have to raise $2.2 billion by cutting spending, increasing taxes, or both.

And in Ottawa, we all faced a federal government leading the way in terms of fiscal irresponsibility, or at least fiscal fibbing.

Days before the election in October of 2008, the prime minister said: "We will not be running a deficit. We will keep our spending within our means. It is that simple. The alternative is not a plan. It is just the consequence of complete panic, and this government will not panic at a time of uncertainty." One year later, the country was sinking into new debt at the rate of $6 billion a month, on track to record the worst-ever annual deficit of

$56 billion, and a legacy that will, according to the Parliamentary Budget Officer, see the national debt hit more than $620 billion by 2015.

Caught in a vice of evaporating tax revenues and the need for more spending on unemployment and job-creating stimulus, the destruction in national finances showed just how fast a nation's financial safety net can shred. Only three years earlier, Ottawa was chalking up record budget surpluses. Based on that, the Conservative government embarked on a major spending spree at the worst possible time, while chopping the national sales tax rate against the advice of almost every mainstream economist. After the market meltdown, predictably, its balance sheet also melted.

What does this mean?

Watch the bond market

One certainty, of course, is a mess of new government bonds. That's where deficits are financed when taxes don't meet expenditures, in the bond market. Government of Canada bonds are always hot sellers, since they're backed by the country's ability to endlessly tax its citizens. But they also have to compete with debt from other countries, as well as provinces and corporations, and that means at rates that continue to attract investors.

This puts more upward pressure on interest rates, drives bond yields skywards and ends up jacking mortgage costs, since home loan rates are set in the bond market.

However, this may be the least of our worries, if history's any guide.

The last time the feds fell off a budget cliff was in the early 1990s. Brian Mulroney was the prime minister. Michael Wilson was the finance minister. I was an MP.

The deficit was approaching $40 billion, and 32 cents of every dollar the government spent was being sucked off for interest on the burgeoning national debt. If nothing changed, that would become fifty cents. So something did change. It was called the GST.

One morning Wilson grabbed me out of national caucus and took me to the small room where MPs fetched their coffee and cookies. He was agonizing over how the new tax should apply to real estate and new houses in particular. To be fair and consistent, he said, they must be taxed at the full 7% rate, but he worried about the impact on consumers and the market in general.

"What should we do?" He stared down at me, holding in his hand an eyes-only Department of Finance briefing document that I then knew made the case for a full-bore tax load on everything.

I argued as forcefully as I could for exempting new home sales, saying it would be the death of the development industry. Wilson listened, made notes with his golden ballpoint, thanked me, and we walked back in as the Prime Minister was taking the podium. In the end, the government came up with a compromise, rebating much of the tax on a sliding scale.

Still, the GST had a dramatic impact, deepening a recession when it hit, and forever decimating the Progressive Conservative party which brought it in. Consumer prices took a jump, consumer spending retreated and the tax started raising $1 billion a month. Six years later, the deficit was gone.

So now that another fiscal crisis has descended, now that the deficit is $56 billion, not $40 billion, and now that we already have the GST, what can we expect? Less, and more. Less spending, fewer services, reduced government presence, smaller transfers to other levels of government, diminished incentives for small business and cuts in grants and subsidies. Most importantly, there will be no personal income tax cuts, no more

GST cuts and no reductions in corporate tax levels to make us more competitive.

In fact, there will be more tax. Inevitably, sadly and at great cost to those who don't see it coming. Reluctantly, the feds could raise the GST rate, reversing some of those treasury-killing cuts. The marginal tax rate on higher-income earners could well be increased by a point or two. User fees will surely be increased for everything from passports to immigration processing to the price of a stamp.

There's simply no option. Economic growth alone won't get us out of this mess. In fact, 60% of the country's economy is made up of consumer spending, so with higher prices, higher taxes and hopped-up mortgages on the agenda, how could we possibly goose the economy enough to get the feds out of this mess? Or the provinces? Or your city?

For example, if you're one of the six million people living in the GTA, you're suddenly on the hook for record deficits by all three levels of politicians. And the school board. If you think your current level of tax is not going to change, you're just not paying attention. So, one of the defining features of the half-decade before us is a constant threat by government to your personal wealth.

The money road, you will find, is a twisted path through the minefields of taxation. And while we all need to pay our fair share, only the foolish or inattentive among us will pay more.

Tax avoidance is still legal. Do it.

While tax evasion is illegal, tax avoidance is entirely legal and a goal everyone should aim for.

- This book guides you into those streams of income which are the least taxed.

- It demonstrates how to earn significant amounts of cash, and yet pay only half—or less—as much tax as your neighbour who goes to work each day and busts his butt to bring home a paycheque.
- It's a guide to making retirement savings plan contributions without money. How to use the new tax-free savings account to shield your investments and also generate tax-free payments to you directly from the government.
- This book provides guidance on how to remove cash from your RRSP or your RRIF without paying any tax.
- How to income-split with your spouse, or your kids.
- It shows how to use life insurance to create a perfectly tax-free pension for the rest of your life.
- It also lays out the process to achieve a tax-deductible mortgage on your home.

Some of these things are simple to accomplish and only a few pages will take you there. Others require professional help to get the right investments in place and ensure you are bullet-proof if challenged by the revenue agency. But all are worthy of your attention, given what lies ahead.

Some will argue the tax-saving strategies in these pages are unseemly for an author who was once in charge of Revenue Canada. Maybe so. But unlike them, I've been in government.

One day the deputy minister brought a pile of ministerial orders to my Parliament Hill desk that required signatures. Two inches down I found a document authorizing the seizure of a fleet of taxi cabs in Victoria. I asked the deputy what gave. Was the federal government now in the used car business?

"The fleet operator in question hasn't paid his corporate taxes," he said, "so we are taking his vehicles."

"No we're not," I said, and stroked the document through. "If we grab his cars the guy will never be able to pay his bill." The deputy retreated in a huff. And I was sure he'd never hacked a cab, or met a payroll.

■ ■ ■

The crisis nobody's talking about

The years just ahead will bring a demographic mess. As the Baby Boomers move into their sixties, expect big changes in the real estate market, a surge of scared money into equities and the media to be overflowing with stories of a looming retirement crisis.

Aging Boomers are a global football. Every developed country is trying to figure this one out—how to keep economies growing when so many people are greyer, and how to cushion the advent of a time when life expectancy means folks spend up to three decades after work.

There's nothing more certain—not interest rates, government debt or higher taxes—than aging. Canada has one of the biggest Boomer populations in the world, about nine million people, or almost a third of the country. This means the number of seniors you see in the grocery store and on the street is about to double, to an unheard-of 25% of the nation within twenty years. Of all those folks, seven in ten will have nothing much to live on except the public pension system—one of the stingiest in the world.

Simply put, the number of those among us on subsistence incomes is about to explode. Their living standards will tumble, and discretionary spending will dry up fast. No longer will retailers and manufacturers count them as customers for new cars, flat screen TVs, iPhones or timeshares in Florida or Muskoka. This economic hit will be felt exactly when demands will grow for government to step in and save the biggest mass of voters from their own financial demise. And make no mistake, we have no one to blame but ourselves.

Those Boomers (and I'm one of them) have grown up in a time of almost constant inflation, endless economic growth, technological advance and wall-to-wall progress that seemed to obliterate the need for personal responsibility. Back when the public pension system was being set up, the Boomers were in grade school and the country was rocking. Growth was rampant, corporations expanding, private pension plans were being set up right and left, moms were streaming into the workforce as never before and workers were being given a cool new savings vehicle called the registered retirement savings plan. The future seemed obvious and the CPP (Canada Pension Plan) was designed for just one function—to supplement other forms of retirement income, namely those corporate pensions and RRSP savings.

Never, ever, did policymakers dream 50 years ago that the bulk of those kids teeming into the public schools would end up like this. Three-quarters without corporate pensions. Millions discovering they'd been cheated when those pensions were underfunded. Two-thirds having missed most, if not all, of their available RRSP contributions. Only one kid per class ending up being serious about retirement savings. Most learning that at age 65 they couldn't afford to retire in comfort, or retire at all.

How could they have envisioned in the sixties that a generation born into such education, promise and prosperity would borrow so much, spend so carelessly, save so little, invest so reluctantly or fail so spectacularly that those tiny supplemental public pensions might become their only salvation?

It's hard to underestimate the changes a few decades have brought. For example, when my father was a young man in southwestern Ontario, there was a horse-drawn stagecoach connecting his village, where his father was a blind, country hardware store operator, with the nearest city. By the time my father died he had two bionic knees and a six-figure government-indexed pension.

From horses to space travel in one generation. More importantly to this book, from feudalism to the welfare state, in a single lifetime.

Once again, a fend-for-yourself society

Incredibly, we may now be back on the path to a fend-for-yourself society.

Boomers have always had a profound, out-of-proportion effect on the economy. It's about to get worse. In the fifties we overran the public schools and sowed the seeds of government debt. In the sixties we inflated the universities. In the Seventies we started families, then a real estate boom. In the eighties we flooded into mutual funds and sent equities spinning. In the nineties we fell for dot-coms and the NASDAQ and created wild market excess. And then came the second real estate wave, of suburban McMansions and recreational properties.

Now this giant generation is coming to the realization of just how much trouble it's in.

House-rich and cash-poor, Boomers have a depressingly low rate of savings and most of their net worth in real estate assets that can only grow more illiquid. Worse, the recession, which ravaged the economy in 2009, hit older workers proportionately harder, and men far more than women. Tens of thousands of guys in their fifties will likely never work again, especially if their careers had anything remotely to do with manufacturing, exporting or cars.

This group is also learning fast that the cradle-to-grave security my father discovered may in fact have been buried with him. Indexed pensions are fast disappearing, as are defined benefit retirement schemes and most corporate plans of any kind. The vast majority of Boomers have no pensions to look forward to over the next ten years, and many had their few financial investments punted when the government attacked income trusts or the stock markets tanked.

So as nine million people move into this phase, amid faltering income opportunities, governments shackled by debt and a crumbling pension system, modern society seems destined to suffer its first retirement crisis.

The numbers tell the tale. It's ugly. Millions in my generation are staring at relative poverty, or at least a massive drop in income from their working years.

"The statistics speak for themselves. We've got eleven million working Canadians with zero company-sponsored retirement pension plans... (RRSPs are) very underutilized and skewed to higher-income earners. I don't think it's a great leap to say, clearly, the system is not working," David Denison, CEO of the CPP Investment Board said, as the Nortel pension debacle spilled over onto the floor of the House of Commons.

One thing the Boomers do have, however, is real estate. Lots of it. And mostly the wrong kind. Overwhelmingly, this generation owns large, suburban properties with multiple bedrooms, double or triple-car garages, Scarlett O'Hara staircases, hot tubs and utility bills many small nations would recognize. The bulk of these homes are also paid for, which means most of the net worth of Boomer couples now sits in a single asset at a single address. So much for the rule of diversification.

In an age of rising energy costs, smaller families and an exodus from the burbs back to the cities, this could hardly be a worse scenario. But, it gets worse.

Why the Boomers could destroy real estate

Over the coming decade, the Big Generation will have absolutely no alternative but to try to turn real estate into cash. This money will be needed for immediate income, but also for growth, since life expectancy is catapulting higher. The average Boomer, at age 60 for example, has 25 years or more yet to finance—years often devoid of either earned income or meaningful pension payments. That means the money from real estate needs to be turned into lifetime investment income. The consequences for equity markets are obvious—a 20-year infusion of capital that can't help but propel assets higher.

But before that happens, those suburban houses have to hit the market and be turned liquid. One more big reason that smart money wants very little to do with real estate in the years ahead of us. After all, imagine what will happen to housing supply and demand as one, two or three million more properties turn into listings over the next 60 months. This is likely to take place just as interest rates increase and taxes start to rise, along with a steady, long ascent in energy prices.

House values are significantly impacted by supply and demand, and the Boomer dump could well end up being the mother of all real estate events, driving down not only the value of competing suburban properties, but the entire market. This will be especially so after the housing bubble conditions I've already described—the result of Mark Carney's experiment in super-cheap interest rates. Boom, then bust. Hardly the time to be trying to unload your big house. And a time you want to avoid.

Clearly, there are no alternatives to a real estate fire sale. With Boomers now streaming into their sixth decade, it's obvious time has run out to grow savings enough to finance the future. There's no way stock market gains or secure fixed-income investments can make up for 30 years of new cars, new Nikes, flipping houses or affording your kids.

Reality is, the Boomers have no backstop. The move into the last quarter of their lives comes as governments stagger under record debt, the economy's wounded and tentative, interest rates and taxes are on the rise, peak oil and climate change cloud the horizon and the country's long-time saviour, America, fights its own mounting demons.

Are you ready for this journey? The money road runs clear through the middle of the storm.

How to avoid collapse of suburbia

Total disintegration is not inevitable. You can steer clear of it.

- This book gives you defensive strategies. How to avoid the coming collapse of suburbia. What kinds of real estate still have a future.
- How to sell a property as competition mounts and prices decline.
- If you are a Boomer, this book helps with strategies for maximizing the return on the savings that you have, to take advantage of rising rates and erratic changes in equity markets.
- It describes how to use investments that will lock in gains while avoiding losses, that will protect your principal and yet give far higher returns than traditional lose-lose products such as guaranteed investment certificates or savings bonds.
- It will assist you in indentifying those places where your money's likely to get superior returns.
- How to pick mutual funds, how to use exotic yet profoundly useful tools such as puts and calls and futures.
- It lays out the basics of technical, fundamental and corporate analysis so you can download company financial statements and starkly assess the prospects for growth for yourself.

- It describes why we're on the verge of a range-bound stock market in which finding growth assets is critically important. Equally, why those who passively invest in index funds or ETFs may be in for a nasty surprise.
- And why commodities—oil, gold, agricultural products— are likely to give profoundly satisfying returns over the years ahead.

If there's one thing the Boomers have shown all of us, it's the misunderstood nature of risk. By trying to avoid it, this generation has turned into not only a disappointment and a giant potential drag on society, but one of the greatest financial flops in history.

To most people, risk means losing money in a bad investment that tanks. It might be Nortel crashing from $130 a share to penny stock status, and then nothing. Or gold-mining fraudster company Bre-X, whose stock went from 12 cents to $280, and back down just as fast. Or any one of a slew of Internet stocks, like Pet.com, which milked investors of $82 million in an initial public offering, then promptly went bankrupt.

Those are sad tales, and they sucked in untold squads of investors, many of whom were do-it-yourself victims. But while those stories made a big media splash, the failed companies stung a relatively small number of people. What they did do, however, was freak out millions of others who decided they were far better off to retreat into the perceived safety of residential real estate or to steer clear of stocks and mutual funds, and sock their money into fixed-income instruments like GICs.

It was a big mistake, as we can now see. And that's simply because the greatest risk we all now face is not losing money in a bad investment, but outliving it.

The biggest risk now: running out of money

Maybe I'm typical. Probably am. My father died in his 84th year, and likely could have held on longer without the cigars and the scotch. My mother passed at 90 (she also smoked cigars, but dainty ones). My wife's father was gone at 75, but that was after learning to smoke as a soldier in World War Two—and never really quitting. Dorothy's mother is still kicking at 80. Our family doctor (he's over 65 now) says we should both be good for late 80s. Or more.

At age 65, women today live about 25% longer than women of the same age in 1960. Guys now live a third longer. That means people who retired at 65 a generation ago were being carried out the door, on average, within 5 years. Today they should count on at least 20. So while savings of, say, $100,000 was wildly sufficient then to finance retirement at a level equal to 70% of your working income, today it's likely to be at least half a million.

As I documented, Canadian boomers now hitting retirement prove without a doubt they screwed this up. And so do those to the south. US Social Security pays just $12,000 a year, and yet an absolute majority of senior Americans now rely on it for 80% of their income.

And forget about inheritance. My parents did the job I expected of burning through mine. My father needed constant care in his final years—at $8,000 a month. And my mother was rafting down the Amazon six months before she passed on. I still get people who were on that trip with her—people I've never met—e-mailing me pictures of Doris Turner with exotic flowers in her gray hair and a glass full of marguerita on her head. Makes me happy to get them.

While Canadian stats are hard to find, there is some evidence in the US that inheritance is not what it used to be. Of two and a half million deaths in 2003, for example, only 66,000 had estates of more than $1 million.

So, the risks are obvious. Yet people don't get it. So it amazes me when I run into 30-year-olds who flee from the idea of an equity mutual fund because to them it screams of Bernie Madoff and stock market Armageddon. If the pathetic cohort of Boomers have proven anything, it's that a failure to invest is the greatest single financial risk—and perhaps life risk—you can take.

Why are we so bad at this? Maybe because we were never schooled in how to pull it off. We learn grammar and chemistry and history, but not how to bank, buy a stock or choose a mortgage. No wonder we end up where we do. A recent survey showed that 48% of people had no idea that investing in a single stock was riskier than a stock mutual fund. Our financial literacy is woeful. And that's got to change.

Why 'safe' investments can now be fatal

This book shows how to achieve diversification, and tells you how many stocks it takes to virtually eliminate risk.

- I'll explain asset allocation and how to achieve it. This one move is responsible for, on average, about 90% of the return a portfolio can give you.
- You'll find out why investing in 'safe' things like GICs and savings bonds is almost as bad as not investing at all, especially outside of a registered plan like an RRSP.
- The book explains how to pick good corporate and government bonds, which can be laddered for a stable stream of income no matter what interest rates do.
- How it's very wise to take your money out of the bank, and invest it in the bank instead, especially through preferred shares, which pay you in tax-reduced dollars.

■ And don't even consider a reverse mortgage, unless you hate your children.

■ ■ ■

Obama and the empire of decline

Finally, the years ahead will have a lot to do with Barack Obama, America, and you.

It was hardly a fluke in 2009 when the Canadian dollar started moving towards parity with the Yankee greenback. Or that the price of an ounce of gold bulldozed through the $1,000 (US) an ounce mark. That's because the American dollar is in a long, steady decline which, other factors being equal, will force up the value of anything priced in it.

Expect this to continue. Also expect the American economy to be slowed, even paralyzed over the next five years, while other countries—China, especially—leap to the front of the line. This is a profound change. Everyone reading this book will have grown up in a time when America was on top, leading technological change, dominating industrial production, remaining the world's most important country, flexing its untiring military muscles and leading the financial business.

But those days are ending. Maybe already over.

The American empire's in decline and no country stands to be impacted more than Canada. As Niall Ferguson, Harvard professor and author of *The Ascent of Money* has written: "Let's face it: If you're trying to borrow $9 trillion to save your financial system...and already half your public debt is held by foreigners, it's not really the conduct of rising empires, is it?"

Sure isn't. Americans gambled on what the future would look like, and it's not turning out too well. The bet was that in a knowledge-based world all those messy, lower-wage manufacturing jobs could be exported to developing countries, slashing production costs. Sure enough, soon Wal-Marts across America filled with cameras, underwear, bar-b-ques, solar panels, lawn furniture and computers made in China. A ton of manufacturing jobs had been lost across the States, but the trade-off was cheap consumer prices.

The de-industrialization of the country helped redefine the economy. Before long, over 65% of all activity was the result of consumer activity. The nation that was a production powerhouse turned into a country where most people worked in the service sector, selling each other stuff. At the same time, a popular culture of debt exploded, fuelled by the real estate bubble that developed after Nine Eleven. In the majority of US cities between 2003 and 2006, many peoples' houses made more money each year than they did, and as values soared, so did mortgage debt.

So long as the asset bubble continued, loans got increasingly easier to pay. All families had to do was refinance their homes, sucking out new equity, which the market had created, and replacing it with low-cost debt. The party continued until interest rates spiked, loan defaults exploded and real estate values collapsed under their own weight. Meanwhile investment bankers had packaged vast quantities of loans together and sold them to investors and pension funds as AAA products. Then all hell broke loose.

The ensuing collapse has been America's mortal wound. The disappearance of companies like Lehman Brothers, Bear Stearns and Merrill Lynch ended the country's control of the global financial system. The near-bankruptcy of General Motors and Chrysler in just a matter of weeks made a myth of American industrial might and product superiority. The decimation of the residential real estate market was the beginning of the end of the American middle class. It's estimated that over $11 trillion in personal wealth was destroyed. By the end of 2009, house prices in most major cities were right back at 2003 levels, meaning anyone who had bought during that time was a net loser. In some cities, like Cleveland and Detroit, real estate values were identical to those in 1995. So much for the ascending American dream.

Most debilitating, though, is public debt. Applying a killer dose of Keynsian economics, Washington opened up the spending floodgates once it became apparent the country was on the verge of indenture, deflation and depression. The government not only put $70 billion into the car companies, assuming an ownership position, but it then paid customers to buy the products. The 'cash for clunkers' program handed over $4,500 to everyone who traded in a rusting piece of junk for new wheels. The Obama Administration then bailed out AIG and the mortgage giants Fannie Mae and Freddie Mac, along with banks and finance companies. The government also paid people to buy houses, offering an $8,000 credit to purchasers, as well as increasing social program spending—while it was ramping up its star-crossed mission in Afghanistan.

The results were predictable. Trillions in stimulus spending goosed the GDP, but also created an economy hooked on handouts. The economy grew enough to slough off the 'recession' label, but without actually creating jobs. In the absence of those, it was impossible to revive a consumer-led economy. So the lasting legacy was debt.

Back to Niall Ferguson, who's compared America in this decade of the new century with Britain about 1900. Then, in the twilight of the empire, the UK failed to recognize the rising dominance of Germany, just as the US may now be dismissing China. But it's impossible to do so. With so many machines unbolted from their moorings in factories in Ohio and Michigan and Pennsylvania, and shipped to China, it's likely impossible the US can regain industrial dominance. Worse, it's deep into the ranks of the debtor nations, expected to have trillion-dollar deficits for years to come, while it amasses the greatest foreign indebtedness of all time. Ironically, it's the very country that filled those Wal-Marts in the US rust belt with cheap goods that now holds both the exported factory jobs of its unemployed workers, and trillions in American debt.

"When China's economy is equal in size to that of the US, which could come as early as 2027...it means China becomes not only a major economic competitor—it's that already, it then becomes a diplomatic competitor and a military competitor," Ferguson writes. "There's no other way of interpreting this than as a challenge to the hegemony of the U.S. in the Asia-Pacific region."

The age of gold, oil and Canadian vultures

But this is about you, and me, and Canadian investors. With the US middle class in trouble, after a recession that claimed seven million jobs and scores of companies, leaving our biggest trading partner seriously in hock and its currency on a downward journey, there are consequences for all of us.

Among them will likely be a rising, strong Canadian dollar. This will reflect the weakness of the US note, and also the significant gains we should all expect in commodity prices—gold, oil, natural gas and agricultural products, among others. In fact, the greenback's woes alone will be enough to push oil and bullion higher, and fuel the belief of many that gold has more potential to become an alternative global currency. It will make US imports cheaper, let Canadian vultures swoop more easily on distressed American real estate and help businesses that need to retool with imported machinery.

But our fat loonie will be hell for many others. Tourism will take a further hit as US tourists stay home with their shrinking dollars. Exporters of raw materials like softwood lumber will risk being priced out of key markets. In fact, a persistently high currency, combined with a weakened America, is news this country doesn't need.

In a late-2009 report, CIBC economist Avery Shenfeld warned dramatically of a 'hollowing-out' of the country's industrial base because of the dollar. "Plants that close because they are unprofitable at current exchange rates might permanently relocate elsewhere," he said. "They won't suddenly come back if the currency later cheapens."

Exactly. I've walked on shop floors where the evidence is undeniable. One, an aircraft parts manufacturer outside of Toronto, was in the final stages of disassembly when I went through in the autumn of 2008. The workforce of 450 had been reduced to about three dozen men and women whose job it was to crate the hundreds of drill presses, stamping presses and computer-guided lathes. As he showed me around, the owner was too emotional to even talk to his crews. When I asked him where all this stuff was going—sold for an average of 18 cents on the dollar—he said only, "Guangzhou."

The reality is that just under 40% of our economy is made up of exports. The rising dollar seriously erodes the competitiveness of Canadian goods, and is a job-killer. At the same time, our indebted and hobbled neighbour to the south—where 70% of our exports have traditionally gone—is hardly in a buying mood. The combination is dire. It points to a slower pace of growth, painfully high levels of unemployment and serious troubles in places highly dependent on foreign markets—like northern BC.

Invest in the future, not the past

On the journey ahead, this is serious roadkill. You need to know.

- This book shows you how to easily and effectively move investments out of US companies and into those which have a far more promising future, such as burgeoning enterprises in China and India.
- You'll also see how to easily harness the power of foreign exchange markets through the relative safety of currency ETFs (exchange-traded funds).
- You can also benefit from the insatiable Chinese thirst for energy, particularly oil, without having your money ever leave Canada.
- This book also underscores the danger of having most of your net worth in a house in the wrong place at the wrong time. Those parts of the country dependent on exports are entering a protracted period of decline, which will see home prices tumble in many cities and regions. In places like Windsor, Ontario, it has already happened, with the value of middle-class homes often being lower than the price of new minivans.

Let nobody tell you the future is unclear. Or the path ahead unknown.

A new era of volatility and turmoil

Money will cost more. Houses will cost less. Energy values will soar, as will doubts and concerns about climate. Taxes have only one direction in which to travel. Large amounts of personal wealth will be lost as real estate values decline. Big gains will be made by those who invest in commodities or profit from interest rate changes. Taxes on income and spending will jump, causing the smart money to flow into new streams. And do not be surprised if we're entering into a new era of protracted volatility,

stagnation and turmoil. Those who do not understand or prepare will pay the price. Those who understand can absolutely
preserve their money and find financial peace.

Large parts of the economy will be in stress. Many of the
people you probably know will be there, too. Pensions will be lost.
Many Boomers will never work again. Some industries will all
but disappear. Our standard of living will stall. Some places just
won't be worth living in.

So, is it impossible to achieve financial security in such times?
What if you're a 55-year-old Boomer with all your money in all
the wrong places? Or a 30-year-old contemplating a future pep-
pered with debt and rising taxes, thanks to the last generation?
Are the easy, predictable times gone?

In a word, yes.

Our destination, financial security

The road ahead is a daunting one, littered with the wrecks of
those who didn't peer far enough ahead to see the obstacles,
and swerve to avoid them. The recession of 2008–9 was a game-
changer, marking the end of several key periods. The economic
power of the Boomers. The ascendancy of America. The credit
society. The housing bubble.

And while it will take more effort and skill, more knowledge
and often more daring to achieve money security in the years
now upon us, it is absolutely possible to get there. This book is
about showing you how.

In the pages that follow, I will detail how to seriously cut the
taxes you pay; how to retire when you want with what you want;
how to make money in real estate regardless of the market; how
to assess, choose and buy stocks and bonds; and how to use both
passive and aggressive strategies to seize control. Take the wheel.
And ride.

TWO

ROADKILL

This time listen to the chart

In the autumn of 2000, I was doing a live television hit from the 'floor' of the Toronto Stock Exchange, amid a glitzy high-tech array of screens in an office tower storefront in the middle of the financial district. (All actual trading is now done electronically, instead of by the mass of worried traders waving their arms that you see in movies.)

'It's different this time.' It wasn't

This was near the frothy top of the dot-com, tech bubble. The stock market was flying high, day trading was all the rage, 20-year-olds with unproven but highly cool business models were doing IPOs worth billions, tech-heavy mutual funds were surging wildly in value, the mantra on Bay Street and Wall Street was, 'it's different this time', and one Canadian company had been sweeping the world in bold, incontrovertible proof of that very fact.

As the camera rolled, the operator was careful to include images over my head of the giant ticker screen as live trades rolled by. Every third or fourth one included the letters NT, followed by a double-digit number. The big news was a decline in Nortel shares, then changing hands in the $95-range, down almost $40 from their high months earlier.

This was huge, since Nortel had come to dominate Bay Street with its immense capitalization. In the summer of 2000, its stock alone, at $124 a pop, accounted for almost 40% of the entire market as measured by the TSE 300. That meant the other 299 companies, including giants like the Royal Bank and Bell Canada, together made up the rest. Everybody had wanted in on this baby—portfolio managers, hedge funds, institutional investors, giant pension funds guarding the retirement assets of millions of workers, star mutual fund managers and countless retail investors stuffing NT shares into the RRSPs, RRIFS, non-registered accounts and even their kid's education savings plans.

Sure, they'd bought far after the stock was cheap, yet every projection was for a Cadillac security to turn into a Mercedes. Investors of all kinds and sizes, ages and risk tolerances were pigged out on NT. And why not? The 'Nortel effect' alone had raised the TSE 300 Composite Index a breathtaking 30% in 1999, eclipsing by five points even the high-flying Dow in New York.

Still, this correction had people asking, was the bloom off the rose? Or was this a giant opportunity to load up on more Nortel, a no-miss security, at bargain prices?

That's what a roomful of Wall Street financial analysts wondered as the luncheon plates were noisily cleared and John Roth took the podium. The lanky, 58-year-old, Alberta-bred CEO faced a sea of doubters wondering why the company's revenue growth had slowed from their street estimates. Sales of its leading optical equipment had jumped 90% in the last quarter when Nortel had led them to believe 120% was likely.

Roth was unequivocal. The business has stabilized, he said. Overall company revenues are solid, and will grow by 40% in calendar 2000—twice what he had predicted to analysts only one year earlier. Just stand by me, he said.

Meanwhile some people were very worried about Roth, Nortel, high-technology and mostly that herd investor psychology. They spent considerable time looking at trading patterns, price movements, buy and sell orders and the sheer gluttony that NT had provoked. The charts, they said to anyone who would listen, are trying to shout something important.

On October 25th, 2000, Roth issued a profit warning that hit the markets like a cyclone. While he reiterated Nortel would make over $8 billion every three months, the company was proving it might actually be mortal, subject to the laws of supply and demand and competition. That day NT stock collapsed by 35%, from $96 to $71. That cratered the Toronto market, which by 4 PM was down a stunning 840 points.

From there, things just got worse. A years-long surge in buying became a tidal wave of selling, as the company revealed more and more rotten news about sales, earnings, debt and corporate performance. In January 2001, Roth once again tried to stem the decline, telling another room of analysts and the financial media that Nortel would enjoy revenue growth of 30% by the time the year was over.

A month later, one Thursday afternoon after the market closed, the Brampton, Ontario-based company revealed sales would be $2 billion less than forecast, and, inconceivably, the company would post a loss for the first quarter. Nortel, it said, would immediately slash its workforce by 4,000, bringing total job cuts up to 10,000.

Investors were gobsmacked yet again. Those who didn't act at the opening bell on Friday saw their wealth devastated as tens of billions of dollars vaporized. After closing at $46 on Thursday afternoon, NT opened on Friday at $30 in a barrage of trading that shut down the exchange several times during the day, the first time at two minutes after the opening bell. The TSE 300 closed down 574 points.

But still, Nortel was supported by those brokerage houses, analysts and institutions who had shoved billions into its stock on behalf of their clients and investors. CIBC World Markets changed its NT rating from an outright 'buy' to a 'strong buy.' Merrill Lynch went from 'buy' to 'accumulate,' while TD Securities told its clients they should stop buying the stock but maintain it as a 'hold.'

Those who listened were soon filled with regret. By the end of 2001, NT had lost 60% of its value, and was trading at $12. Half of its 90,000 workforce had been fired or laid off.

John Roth stepped down in disgrace. But comforting his departure was the fact he'd sold a large part of his own stock options in 2000, just as he was reassuring markets and telling investors to hang on. His personal profit that year was $135 million. He retired to an estate in the horse country outside Orangeville, Ontario, where word soon spread among locals of the profligacy of his spending on landscaping and fountains.

Nine years later, shortly after New Year's Day 2009, eleven Nortel directors sat down in a nondescript office in an unremarkable low-rise building near Toronto's Pearson airport. The economy was in the throes of a global recession, the markets had tumbled, fear had replaced greed as the motivation of most investors, Nortel's remaining cash reserves were threatened by an immediate bond interest payment and the company's remaining 25,000 employees were living on a knife's edge. NT stock was changing hands at 40 cents.

Faced with the fact that an orderly liquidation would trigger demands not only by creditors and debtors but the legal obligation to set aside hundreds of millions for severance and pension payments to its workers, the directors voted to force Nortel into bankruptcy—just days after having been turned down for a federal bailout by senior ministers of the ruling Conservative government.

It was over. Nortel stock went to 11 cents, and its key assets were eventually sold to communications giant Ericsson for little more than $1 billion. Briefly, it was controversial—the entrails of a Canadian titan ending up in Sweden.

How to avoid being investor roadkill

What does this tale tell us? Obviously, that fortunes can be made and lost in the market. Those who bought Nortel on the way up, and sold near the top pocketed an astonishing capital gain. Those who bought early and sold when John Roth's words rang hollow, ended up—if they were lucky—with most of their cash back. Those who bought at the top, or when some Bay Street brokerages were still touting the stock in 2001, were decimated. And tens of thousands of employees not only lost their jobs, but also saw much of their pensions erased when Canada's greatest technology success bit the dust in the darkest hours of the worst market since the 1930s.

How could you, as a retail investor, have avoided this?

In many ways. You could have done as I did, and relied on a professional portfolio manager. In June of 1999 I cut a cheque, and with it turned over everything I had to invest, to be put into a discretionary trading account. In doing so, I hired a smart guy who had taken me months of research and interviews to find. As I gave him authority to manage my money as he saw fit, without the need to discuss investment decisions in advance, I asked him about Nortel, then at its apex. "This will not end well," he said. We never discussed it again.

Or, you can arm yourself with the knowledge and tools necessary to chart your own path. Forget the media, Bay Street hypesters, the stock-pumpers, the breathless talking heads on BNN or CNBC, the mutual fund salesguys or financial columnists who actually believe corporate press releases. Instead, you can do your own research. Arrive at an independent conclusion. Make your own decisions. Know enough to know what to ask.

If you want to be in control, there are things you need to know. Like how to tell when others around you are delusional, blinded by fear or greed. One good way to do that is by using technical analysis.

Why history always repeats

Market analysts employ an array of tools, and they all have some value. Like fundamental analysis, which looks at where the economy's headed (expansion, peak, contraction or recessionary trough), what impact this has on various industries (like the car business, which is highly cyclical and crunched in hard times), and individual companies (like Ford, which had better products and management than GM or Chrysler). The idea is to pick stocks that will outperform the market, whether it's rising or falling, and based on where we're headed. For example, cyclical stocks (such as car companies and oil producers) tend to outperform in good times, and tank in bad, while defensive stocks (like banks and utilities) offer less growth but more stability. More on this a bit later.

Technical analysts, on the other hand, couldn't care less what the economy will bring, if Ford has a car than can run on spit, or if John Roth told Wall Streeters exactly what they wanted to hear. Instead, the only thing that matters is how a stock has done on the market, based on the belief that people never change.

In other words, technical analysis is measuring how much fear or greed's in the air. This is done in part by studying price changes, trading volumes and the amount of time it takes for patterns and trends to appear. Based on that, there are three assumptions made:

1. history repeats,
2. trends persist and
3. markets move based on known facts. In other words, there's no point worrying about information that can't be known, since market action itself tells you all you need to know.

There's another crucial assumption: one thing never changes about the stock market—people always think the same way. This yields a few more conclusions. When a trend shows up in a stock (or a market as a whole), it's there for a reason, and will probably persist. So, until it reaches an extreme point, smart investors should just follow until technical analysis clearly shows that extreme moment has been reached (like Nortel at more than $120 a share). The extremes always have one of two things in common—fear or greed. For example, markets reached maximum despair and capitulation in the winter of 2009 when the media was full of stories about a new depression and a collapse of the financial system. Conversely, they were euphoric and greed-bound in 1929 (just prior to the sell-off that October) and in 1999 (when dot-com mania swept NT into unchartered territory).

Technical analysis says investors should not argue with a stock price or try to hedge against future movements, because it's doing so for a reason. If more people want to buy than sell, the stock will rise and keep on rising, until investor psychology changes. And when it does, that will show up on the analysts' charts or in their moving averages. The key to winning, then, is to anticipate the herd.

How to tell when a bull will be a bear

How do you know when a bull trend is about to turn into a bear? When your profits will morph uncontrollably into losses? Could there have been any clear warning signs Nortel was going to implode in a tsunami of sell orders? If so, why did so few people see them?

Technical analysis says there are always levels of resistance, above which buyers won't enter the market because they think a stock costs too much, and levels of support where investors think a stock is so cheap they must buy. By plotting prices and volumes, they seek to identify these points and therefore trace investor sentiment. If a stock price breaks out of an identified trend—and smashes above or below one of these markers, then that signals a new phase that can be either bullish or bearish. In other words, that's the moment a buy or sell decision should be made. A psychological barrier has been shattered—perhaps like the evening referenced above when Nortel issued a profit warning. Despite the assurances of the market pros, investor greed had been shattered. It was all over. Zip. Get out.

How can you know this? Actually, the answer is there in front of you, online and for free, every single day. Just go to a media site like the *Globe and Mail*, or to any one of a host of discount brokerage sites and access their stock charts. Then look for patterns that signal the winds are about to change.

There are two special formations to be on the lookout for, both called 'head and shoulders' (see Figure 2-1). A bearish head and shoulders forms at the top of a market, while a reversal or inverted head and shoulders indicates a market bottom. The key is to look for a stock that breaks out of this pattern, because history tells us that three times out of four, it will form a new trend which is likely unstoppable.

Fig 2-1 *Head and shoulders formation*

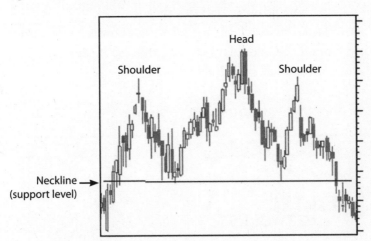

A head and shoulders formation indicating downward momentum as investors push a stock price below its previous level of support.

This is not a happy chart. Figure 2-1 shows a stock that's risen in price (left shoulder), dropped back to a support level, jumped to a new high-water mark (head) before falling again to the point when it looks cheap, then retested its high (right shoulder) before breaking below the neckline. The greater the volume of trading on the right shoulder, the more momentum the downward move becomes. This signals a fundamental shift in investor sentiment, because at the neckline, most people no longer think the stock is as cheap as it's going to get—which means they're right.

The same pattern in reverse tells an opposite tale, when a falling stock hits a support point (as cheap as it's going to get—the new neckline), jumps up to a point of resistance, falls again to that same bottom level, then rises again, this time right through the resistance point. This tells you that investors have suddenly decided this company has reached a point where it's too much of a bargain to ignore. Sentiment changes, buyers move in, and the momentum turns decidedly bullish. The greater the trading volume, the more advance that lies ahead.

Now, back to Nortel. Figure 2-2 shows how the stock price looked from its halcyon days of the 1990s, to its apex in 2000, and then into the sewer in 2009.

Fig 2-2 *Nortel Network's stock price history*

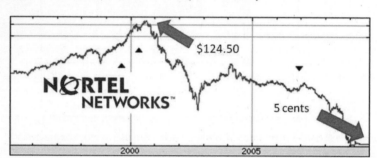

This is the stock's journey from high-tech darling and growth company, to market-dominating behemoth, to wealth-buster and finally near-worthlessness. Millions of investors eventually lost billions of dollars because they bought at the wrong time or, more importantly, failed to bail when the writing was on the wall.

Smart investors might well have avoided that mistake, using technical analysis. In fact, their chances of reaping profits and leaving the losses for others could have been greatly enhanced, this theory says, by looking at the chart in Figure 2-2, taking out their pencils and drawing a few lines.

All that matters: what investors think

As I mentioned earlier, to a technical analyst it actually didn't matter what John Roth said, whether high-tech stocks in general had become overvalued, or what impact Nine Eleven would have on the North American economy. All that mattered was what investors thought—the people whose dollars were driving the stock price. If they were bullish, NT shares would rocket higher, ·but if sentiment became overwhelmingly negative as reflected in telling patterns forming on the chart in Figure 2-2, then the moment of retreat had clearly arrived.

Of course, this 14-year graph contains a huge amount of information, but I would say investors were given three clear warnings it was all going to end very, very badly. The first came in 2000 when Nortel shares bounced off their all-time high, and again in early 2004 and 2007 when the chart indicated two more exit points before the lights were set to go out. All three have classic head-and-shoulders formations.

Fig 2-3 *Nortel Networks, head-and-shoulders formations*

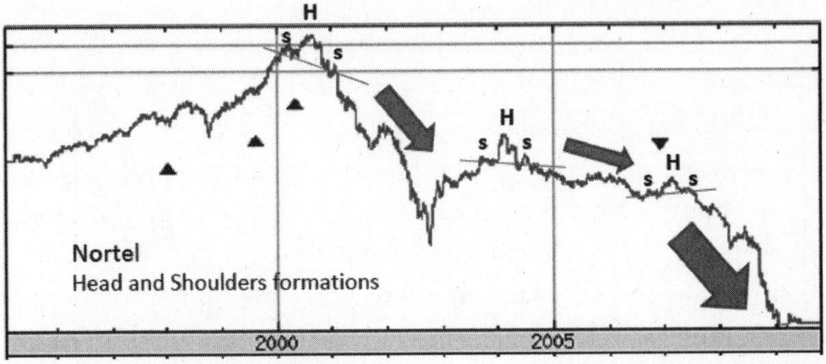

Three distinct head and shoulders formations could have given astute investors three chances to flee this sinking ship.

You can see that in the simple chart in Figure 2-3. Once Nortel shares hit the top after a more or less straight run up for more than five years, then fell to test a support level (right shoulder) established by a previous dip (left shoulder), and plunged right through, it was time to bail. But in case you missed that, a second opportunity to sell came twice more over the next few years, before all hope was lost.

All this chart says is this: Let the market do the talking. It alone will give you the best hints as to what's coming next, based on the simple belief that investors move in herds, and it's investor sentiment—more than corporate profits, interest rate changes or acts of terrorism—that dictates market action. And because humans never change, technical analysts believe there are repeating patterns (like the head-and-shoulders) that form the guide to the future. So, technical analysts look at just the supply and demand for a stock (which is reflected in the price and the volume of shares traded) while fundamental analysts (more on this below) try to determine what causes the price movements themselves.

Fig 2-4 *Moving average*

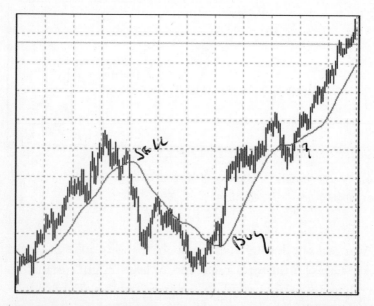

A moving average smooths out stock price movement, helping to indicate buy and sell points.

Here is a second tool of technical analysis, also simple to use, and which has proven to be uncannily effective in determining the best moment to jump into, or out of, a stock. It's called moving averages. Think of this as a stock market smoothie—a chart that takes highs and lows recorded on a daily basis, smoothes out the jagged profile, and gives you a more balanced view of where this baby is headed. Moving averages are used as a supplement to the kind of chart analysis I have just described, to identify trends and provide warning signals.

The moving average is arrived at by adding up the closing prices of a stock over a certain period of time (the most common is 200 days, or 40 trading weeks), then dividing the total by the number of days. This measure of stock movement is used extensively and, once again, you can plug into the data free of charge on any one of scores of web sites. Figure 2-4 shows what it looks like.

You can see that all the 200-day moving average line does is reduce the daily highs and lows of this stock and gives us a more balanced view. Clearly this particular company is on the upswing, but how would an investor know when to jump in for maximum gains (there are obviously two legs higher), and when to bail out, taking profits before the stock price took a dive? (You can see the months-long crash in the middle of this chart.)

A graphic signal when to buy or sell

Technical analysis says that the moving average will answer these questions (at least most of the time). Here are the rules.

- When the stock price (on a daily basis) is trading above the moving average line, hang on to it.
- When the stock price dives through the moving average line from above, then it has clearly broken the trend previously established, and it's time to bail.

- When the stock price then stays below the moving average line, it's a good idea to stay out.
- But when the daily stock price punches through the moving averages line from below, it's a buy signal, since chances are a new trend is in the process of being established.

Okay, let's go back to Nortel, and see if we can spot the buy/sell signals indicated by moving averages. In this case (Figure 2-5) we'll use three averages—short (50-day), medium (100-day), and long (200-day). Here is how NT shares looked over a two-year period after the big dump of 2001.

Fig 2-5 *Nortel Networks, moving averages*

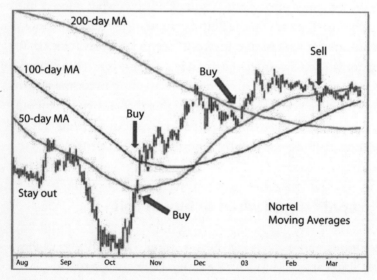

When a moving average line intersects the price line, a buy or sell event may well be signalled.

You can see on the left that the stock was trading far below its three moving averages—a clear signal that you shouldn't have had anything to do with it. Then in mid-October, it punched up through the short-term moving average, which in technical analysis is a clear buy signal. A week or two later that trend was confirmed when the stock rose up through the medium-term, 100-day moving average. Then in mid-February the short-term moving average indicated it was time to sell, which was confirmed by the medium-term average on the extreme right of the chart towards the end of March. Longer-term investors would have been more cautious, waiting until the 200-day line was breached in December, and hanging on for a longer ride.

The information investors need to survive

This is the kind of information active traders need to survive. In the case of this company, following the instructions of the short-term moving average, you would have been an NT owner for about five months, and pocketed a respectable profit while avoiding the corporate misery to come. If this kind of analysis turns you on, the next step is to learn about oscillators, which are indicators giving a road map based on the relationship between two moving averages. The most common is the MACD (moving average convergence-divergence), which measures the difference between two short-term moving averages and then provides a signal line. This is useful as an early warning that a market may be losing momentum, as investors start to have serious second thoughts about a stock. If you know what they're thinking before they do, you win.

A final word on technical analysis: listen to what the barber tells you, or the taxi driver, or the guy in the next cubicle at work, or the parents at a kid's neighbourhood birthday party, or just turn on BNN for a couple of hours. This is the theory that whatever most people believe is probably garbage. If you bet against them, in the vast majority of cases, you'll win.

Of course, this was true in the instance of Nortel—in fact with most of the profitless, high-flying dot.com stocks at the same time which had unbelievable P/E ratios (stock prices in relation to corporate earnings), paid no dividends, had little if any track record, and were pure glamour stocks. When everybody wanted them, and were willing to pay ever-higher prices, the things were clearly about to crash and burn.

The same has been true for almost every asset people covet. I remember in the late 1970s when investors in Toronto lined up for two blocks down Yonge Street to get into a trust company office to buy gold bullion at around $1,000 (Cdn) an ounce. The metal had shot higher (along with silver) and was trading at its historic apex. There was little fundamental reason for this, other than a bout of inflation at the time, but the technical reason was clear: demand exceeded supply. In a few months, gold cratered. In fact, it stayed under the $1,000 mark for the next two decades, before rising again in the midst of the financial crisis of 2009. Investors who missed the signal were left with big capital losses and expensive doorstops.

The herd gets it absolutely wrong

The same's held true with real estate, also prone to excessive boom-and-bust cycles. In late 2009, housing prices across Canada soared by more than 20% and in Toronto and Vancouver by up to 40%—an extraordinary phenomenon during a time of deep recession and unemployment touching 1.5 million people. The bubble was fuelled by record low mortgage rates and lax lending standards, of course, but the real lubricant was investor sentiment. Just as people surged into Nortel stock at its most expensive, or gold when it became extraordinarily priced, so buyers flew into bidding wars for houses at the highest values in history, believing if they didn't buy then, they'd be priced out forever.

I have no doubt, as this book spells out, that the herd will once again be wrong. And contrarians proven right.

In fact, contrarianism is a key part of technical analysis. It suggests you buy when others sell, and that you flee when public sentiment is totally in favour of gorging on the latest asset, whether it's stock in Research in Motion or bungalows in North Vancouver. So, pay attention to bullish and bearish indicators— you can find those on the web with a simple Google search. In general, when a majority of people expect prices to rise, then we're usually at the peak of a boom period for a stock or the market in general. One theory says when three-quarters of investors are bullish, the market is overbought and ready for a correction. Conversely, when only a quarter of people think it's a good time to invest, we're likely close to the point of capitulation when there's no place to go but up.

The most recent example of that came in the dark hours of February and March 2009, in the aftermath of the collapse of Lehman Brothers, Bear Stearns, the US mortgage giants Fannie and Freddie, the implosion of AIG, massive corporate layoffs, the looming bankruptcy of the car companies and daily stock market carnage. Just when the Dow and the TSX had lost half their value and it looked like the financial system was close to collapse, Canadians decided to barrage their investment advisors and the banks in a torrent of mutual fund selling. In doing so, millions of people locked in billions worth of losses, sold at the worst possible moment, and made the decision to get out of the market. In doing so, they displayed the same behaviour in reverse as couples bidding $930,000 for the average detached home in Vancouver just months before the heady 2010 Olympics. Both were being irrational, emotional losers.

The contrarians watched. Waited. Then moved.

Never argue with the fundamentals

When the tech bubble collapsed, the economy slid into a recession. In March of 2000, pumped up by dot-coms, the NASDAQ was at 4,572. By September of 2002, it languished at 1,172— having lost a stunning 75% of its value. Even by the end of 2009, the technology-laden index, home to titans Apple and Google and Microsoft, was mired at the 2,000 mark. This was one of the greatest bubble bursts of modern times, wiping out the accounts of a whole new army of day-trading warriors.

But how could the bellweather index of technology companies crumble like that when obviously every day society gets more wired, more hooked on online applications, and utterly dependent on the innovations and products these firms provide?

Did the stock plop then cause the economy to tank, or was it the other way around? And how about the crumble of the Dow, the TSX and virtually all major markets around the world in the meltdown of 2008-9? With the DJIA shedding hundreds of points a day, and companies like Caterpillar laying off 20,000 workers in a single media release, were the financial losses because of deteriorating economic factors, or had the world moved to a point where stock markets dictate whether people have jobs and families have secure futures?

In reality, North America was entering a recession in 2000 (see Figure 2-6), after several years of rampant growth, market advances and then rising interest rates. Investors who were suddenly used to fat gains with little thought plowed obscene amounts of money into unproven Internet companies with a zero track record of earnings, at precisely the wrong moment. The economy was contracting anyway, but the combined actions of so many profit-obsessed investors made it all happen with more swiftness and pain. Had people stood back and looked at the rising cost of money, inflationary pressures, corporate earnings and a business cycle that was long in the tooth, they might have acted differently, sparing themselves biblical losses.

Fig 2-6 *NASDAQ, 1999–2009*

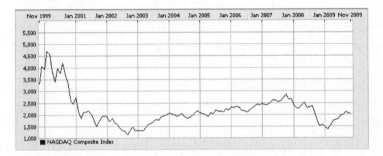

The technology-heavy NASDAQ lost 75% of its value, and never recovered

Likewise, when the world fell off a cliff in late 2008, should it have been such a shock to the media and the minister of finance? Hardly. Six months earlier I wrote a book on the looming threats to Canadian real estate that spelled out a host of perils— almost all of which were already starkly evident in America. Interest rates had been rising, consumer credit was off the chart, government deficits were increasing, stock markets were at the peak of their cycle and another massive asset bubble had been created. This time it was not the work of 21-year-old dot-com CEOs and their new Vipers, but average families who'd pushed real estate values into the stratosphere. Rapacious investment bankers and sloppy politicians just finished it all off by selling bum mortgages as triple-A investments, and allowing lending standards to slip at precisely the wrong moment.

Once again, had investors and homeowners backed up and looked at the big picture, they might have seen how fragile and over-extended the world was. As in 2000, we were massively prone to shock. In three words, the fundamentals sucked.

So, where are we now?

An economy now prone to shock

That's what fundamental analysis tries to answer, and it's worth paying attention to. Technical analysis tells us what markets are doing and how individual securities are being affected, giving important clues as to what comes next, based on the actions of emotional investors. Fundamental analysis tells us why. You need both.

This is simply a top-down approach, looking at the context in which you're investing your money. Instead of focussing first on an individual company or stock (like Bank of Montreal) or even an industry (banking) or a sector (financial services), it's key to check out what's going on with the whole economy. That way you might know better what lies ahead—recovery or recession, inflation or deflation, cheap money or escalating interest charges. Sounds daunting, but not so if you know what to look for. The media's full of this stuff daily—stories on leading indicators, monthly inflation, interest rates and government legislation.

There are three main elements to track.

1. Fiscal Policy
2. Monetary Policy
3. The Business Cycle

1. Fiscal policy

What the federal government does affects us all, sometimes deeply. For example, on Halloween 2006, the finance minister lowered the boom on income trusts—wildly popular investment assets that paid a regular stream of income from businesses that had turned themselves from corporations into trusts. By doing so they passed on their earnings, and their tax bill, to those people who bought units—something Ottawa alleged cut into its revenues. So, at a stroke, these entities were nailed with a looming tax which affected the valuations of all trusts. Investors collectively lost tens of billions of dollars, and howled in protest.

That's fiscal policy at work. This is why you should pay heed to federal budgets, which almost always contain some kind of tax changes. A good example of that is the Tax-Free Savings Account, the centrepiece of the 2008 Budget, and in existence since the beginning of 2009. This was introduced as a way of encouraging Canadians to save money, since the maximum $5,000 annual contribution can be invested and the growth on that money sheltered from tax. But since interest rates were plunging at the time, relatively few people felt the TFSA and the meagre returns on savings were worth the effort.

Big mistake. Smart (and usually wealthy) investors quickly figured out that if they dumped assets into TFSAs, such as stocks, bonds, mutual funds or derivatives, they could fully escape capital gains or any other form of taxation. They even figured out how to profitably over-contribute, and also that if you took tax-free growth from a TFSA and stuck it in an RRSP, the government would send you back a cheque for half the deposit, tax free, which could be plopped back in the TFSA. Yeah, money for nothing. (More on TFSA, and how to play this thing, in the chapter on tax strategies.)

Fiscal policy's other big impact is government spending. Obviously this is now a key determinant of where we're all headed. As you know, governments around the world, Canada included, have ratcheted spending to an all-time high in a desperate attempt to turn back deflationary pressures and replace them with the devil we know better, inflation. The result in Canada by the time of the first federal budget in 2010 was the biggest annual deficit ever—approaching $60 billion.

This is classic Keynesian economics—named after famous Depression-era economist John Maynard Keynes. The logic is simple: governments should spend big time when economies falter to stimulate activity and help people out, especially the newly-unemployed, then cut back during boom times to quell inflationary pressures and investing excess. Spending is often combined with tax policy to achieve the goal faster. That happened during the crash of 2008-9, when Ottawa brought in the home renovation tax credit along with infrastructure grants, and the Obama Administration flooded the country with bailout money including paying people $4,500 to buy new cars (the 'cash for clunkers' program) and doling out $8,000 tax breaks to first-time homebuyers (later extended to existing homeowners through $6,500 credits).

But spending's a big problem when governments don't have the money. So, they borrow it, almost always in the bond market, where a flood of new issues creates more competition for capital and ultimately results in higher mortgage rates. In fact we're consequently awash in debt. While consumer indebtedness in Canada has reached its highest level ever (family debt equalled 140% of disposable income in 2009), we're now setting records for public debt as well. As mentioned, the annual budget shortfall (called the deficit) in Canada reached its highest point on record in 2009, and we're likely to stay in the red until at least 2015. According to the Parliamentary Budget Officer, Canada's national debt is on its way to $620 billion, up 35% from 2008. In the States, government financing is a nightmare, with a $1.4 trillion deficit in 2009, and the projection of trillion-dollar shortfalls for the next decade.

So what?

More tax, less spending, and stagnant growth

It means this aspect of fiscal policy will be a huge drag on the investment environment to come, and one reason it looks like we're entering into a protracted time of range-bound markets— where picking individual securities (rather than buying an index fund or an ETF that mirrors the market) will be key to staying on the road. Here are a few things that debt-bloated public finances mean.

- **No new tax cuts.** Forget about any more reductions in the GST, decreases in personal exemptions, a chop in any one of our four income tax brackets, a capital gains tax holiday or a further slice in corporate taxes. The recession of 2008-9 and the after effects have been devastating for government finances. In Ontario, for example, corporate tax revenues plunged by 50% in 2009, leading the country's richest province into a staggering $24 billion deficit. There will be no more tax breaks for a long, long time. In fact, just the opposite.

- **Higher consumption taxes.** Despite the protestations from politicians, it seems an increase in consumption taxes, like the GST, is inevitable. This will happen when it becomes clear the economy can't grow fast enough to goose government revenues and solve the slide into unacceptable levels of debt. Ottawa would move to hike the GST before it considers boosting income taxes, since taxing income instead of spending only makes family finances worse, robs disposable income and torpedoes an economy that is 60% dependent on consumer spending. In fact, it's already happening. The introduction of the HST—the 'harmonization' of the GST with provincial sales taxes—in both Ontario and BC in 2010 gives a taste of taxes to come. This move broadens the tax base, adds up to 7% to the cost of many things most people buy, slaps a hefty new levy on services like real estate commissions, fixing your plumbing or preparing your taxes, and makes real estate considerably less affordable. All this may help government coffers, but not bank accounts on Main Street.

- **Less spending.** It's the flip side tomorrow of excessive government largesse today. Ottawa and Washington, the provinces and the states have no room for more programs and will struggle mightily to maintain the ones most people take for granted. In the next five years at least, it could be impossible to sustain health care, public pensions and education spending (the priorities). Many programs, grants and incentives currently in place for small businesses, the self-employed, for example, will disappear. As the economy inches ahead from its recessionary lows, government stimulus will be shed, leaving a zero net effect. Just look at the pain California has gone through.

- **Higher rates.** This is a certainty. Interest rates were sliced to the bone by the Bank of Canada and the US Federal Reserve in 2008 when it looked like we were all going to live through a rerun of *The Grapes of Wrath*. By taking the overnight lending rate to 0.25%, our central bank brought out its nuclear weapon. But in making borrowed money so cheap (mortgages were available for as little as 1.5% in 2009), the bank rate fuelled an orgy of loans which led to the formation of a new housing bubble. Besides, it's a tad bizarre to believe a new wave of borrowing can restore an economy that tanked in part because of excessive consumer debt. In any case, there's now only one direction for rates to travel in, thanks to government spending and the impact that will have in the bond market for years. (More on rates below.)

■ **Lower corporate earnings.** And how could it be otherwise? Higher taxes on families will lead to less disposable income, lower spending and fewer sales for companies in key sectors. Increased interest rates hike the cost of corporate borrowings—bank loans, lines of credit, debentures and bonds—which comes right off the bottom line. Lower government spending removes an artificial stimulus from the economy—but a stimulus nonetheless. Interest-rate sectors like banking will be impacted. The equity market as a whole will likely move sideways, bolstered more by rising commodity prices than anything else.

■ **Inflation without growth.** That's also known as 'stagflation' and it seems ready to revisit. The last bout we had was in the 1970s when rapidly rising energy prices (remember the way OPEC grabbed us by the shorts?) led to higher living costs, but at the same time low economic growth. The stock market flopped around like a dying fish for several years, ending 1975 almost exactly where it started in 1970. That could be the model for the half-decade to come which, as I mentioned, is known as a range-bound market. This is why those investors loading up on 'passive' investments like ETF could be very unhappy people by 2015.

2. Monetary policy

Why the Bank of Canada flipped out

Wisdom has it that just two factors account for between 80% and 90% of all market action—corporate earnings, and interest rates. And rates have a huge impact on earnings, which makes this the single most important thing to keep your eye on. Needless to say, we've just lived through one of the most unusual periods in history for the cost of money. It's doubtful your children or grandchildren will see this repeated. Remember these days.

While the federal government sets fiscal policy (taxes, spending), monetary policy is left to the Bank of Canada, which is supposed to operate at a safe distance from elected politicians, and is run by a Governor (appointed by politicians, of course). The central bank doesn't make consumer loans or mortgages or take deposits, but it sure affects those which do. It regulates how much money is in circulation, oversees the creation of money, tries to ensure a stable and orderly path for the Canadian dollar and sets benchmark interest rates. It does this by regulating the rate at which the big chartered banks loan each other hundreds of millions of dollars each night (to settle transactions between their customers). It's a very staid, secretive, conservative institution.

But sometimes it flips out.

That happened following the crash of 2008 (see Figure 2-7) when Governor Mark Carney (a former Goldman Sachs investment banker) followed the lead of his US counterpart Ben Bernanke, and sliced the bank rate to 0.25%. That is as low as it's possible to go, and was a staggering decrease from the 4.5% mark at the beginning of the year. In short, Carney was a radical, and did everything he could but give money away.

The imminent danger was a deflationary spiral caused by the collapse of the American housing market, which cascaded into bankruptcies on Wall Street, a global stock market dump, an immediate wave of mega-layoffs and faltering consumer confidence. By dropping the cost of money, central banks aimed first at flooding the financial system with boodles of cash to prevent banks from seizing up and second to stimulate an economic rebound through new consumer borrowing and spending. A decade of over-borrowing and spending had created over-valuations of both stocks and assets like oil (it peaked near $150 a barrel in the summer of 2008) and real estate. Banks, especially in the US, had rolled the dice with subprime mortgages with several becoming seriously over-extended. By raising interest rates in 2005 and 2006, governments tried to cool off the party, but it was too late. So once it all hit the fan, the US Fed and the Bank of Canada quickly reversed themselves and went into crisis mode, slashing the cost of money.

Fig 2-7 *Bank of Canada and US Fed key rates*

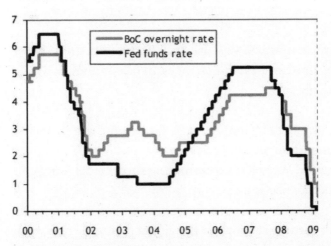

After jacking up lending rates in the boom years of 2005–8, central banks in the US and Canada dropped them to almost nothing in 2009 to stave off the threat of a new depression. The result in Canada was a borrowing orgy and a real estate bubble.

This is monetary policy at its most extreme, and it's easy to see the impact it had on stock markets and prescient investors (see Figure 2-8).

Fig 2-8 *Boom and bust on Bay Street*

| Nov 2004 | Jan 2006 | Jan 2007 | Jan 2008 | Jan 2009 | Nov 2009 |

16,000
15,000
14,000
13,000
12,000
11,000
10,000
9,000
8,000

S&P TSX

Investor Euphoria

Bust Rates fall to all-time low

Boom Rates rise to cool economy

Investor Despair

Rebound

■ S&P/TSX Composite index (Official)

Emotions at work: Investors bounce from euphoria to despair, almost always buying and selling at the worst moments.

Remember: up to 90% of market action results from corporate earnings and interest rate changes. In fact here are two rules worth remembering.

- The number 1 determinant of the future price of bonds is interest rates.
- The number 1 factor determining future stock prices is corporate profits.

So after the initial shock of the global financial crisis, with the stock market having lost a stunning 5,800 points, or 40% of its value, the moment of greatest investor despair was reached. It was then that Canadians stampeded to bail out of mutual funds, dropping fund sales to the lowest level in five years—precisely at the moment when they would maximize their losses.

And that brings us back to contrarian investing—when most people are convinced one thing will happen, and there are analytical reasons to think they're wrong, they usually are.

In this case the drop in the price of money, in a concerted and coordinated move by central banks around the world, was enough to convince smart and courageous investors the bottom had been reached. So, those who started piling back in during March or April of 2009 had a massive profit on their hands by Christmas. Concurrently, oil and gold jumped in value as the price of money fell, reacting to a signal from Bernanke, Carney and other central bankers that they would pull out every stop to bring back the good old days of inflation. That was bullish news for corporations whose borrowing costs plunged to all-time lows. It was also powerful news for the bond market, since the tumble in rates made existing bonds more valuable, pounding their prices higher—and giving a pleasing capital gain to investors.

How a near depression turned into a bubble

So, monetary policy affects both interest rates and company profits. In turn that moves stock and bond markets. It has the ability to turn a consumer funk into heaps of new mortgage, credit card and line-of-credit debt. In the events of the crash of 2008–09, it and government spending were the two tools used to ensure that a mother of a recession did not turn into the son of the Great Depression. And while unemployment languished, Canada developed a rate-induced housing bubble, and the loonie jumped too much too fast, the overall goal was accomplished. Most importantly for the purposes of this book, if you saw what the Bank of Canada was doing, and understood the consequences, then you knew how to invest. That's why in the winter of 2009, near the ebb of investor confidence, I told my blog following that equities would lead the economic recovery by a factor of months. And that's precisely what happened.

So, what's next? If you knew that, you'd obviously have a head start on people who just aren't paying attention, which is most of them.

After hitting 0.25%, interest rates in Canada had but one direction in which to travel. As economic recovery took hold, and in the wake of massive stimulus spending by countries around the world, inflationary pressures were destined to return, forcing central bankers to dampen borrowing and price hikes with rate increases. At the same time, governments drowning in debt were flooding the bond market with new financings, and the ensuing competition for money drove interest rates higher. Then there was that irrational real estate bubble that ballooned after mortgages at 2% and 3% sparked bidding wars in Toronto and Vancouver. Governor Carney started to fret over that about the time somebody paid $999,000 for an unrenovated, frame, one-bedroom cottage in North Vancouver, and a broken-down bungalow in east-end Toronto attracted 21 offers and sold for 142% over the asking price.

It's a safe bet to believe interest rates will be travelling higher for several years to come. How fast or slow the escalation ends up being depends on a bunch of things it's hard to know—like whether or not the US dollar will recover, or in fact continue the path of decline it's been on for years. Carney and his political masters are also quite aware a rapid jump in mortgage rates has the potential to do to Canadian real estate what the subprime mortgage bust did in the States, crashing home prices and dousing consumer confidence. Finally, the last thing a federal government with $50 billion in new bonds to float wants is radically higher interest rates on its debt.

Why to expect interest rates will triple

A rational investor would therefore conclude the prime rate, which hit an historic low of 2.25% in 2009, will probably double within two years, and triple within five—to between 6% and 7% by 2015, all things being equal. You'd also conclude the economic recovery taking hold would be accompanied by a serious drop in the jobless ranks by the middle of this period.

Here's what that means.

- An increase in mortgage rates of up to 4% by the time a lot of 2009 buyers come to renew their home loans in 2014. Ouch. This is why residential real estate has a lousy immediate future.
- A big drop in bond prices as yields shoot higher. Fixed-income investors will demand a higher rate of return, and as governments barrage the bond market with new issues, existing bonds become less attractive. This means a capital loss for people holding bonds, especially long-term securities.
- Upward pressure on the Canadian dollar, since higher rates and increased commodity prices (especially oil) attract capital here, pushing up the currency. Not good news, of course, for an exporting nation, so expect more grief in the manufacturing and tourism sectors.
- Still, a gentle uptrend in rates, while the economy regains ground, is about the best that equity investors can expect. Higher bond yields pose more competition for stocks, but that should be more than outweighed by an expected jump in corporate earnings.
- Inflation is a wild card. Some people believe trillions in new government spending and debt, principally in the US, will result in a form of hyper-inflation reminiscent of pre-war Germany. Many of them think gold will rise as an alternate form of wealth as the greenback is destroyed by Washington's printing presses. But I think that is massively unlikely.

The crash of 2008–9 took North Americans to the brink of deflation. In fact, for months during 2009, Canadian consumer prices were negative, while the economy was contracting and unemployment rising. The jobless rate in the US passed 10% in late 2009 for the first time in two decades, while the effective unemployment rate (including discouraged workers) touched 17%, within striking distance of Depression-era levels.

So, hyper-inflation is not a likely scenario within five years of that experience. Instead, investors should expect central banks to keep the cost of living within a fairly narrow band, possibly 2% to 4%. Again, this is good news for investors and for markets.

Higher inflation breeds rising interest rates, increased costs for corporations and lower earnings. Inflation gooses inventory and raw material costs, leads to wage and salary demands and, in turn, higher consumer prices and lower sales. That all means less profitability and depressed equity markets—and it is something central banks do not want to happen in normal times, and certainly not within a few years of near economic meltdown.

So, remember there's an inverse relationship between inflation and corporate earnings. In the years ahead of relentlessly but slowing rising rates and contained inflation, of economic expansion and rising commodity prices, markets have every reason to advance.

Unlike fiscal policy, the aging Boomers, a pension crisis or a housing bust, monetary policy is about to be your friend.

3. The business cycle

Why real estate took 16 years to recover

In the late eighties I sold a commercial property at an inflated price to a hotshot entrepreneur and took back a fat mortgage at the now-obscene rate of 13%. Sadly, my genius good deal did not last when the guy came to me two years later, in the midst of a painful recession, and told me he was unable to keep up his payments.

We struck a deal. In return for my half-million-dollar mortgage, he gave me the keys to a swishy new condo on the waterfront in Toronto, bought two years earlier (at an inflated price) for about the same amount. At the time, the real estate market was moribund. Prices had fallen off a cliff after hitting an all-time high in 1989–90. Buyers were non-existent, and over-building in the condo sector during the boom years meant there was a massive glut of units, forcing their prices down even more than that of single-family dwellings. The tenants in that condo—a working couple, both of them bankers—paid the going market rate, which didn't even cover the taxes and condo fees on the unit. All the capital tied up, in other words, yielded a zero rate of return. I had to hold on to that unit for almost five years until the market revived a little, mortgage rates fell and buyers returned—to finally get my money back. At least some of it.

That's why the business cycle deserves serious respect.

In this instance, I'd sold an inflated asset at the peak of the cycle just as the Bank of Canada was desperately trying to cool things off with higher rates. It worked, since the boom was followed by a sharp contraction, leading to a recessionary trough, marked by falling prices, slumping profits and lousy stock markets (the TSE went sideways for four years, from 1989 to 1993). In fact, it took 16 years for real estate prices to retest their previous high, meaning investors who bought at the wrong moment—when values were most extreme and mortgage rates punishing—paid a heavy price for getting on the wrong side of the business cycle.

Smart investors will always pay attention to this, but most people don't. Sadly, your relatives and the people you work with tend to think that whatever the current condition is will last forever. That means in boom times of rising prices, buoyant markets and optimism, folks are willing to buy houses or mutual funds (or Nortel or Google stock) whatever the price, risk going into debt and save nothing for the future. In times of falling prices, desperate sellers, declining markets and gloom, they stay home, buy nothing but food, socks and dog chow and deepen the despair.

If not always predictable, business cycles do follow a similar pattern. If you know this, and can recognize where we are on the curve, you can avoid the traps so many fall into. Normal growth, for example, often leads to economic expansion—good times, in which consumer demand is growing, companies are producing more product to meet that demand, profits are rising, jobs being created, new ventures being formed and the stock market tracking higher. Interest rates are stable and the cost of living is predictable.

This often leads to imbalances (see Figure 2-9). For example, if consumers clamour for a new kind of vehicle (like SUVs), then surging sales can lead to humming factories, wage demands by workers and higher product prices. At the same time, buyer optimism based on a growth in family income could fuel house sales. Demand creeps past supply, and prices vault as a result.

At a certain point, this hits an extreme level—the peak of the cycle. Wage demands, higher car prices and rising real estate values have created inflationary expectations. Inflation means the value of the money in circulation falls every day, since a dollar buys less. Inflation seriously erodes the quality of life for people on fixed incomes, like pensions. It kicks the stuffing out of invested money and sideswipes the bond market. It leads to lenders demanding a higher rate of interest on the cash they put out.

Fig 2-9 *The business and investment cycle*

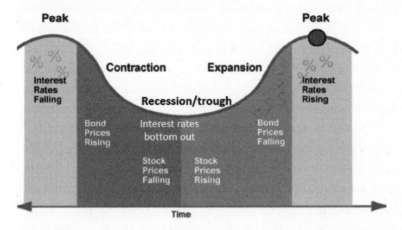

By keeping an eye on the business cycle investors can practice sector rotation, moving in and out of cyclical and defensive stocks.

At the peak, the central bank hikes its key interest rate in an attempt to cool things off, dampen demand for cars and houses and slow the inflationary momentum. Businesses start to feel the chill, sales decline, and some of those newly-hired workers are let go. Inventory begins to build up, so stores have sales. Listings outstrip buyers, so real estate values decline. Corporate profits dip so, combined with rising rates, it results in protracted stock market declines.

The economy actually shrinks, and if this period of contraction lasts long enough—six months is the normal measure—it's called a recession. The big story becomes unemployment, as companies adjust to plunging sales by trying to slice overheads. More jobless people means fewer consumers, so sales of cars and houses, sofas, beds and flat screen TVs tank. Companies recently formed may fail.

This stage, the trough of the cycle, is the moment of maximum despair (think March of 2009). The economy suffers from overcapacity and dwindling demand, so inflation dissipates. The central bank usually chops interest rates since expensive money is no longer needed to slow things down, and low rates are desirable to help stimulate new demand. As rates fall, bonds rally and soon thereafter stocks start to rise in anticipation of a recovery.

The recovery gathers slowly, held back by lagging unemployment since jobs are always thrown overboard faster than they are created. As prospects brighten consumers unleash some of their pent-up buying demand on cars and houses which are still depressed in price. Companies start to increase production to meet new demand, and interest rates may rise briefly to keep renewed inflation in check. However, slow job growth dampens wage pressures, and it looks like normal growth has been resumed.

And then it begins over again.

If that pattern looks familiar, it should. The cycle was played out when I sold my commercial building amid inflated prices and high rates (peak), when my debtor reneged on his obligation due to lousy business conditions (contraction), when real estate values hit bottom and buyers for my condo dried up (recession) and finally when rates declined, activity picked up and buyers started nosing around again (recovery). We also saw this play out dramatically in the last couple of years, with boom times and record markets (2007) turning into bust and widespread losses (2008), then despair and fear and capitulation amid low interest rates and surging layoffs (early 2009) then recovery and rebounding markets in the months that followed.

How to know what comes next

So, how can you know with some assurance where we're headed next on this eternal economic roller coaster? And then, what does a nimble investor do about it?

For most of us, all the data we need is online, current, constantly updated and mercifully free. Start with the 'leading indicators' published by Stats Canada (just Google 'Statistics Canada composite leading indicators'). This list of ten key measures of the economy is an early warning of what's coming, since the indicators are intended to give ample warning of an impending peak or trough by tracking what businesses and consumers are investing in, or spending.

The business sections of daily papers (those that are left) often will run a small story telling you if the indicators are up or down, but why not have a look for yourself? Every month Stats Can will tabulate the changes in these key areas, as seen in Figure 2-10.

Fig 2-10 *Stats Can's leading indicators*

Indicator	What it means
S&P TSX	The all-important Toronto stock market's key index of the 60 biggest companies—a daily scorecard on investor sentiment.
Money supply (M1)	The total of hard currency in circulation in our pockets, and in the bank in chequing and other accounts. More Money = More Inflation
US leading index	If the American economy slows, chances are ours will too, given the importance of exports to the US.
Durable goods orders	New factory orders for refrigerators, furniture, business equipment, indicating how busy manufacturers will be performing.
Shipments to inventory	This ratio shows the volume of finished goods being shipped from producers to end users and retailers.
Average work week	The number of hours employees are being offered on the job. The more hours, the more work being processed and the more economic activity.
Employment	In businesses and services—the number of people entering or leaving the workforce on a monthly basis.
Furniture & appliances	Sales of big-ticket household items, which is an important indicator of consumer confidence.

Retail durable goods	This tracks the sales of other items at the retail level, which also indicates whether consumers are shelling out or pulling back.
House spending	A key indicator, since real estate represents the biggest purchase of most families' lives. This index includes both housing starts (construction) as well as house sales.

So, quite a list. And each month the statisticians in Ottawa attach a number to this index, giving an overall scorecard as to whether the economy is growing or contracting. Because each of these indicators is 'leading', the whole thing is forward-looking, allowing a rational investor to plan what assets to buy or sell in order to maximize returns. It's important to also understand the business cycle and the equity cycle (or stock market) are closely related and follow almost exactly the same path—but with markets in the lead. That's because investors are always trying to anticipate changes, instead of simply reacting to them—when it is almost always too late. More than anything else, this defines the difference between investing success and heartache.

A case of driving on the wrong road

Let's say in September of 2007 you drove a Hummer (shame on you), loved the beast, and felt General Motors was on a roll with its extensive fleet of SUVs—exactly the kind of vehicles that North American drivers wanted. Besides, the economy was in great shape, despite rising gas prices and some nasty media reports of a tumble in the American real estate market. So, you bought a mess of GM stock.

Perhaps a closer look at the business cycle, and five minutes' study of the economic indicators would have shown a different story and led to a radically altered investment decision (see Figure 2-11). Peaking markets, rising money supply, rising interest rates, falling demand for housing and durable goods demand outpacing supply, just as energy prices were spiking. We can see now in our rear-view mirror, this was the worst time in living memory to be a new GM shareholder, and that economic indicators were flashing yellow as the economy hit the peak of a business cycle. Besides (as we'll see later) an analysis of the company's financial position showed a behemoth with a gargantuan amount of debt that could only be sustained with ever-increasing sales volumes.

Fig 2-11 *Running out of gas: GM stock*

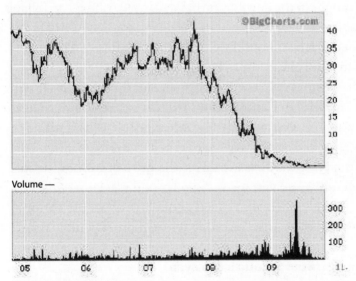

From more than $40 a share at its SUV-induced peak, General Motors stock started on a steep slide well before the economy fell off a cliff in the third quarter of 2008. Why? Because this a cyclical stock, on the wrong side of the business cycle. As it turned out, GM became a penny stock after crisis hit.

At the best of times, GM is a cyclical stock—rising faster than the market in good periods and sinking deeper in the bad—but in days of capitulation, such as the winter of 2008-9, it turned into a disaster on wheels. A Hummer-driving new investor in late 2007 would have been left with only a used truck two years later after the company filed for bankruptcy protection, was bailed out by Washington, and saw its shares battered and diluted down to penny stock status.

While the events of the past few years were unique and unprecedented (at least since the 1930s), they should not have been entirely unexpected. Investors who followed the leading indictors, who looked at how the economy and the business cycle were evolving and paid attention to technical analysis—and who talked regularly to trusted professionals—might well have avoided being caught in the downdraft that destroyed trillions of dollars in wealth.

But this is not about the past. Rather, the future. The money road stretches ahead, yet to be travelled.

The business cycle will continue, and the equity cycle will always advance it. Central banks will use interest rates to heat up or cool off economic activity. Most people will continue to react with greed or fear to what they perceive is happening. This emotional flood will vastly affect the price of houses, stocks, mutual funds and vintage Vespas. Thus, if you know where we are or, better, where we're likely going, you can use rational analysis and contrarian investing to crash-proof your wealth.

Where to invest through the cycle

Here's what I mean. Figure 2-12 represents some of the sensible choices an investor can make at key points in the cycles.

Fig 2-12 *Investment choices geared to the equity cycle*

When the economy's here...	...and the markets are here	Invest here
Trough	Early bull	Banks, financials, transportation stocks (cyclical) Sell bonds

Early recovery	Middle bull	Technology (growth companies), capital goods
Late recovery	Peak	Industrial companies, energy, short-term paper
Peak, boom times	Early bear	Defensive stocks (health care), precious metals Buy short-term bonds
Contraction	Middle bear	Utilities, long-term bonds Reduce stock exposure
Recession	Late bear/early bull	Reduce bonds Increase stocks, especially cyclical

A key point to be aware of is what kind of stocks, companies or mutual funds you're investing in.

- **Defensive companies** are often mature ones with stable earnings, a good track record and that churn out products people want and buy whatever the economy's doing (like hair spray, pet food, financial services or natural gas).
- **Cyclical companies** rise and fall along with the market and the economy as a whole, exaggerating those trends because they make things people buy when they are feeling confident (like Hummers, until they bit the dust).
- **Growth companies** are those with high earnings, low dividend payouts and a glamour element (Google, Apple, RIM), which tend to be more volatile. They have the potential to be rewarding, whatever the economy, but only if well run and well financed.

How much difference does it make what kind of companies you invest in during a business cycle? A huge amount, if history's any guide. From peak to trough and back again, the TSX swings on average by about 55%. During that swing, the return on a defensive stock might only vary by about a third, while investors in cyclical companies can get whiplash with stock values lurching by 100%. Needless to say, defensive companies outperform in times of recessions while cyclical companies lead the pack during economic recoveries and periods of sustained growth. This is exactly why it makes sense to shift your portfolio as conditions change—a technique professional portfolio managers use, called 'sector rotation.'

Of course, combined with these equity choices, you can also mix in short-, medium- or long-term bonds to take advantage of interest rate changes, with risk-free investments like T-bills (when times are really scary) and investments such as dividend funds, income trusts, royalty trusts to provide you with income, or perhaps a guaranteed lifetime return (with annuities, or universal life). Then there are GICs, principal-protected notes, ETFs and index funds, derivatives (puts, calls, futures), hedge funds and tax shelters in which to stuff them all, like RRSPs, RRIFs, TFSAs and RESPs. That alphabet soup is explained in the chapter on tax strategies.

The two things that will move all markets

In short, there's a whack of choices and almost all of them are affected in one way or another by the times in which we live, and the environment in which you invest. That's what crash-proofing means. Without a doubt, the next five years will bring a mess of challenges as we live through the aftermath of the worst crash since the thirties. Taxes, interest rates and the Boomers, for example, will all be problems you need to navigate around.

But while markets will rise and fall, sometimes with drama queen effect, and the economy will expand and contract like the breathing, living thing it is, there's one element that will never change: emotion. Overwhelmingly, greed and fear will dominate investments, spill over into the daily headlines, and cause most people to be reckless or careless.

Understand that, and you're well on the road.

Three

AGAINST THE WIND

In praise of contrary

Why most people don't even see this coming

Every fall the feds buy TV time to showcase falling leaves and landing geese in an effort to get us coveting Canada Savings Bonds (CSBs). From time to time, these have been winners, especially during the interest rate crisis of the late seventies and eighties, when investors scored double-digit returns (but when a one-year mortgage, yikes, cost 12.75%).

However, no more. In fact, the 2009 bond issue will likely go down in history as the most bizarre. The offered rate on CSBs was 0.4%—less than one half of one point. Not only was this lower than the core inflation rate (which means anybody 'investing' was losing money), but the interest these things pay is taxed as regular income. That means for somebody making a middle class salary of $70,000, roughly 40% of the return given by Ottawa is taken away again. The net yield on the 2009 CSB, given those two factors, was a decidedly unpatriotic −1.5%. No wonder the geese migrated.

Despite that, Canadians handed over almost $2 billion for CSBs. Hello? What were these people thinking?

Probably, they weren't thinking—only reacting. After all, the bottom had just fallen out of the stock market, trashing RRSPs (registered retirement savings plans), mutual funds and a sense of security. Suddenly the headlines were full of stories about exploding hedge funds, dangerous derivatives, securitized mortgage defaults and financial shysters like Bernie Madoff. As a result, cash haemorrhaged out of equity mutual funds and into money market funds and Posturepedics across the nation. People panicked, sold their investments at the moment of maximum loss, then plopped cash into CSBs, 'high-yield' savings accounts, short-term GICs (guaranteed investment certificates) or other places where it was destined to lose them more purchasing power. Some plan.

At the same time, record numbers of Canadians were following the same path so many Americans had taken after Nine Eleven. In the wake of the 2001 terrorist attacks, stock markets swooned, investors bolted, the Fed dropped interest rates to prevent a recession and mortgages suddenly became irresistibly, deliciously cheap. Investors terrified of the 'risky' equity market opted for the safety of bricks and mortar. That eventually led to catapulting home prices and a housing bubble which, when it started bursting in early 2006, morphed directly into the global financial meltdown of three years later.

In the wake of the 2008–9 market dive, this pattern was repeated in Canada. Plunging mortgage rates and an overriding aversion to risk led to record home sales across Canada, soaring real estate prices, bidding wars, little or no down payments and unprecedented levels of new debt—taken at a point in the business cycle when it was inevitable rates would rise.

So, what a combination. Savings bonds and other near-cash investments paying less than nothing. Houses selling for record amounts with extreme leverage. Investors running from perceived risk right into the open arms of real risk. Hard to imagine more passive-aggressive actions than that. Or a surer way to end up in front of a speeding bus.

Our emotion-driven, suicidal behaviour

Given what's likely to come, this is erratic, emotion-driven and financially suicidal behaviour. As I reason in the chapter on real estate, houses as assets are past their best-before date. Meanwhile interest rates, taxes and inflation will rise, creaming that goose-friendly CSB, along with many other bonds. So, obviously most investors are lurching along, reacting to events rather than anticipating them. This could be a great explanation of why three-quarters of the Boomers are not ready for a looming retirement, and their kids are SOL on that fat inheritance.

Financial planners may be as fallible as the next guy, but they've learned this: at least 90% of the returns on an investment portfolio come from asset allocation. That simply means a balance of where wealth is put. And this is why people who lack diversification often flame out. They might have all their money in 'safe' fixed-income investments like bonds, which tumble in value when interest rates jump. It could be invested in six or ten stocks that are all in related industries, and take a dive at the same point in the business cycle (that's called positive correlation). Their whole retirement plan might be in the shares of the company they work for, leaving them exposed to somebody else's management screwups. They might have dumped everything in a single 'hot' stock they heard about in an online chat room or a bar in Kelowna. Or, like most Canadians, they stick everything in their houses, and hope for the best.

Overall, we fall into two distinct groups. One, like my friend Suk, lives to find two or three killer stocks that will soar from pennies to dollars and keep on going. Suk couldn't care less what industry the companies are in, what they make, if they earn any money or who's running them. He doesn't care if they trade on a Canadian or American exchange, if they're start-ups or turn-arounds. "I am one of those people that go for quick big return in short time," he told me in one of his urgent emails, "so if you have any hot suggestions let me know now." Suk's totally willing to leverage up his investment with derivatives—using puts and calls which, I'm sure, he doesn't understand but loves to brag about—or those high-octane 2xETFs (leveraged exchange-traded funds which double stock market moves). Suk is convinced he's just a few trades away from an Audi R8 and a babe on each arm.

Then there's the other group—millions of Canadians, the vast majority, who shun risk like the latest pandemic. They'd never dream of buying a stock, know only those investment products sold in the local bank branch and don't give any thought to how the money they make is taxed. For them, there's no more powerful word than 'safe.' They have no idea they can invest to get market growth and a guarantee on their money at the same time, or that it's possible to write off their mortgage interest or have a tax-free pension. Like my parents did, they stick with two assets only: a house and interest-bearing deposits. It's a strategy that may have worked, barely, for a previous generation, but no more.

What both Suk and people like my own folks fail to understand is the nature of risk or, more importantly, how to mitigate it. Day trader Suk is a walking crash waiting to happen. His investments are narrow (high-growth and speculative stocks) and short term, with his danger magnified by the use of leverage. One month-long market plunge can wipe the guy out—and we're in a time when there will be many. The odds of him reaching his goal are hardly better than winning the lottery.

And how about the others, who think my friend's an extrem-ist? Yeah, he is. But ironically, they're just as much at risk. While interest rates will rise—compared to the past few decades we're in a low-rate, low-inflation time when traditional investments like guaranteed investment certificates, savings bonds and high-interest accounts will choke—once you deduct taxes and inflation, returns will be wholly insufficient to build the wealth we all need.

Retire on GIC investing only? Forget it.

Some people disagree. For example, Canadian author and accountant David Trahair devoted a 2009 book, *Enough Bull*, to the premise that GICs alone, combined with a pay-down-your-mortgage discipline, can net you retirement security. Unfortunately, he's wrong. As appealing as it is to think you can get by simply with owning a house and riskless bank products, it's a misleading pipe dream. If it were that simple, millions more of us would be financially secure, instead of investment-starved and freaking out.

For most, the biggest risk is not losing money in a bum investment, like Suk is destined to do. Instead it's running out of money, as a lot of the GIC-and-house gang will discover. The average Canadian now lives to be 80.4 years of age, and an increasing number of those years are in good health with an active (and costly) lifestyle. With two decades devoid of employment income, and the potential that at least a couple of years will require some expensive private medical care, a sizeable whack of invested capital is required.

How much? More than most people have.

For example, $500,000 invested at age 60 at a return of 2.5% (not taking income taxes into consideration) will give an income of $32,000 a year before it becomes zero twenty years later. That may be enough to survive on if you have no mortgage, don't travel and eat a lot of noodles, but it's hardly a goal to strive for. And for most people on their present path, even this is unattainable.

The average RRSP had a market value in 2009 of just $64,000—a mere 12% of the half-million mentioned above. Worse, every dollar coming out of an RRSP is subject to tax (unless you follow the strategies presented later in this book), which is about 40% for most retirement folks collecting CPP and even a small investment income. Even worse, only about half of us have an RRSP, while seven in ten have no corporate pension.

By the way, if that $500,000 invested at age 60 were to get a return equal to the average of the Toronto Stock Exchange (TSX) for the 25 years ending in 2008 (which included the big market meltdown), which was about 7.5%, the annual pre-tax income would be almost $50,000. That's a stunning 57% increase in annual income, for just a 5% jump in annual returns.

And what return were GICs paying, as of 2010? Well, a one-year guaranteed investment certificate equalled that savings bond return of 0.4%, while tying up your money for a long five years, resulted in a yield of 2.1%. Minus taxes and inflation, both were negative. This means $1,000 invested at the top GIC rate would give you a return on principal of just $110 after 60 months. Of that, up to $55 would be payable in tax—and the tax must be remitted each year even though the income is not received, unless sheltered in an RRSP (then the tax is payable when you withdraw funds). Likewise, $120,000 invested for five years would net an increase of $13,200, or $2,600 a year. Check out Figure 3-1 for some figures.

What this means should be clear. It's simply impossible to accumulate enough capital in interest-bearing, no-risk investments, even over decades, to fund a modern retirement lasting 20 or 25 years. Guys like accountant Trahair are as much dream merchants as my testosterone-driven friend Suk is a gambler.

Thus, my inescapable conclusion: if you want this money trip to end well, in financial security, there's no option but to invest in a way that'll give you the best possible return for the level of risk taken. Taking no risk will lead to serious risk. Taking too much risk is reckless.

Fig 3-1 *$500,000 invested and compounded at...*

$500,000 invested and compounded will yield an annual income for x years						
	Number of years					
Rate of Return	*20*	*25*	*30*	*35*	*40*	*45*
GIC 2.5%	$32,074	27,138	23,889	21,603	19,918	18,634
TSX 7.5%	$49,046	44,855	42,336	40,741	39,700	39,006

Source: TaxTips.ca, Canadian Tax and Financial Information
At a contemporary long-term GIC rate of 2.5%, a half million dollar retirement nest egg will yield an income of $32,000 for 20 years. At the average TSX return for the past two decades of 7.5%, that income grows by more than 50%. But that's only half the story. If this money is earned outside an RRSP, the GIC interest income is 100% taxable, while the capital gains from equity markets is only 50% subject to tax. Dividend income (see below) is even more lightly taxed. Obviously investors looking for absolute 'safety' have less to live on.

Fortunately, there's a solution. If you're twenty, middle-aged or cruising into retirement, no difference. Just get on the road.

Your assets, and where to put them

Once you've thought about where we are in the business cycle, where the economy's headed and what financial markets are doing, it's time to make broad choices about how to allocate your money. This is not tough. There are only three main options.

1. Cash
2. Fixed income
3. Equities

Cash

Cash may seem obvious. This includes those CSBs, GICs and high-yield savings accounts I just mentioned. Also lumped in here are treasury bills (T-bills, as they're called—short-term government securities) and bonds (preferably marketable government bonds) maturing in a year or less.

Why hold cash investments at all, when the return is pathetic?

You need cash to live on, so a supply of it is handy for expenses, especially in retirement when your income is lower. Also cash gives you the means to jump on opportunities when they come along—like the next time the stock market takes an emotional dive and shares in great companies such as the banks tumble along with it. Cash is also a necessity in this post-crash world to insulate you from short-term emergencies. For example, would you be ready for a re-run of the 2003 power outage that darkened most of eastern North America? It was a shocking two-day taste of what life would be like without debit or credit cards, functioning banks or ATMs. No cash, no gas.

How much should you have in cash assets? Just 5% of net wealth for most of us, no more than 10% for people who would never drive without their seatbelt on.

Fixed income

The second choice is fixed income. This includes bonds (government or corporate) with a maturity of longer than one year (more in the bonds chapter (Chapter 4) on how to pick them), strip bonds (bought at a discount to face value) and preferred shares (like the ones issued by all the major banks). This part of your portfolio is intended to give you income and a large measure of security. If you time things right, bonds can also provide a capital gain, since the value of bonds goes up every time interest rates go down.

Remember that marketable bonds are not the same animals as Canada Savings Bonds. With market bonds (issued by the feds, provinces, agencies like Municipal Finance Authority of BC or corporations like Telus or Suncor), you can get a wide range of risk and return. Government bonds are the safest, while corporate bonds give a better rate of interest, but with a higher risk of default. Long bonds (maturities of ten years, for example) are more volatile than short bonds because of the potential for interest rate fluctuations over many years. There are bonds that pay you in Canadian dollars, US bucks or other currencies, some of them from Canadian issuers and some foreign. And there are bonds of varying credit ratings, from AAA (Government of Canada) to BBB (corporate investment grade) to CC ('junk bonds' of distressed corporations, often paying five times the government rate of interest).

In times of rising interest rates, bonds get cheaper. You can buy a $100 face-value bond for a discount—for example, $90. The price you pay dictates the return you'll receive to maturity. For example, if you bought a $100 Government of Canada bond with a coupon rate of 6% maturing in ten years for $90, your actual yield to maturity would be 7.4%, or not far off the long-term return of the Toronto stock market. Of course if you held it to maturity, you would be 100% assured of getting your money, while enjoying an income stream. Meanwhile if interest rates fell during that ten years, the bond would become more valuable and could trade for more than $100, in which case you would have the option of selling it and pocketing a capital gain.

Preferred shares are also part of the fixed-income mix because they act a lot like bonds. Companies like the banks issue these and while they are technically stock in the company, preferreds give you a regular stream of income, move up and down in value with changing interest rates and can also yield a capital gain. Like marketable bonds, they're 100% liquid, since you can buy and sell them instantly on the stock exchange. These are more secure than common stock, and bounce around a lot less in price.

Why make 2% when you can make 6%?

There are two serious advantages to preferred shares. First, they pay big bucks, relatively speaking. At a time when GICs were yielding 0.4% to 2.1% for one-year to five-year money, this media release was sent out:

> "Royal Bank of Canada (RY on TSX and NYSE) today announced a domestic public offering of $200 million of Non-Cumulative, 5 year rate reset Preferred Shares Series AR. The bank will issue 8.0 million Preferred Shares Series AR priced at $25 per share and holders will be entitled to receive non-cumulative quarterly fixed dividend for the initial period ending February 24, 2014 in the amount of $1.5625 per share, to yield 6.25% annually."

Obviously 6.25% beats the pants off a 2% GIC, and investing in Canada's largest bank is hardly a major risk. This represents a 300% increase over the guaranteed investment return, but with a big difference: the preferred share income is actually sent to investors in a regular series of cheques, instead of accruing inside a GIC. Dividends put the cash back into cash flow.

And that brings us to the second advantage of preferred shares, which is a humungous tax break. GIC money is taxed as regular income—at the highest rate, like the salary you make through employment or interest on a bank account. In contrast, dividend income is 'grossed up' and then reduced through a sizeable tax credit. Here's how it works.

Let's say you bought 1,000 shares of RY preferred (similar to the above issue) for $20 each, with a 6.25% annual yield. That would give you a $1,250 annual return on the $20,000 investment. For tax purposes you'd gross the amount up by 45%, then claim a 19% tax credit, for a final bill to Ottawa of only $126. That's an effective tax rate of just over 10% for somebody in the middle tax bracket—and 60% less tax than you'd face on the GIC.

This is obviously a serious advantage. So serious, in fact, that if you invested only in preferred shares and had no other income, you could earn $35,000 a year before you were dinged for a single nickel in tax. So why do we have tens of billions of dollars sitting in low-return, high-tax GICs when there's such an obviously superior, low-risk investment vehicle available? Ignorance, I guess. Or maybe too many books written by accountants (who should know better).

As for how much of your wealth to put into fixed-income assets like bonds or preferreds, best determine what income you need, how much safety you want and how much tax you feel like paying. The rule of thumb is at least 15%, and for most of us probably 40%.

Equities

The last of the three major asset allocation choices is equities. This includes the common shares of publicly-traded companies, along with products that are based on (or 'derived' from) them, called derivatives—puts, calls, rights and warrants. In addition, there are mutual funds that just mimic the behaviour of stock markets, such as index funds or ETFs (exchange traded funds) like Barclay's wildly popular iShares, and you can buy both bonds and preferred shares that are convertible into common stock.

Investors don't grab equity products for income or for preservation of capital but for a very defined and essential goal: growth. That usually comes in two ways—through timing the markets, buying low and selling high (using tools like technical and fundamental analysis, described a few pages back), or investing for the long term with a buy-and-hold strategy, which has proven to be successful for the last 50 years.

You can purchase stocks on an individual basis, through mutual funds that hold a mess of them and are professionally managed (for a fee), or you can use those low-cost index or ETF funds to pace the equity market as a whole. Over the last couple of years, that would have put you on a dramatic roller-coaster, but in the period ahead of us—when markets are more likely to move sideways—index investing is probably a bad idea. As for tax, equity returns come in the form of capital gains, half of which escape tax completely. Another reason those investors who choose GICs also choose to pay more.

What stocks to invest in? Well, there are books galore to buy on that topic, but I'll give some guidelines in a few pages. The key is to try to match your investments with the larger economy, and to mine those emotions of greed and fear which leverage the market so dramatically. The four basic choices include: blue chip securities, which enjoy stable earnings in good times and bad (like TD Bank); growth stocks, which lead industries much in demand (like Google); cyclical stocks, which rise and fall more than the market as a whole (like Ford); and defensive stocks, which are less volatile than the market because the companies behind them have stable sales (like Shoppers Drug Mart).

How much wealth to put into equities as a whole—stocks, equity funds, derivatives or ETFs? Without a doubt, this should form the bulk of the investment portfolio for anybody under the age of 40. In fact, a rule of thumb that continues to have merit is to deduct your age from 100, to arrive at a percentage of equity exposure. So, if you're 60, that means 40% could be an ideal level.

But there is an important wrinkle: sex.

Women have always lived longer than guys and while the gap is narrowing lately (fewer of us are apparently dying in grizzly bear hunting, race car and skydiving accidents), women can still expect to outlive men by about six years. Ironically, gobs of studies have also shown women are more risk-averse than men, especially when it comes to saving and investing. They tend to lock in for longer mortgage rate terms (even when variable-rate loans save money) and also to choose fixed-income and the lowest-risk cash investments over growth assets.

It's a deadly combo. Especially now. In this era of relatively low rates and meagre returns on interest-bearing stuff, it's virtually impossible to amass enough capital to finance a life of 78 years, let alone 84 or 90. At the same time, the tax load on interest-yielding securities held outside an RRSP is punishing and, if I'm right, likely to become more so in the years ahead as Ottawa copes with an out-of-control debt. So women have an inherently greater need to hold funds and stocks and ETFs, which is why a female investor should deduct her age from 110 to get the desired growth component.

When it comes to asset allocation, timing matters.

Like it or not, buying five or ten stocks and sitting on them for eons is now a dubious idea. This means buy-and-hold is dead. That was the most favoured strategy in the nineties and even until fairly recently, when all investors had to do was pick a big-name equity fund, then forget about it. Some say the death knell came in the autumn 2008 meltdown when every sector of the market was sideswiped equally by our flirt with a New Depression. And I agree. The big lesson everyone should have learned then comes in one word: diversification.

We all saw stocks take a brutal (if short) drubbing, while interest rates crashed, hurting short-term cash investments but driving bond prices skyward. So, an investor who had a rational mix of the three asset classes could have weathered the storm reasonably well. And what a hurricane it was. In just a few weeks in the 2008–9 market melee, there were more days when the market moved by 5% in a single session than in the previous 60 years of trading.

One message to take away from this book is, "it's not over yet." The threats I outlined in the first chapter will come to dominate the investment choices of those who are serious about avoiding the pitfalls of rising interest rates, an inflated yet stagnant economy, government debt, higher taxes and millions of Boomers making bad and emotional decisions, ruining the housing market while they usher in history's greatest retirement crisis. This will mean drifting stock markets, rising commodity prices and the necessity of crafting a diversified portfolio stressing growth and capital preservation at the same time.

Trying to achieve security through saving is hopeless

Trying to achieve security through no-risk GICs or savings bonds will be hopeless. Jumping into a few stocks or sectors will be downright dangerous. And riding the market higher on a surge of new economic growth is a non-starter. That myth was laid to rest in a major 2009 report written by TD Bank economists Grant Bishop and Derek Burleton.

According to them, the country's growth rate will crash to just 1.6% between 2010 and 2012, and just edge up to 2.1% all the way through to 2019. This will be the result of factors I've already mentioned, namely a rapidly aging population and a massive debt overhang for both families and governments. What this means:

- less government spending, and an obvious end to the kind of stimulus programs that helped rescue us from a deflationary spiral in early 2009;
- an uncompetitive economy as we become comparatively less productive;
- a continued government debt crisis, since economic growth won't be enough to goose tax revenues and pay down deficits quickly. So, pressure to raise tax rates;
- danger for families that don't curtail their borrowing. "Households cannot continue to borrow at rates exceeding income growth and prospective asset accumulation," since this will lead to "heightened household vulnerability and credit risk;" and
- job uncertainty, as a huge debt load hangs over the US, dampening growth in the one economy we are most dependent on for exports—which accounts for more than a third of Canada's entire annual income.

Here's a chart (see Figure 3-2) showing just where the bank thinks the economy's headed over the next ten years, which raises the question of whether or not this could turn into Canada's lost decade.

Fig 3-2 *The economy on a path to stagflation?*

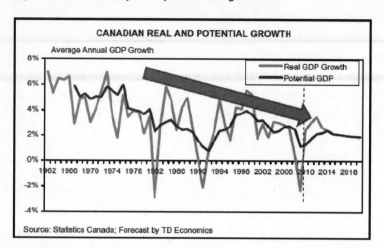

Not hard to see the trend line in terms of Canada's economy. Swings have been wild, especially after recessions in the early eighties, nineties and 2008–9, but the pace of expansion is clearly slowing and TD economists see a flat line stretching as far as 2019. Low growth, when the country's debt has mushroomed, means higher taxes, higher rates and less government spending, just as the Boomers start to cash out of real estate. This is the 'new normal' in which investors must get their asset allocation right.

This is the way to survive what is coming

The implications for people serious about investing and achieving financial security are clear.

- There's no way a real estate asset bubble will be able to withstand this onslaught of moribund growth, with little room for income increases and even moderately rising interest rates.
- As the Boomers hit an average age of 65—about 2015—the flood of house listings should be taking a serious toll on

real estate values. This will be the end of easy real estate profits for at least a generation, with the potential of turning the pride of ownership into a negative equity nightmare for legions of people who bought in 2008 or 2009.

- Barely-alive growth in the economy, an aging workforce and productivity lags will all drag on corporate profits, suggesting stock markets will be range-bound for years to come.

- As growth shifts out of Canada (and the US) and into other countries with younger workforces and less debt, smart investors will be looking to put some of their wealth there.

- Governments will clearly be unable to grow out of their deficit woes, and taxes will rise. Tax minimization and tax avoidance are therefore essential strategies.

- Commodity prices will likely rise as the twin realities of peak oil and climate change become major economic forces over the decade, as money continues to seek a better return, and the US dollar comes under pressure.

- For the first time in the lives of most Canadian investors, their standard of living may decrease, or at least stagnate, as the economy sputters, inflation returns, prices and taxes rise, but incomes do not.

- This will make it harder still to build wealth and achieve security. That's why asset allocation and finding the right portfolio mix is more critical than ever.

Does that mix include commodities, like gold?

You bet. In fact, in the wake of the 2008–9 crash, bullion took off, crashing through the $1,000 (US) an ounce barrier just as oil again neared $80 a barrel. Gold is seen by many as the ultimate defence against the waffling value of paper currencies issued by increasingly bankrupt governments, most notably the United States. Not hard to understand that. The American budget deficit in 2009 was an unprecedented $1.4 trillion under Barack Obama, and the Congressional Budget Office predicts trillion-dollar shortfalls until 2018-9, at which time the American national debt will double to $22 trillion. Obama, in fact, could add more debt in two terms as president than all other presidents combined who went before.

The fear of many is that fiat currency (money created by government at its whim) will become so debased that its intrinsic value will be diminished, if not destroyed, by government action. Indeed, there is some merit to this, since the US central bank engaged in 'quantitative easing' in the wake of the financial meltdown—creating new currency digitally that was used to buy back debt the government itself had previously issued. This added more liquidity to the system, helped the financial sector stay afloat and provided loan capital to small businesses and homeowners, but it also watered down the concept of 'money.' After all, this was cash that was never actually printed, and yet was spent by the government. It's a far cry from when governments would not dare issue a dollar that was not 'backed' by a physical asset.

So, believers in gold (and they are a rapidly growing army) are convinced Washington will take the easy way out of its debt trap, printing more and more cash, using it to skew the bond market, exporting its troubles to other countries through a purposefully devalued greenback (and cheaper exports) and, in the process, unleash inflation so intense it will rival that of pre-WWII Germany. This is behind the conviction that gold will achieve $2,000 an ounce in the coming years, and possibly soar much higher, making it the only repository of true wealth in a world awash in paper notes and the promises of politicians.

The gold rush was given a big boost in late 2009 when India bought 200 metric tonnes of bullion from the International

Monetary Fund (the largest central bank purchase in 30 years), and amid rumours China was promoting a gold-backed currency alternative to the sinking US dollar. This should remind us that Canada once had reserves of 30 million ounces, all of which was sold years ago. What backs our loonie now is a mess of US dollars and the power to tax citizens.

So, does exposure to gold make sense? Should you own some?

Why every investor should have some gold

Yes. While it's hugely unlikely Washington will allow anything approaching hyper-inflation to occur or suffer a continual erosion in the value of the dollar—still the reserve currency of the world—there's little doubt growing numbers of people think this is exactly what will happen. That brings us back to the basics of technical analysis:

- once a trend exists, it tends to persist and
- greed and fear and investor sentiment are unstoppable forces.

There was clearly so much momentum behind precious metals coming out of the collapse of 2008-9 that rational investors should expect it to continue. This alone is enough to take the metals to historic highs in the years ahead and make it attractive to Canadians, especially as another real asset—real estate—takes a drubbing for the reasons this book spells out.

But even if American fundamentals were to rebound, the Yankee dollar soar and gold be knocked back as a result, the metal remains an effective hedge against inflation as does oil, which rose from just $32 in the midst of the recent meltdown to $80 less than a year later—a staggering climb of 150% (and more proof contrarian investors are often geniuses, and sowing the seeds of the next big economic shock). If forecasts for the next half decade are half right, we should expect more inflation as Asian economies boom, the West floods financial markets with trillions in new debt and energy costs rise. Given that, there's little doubt paper money will fall in value and commodity prices jump—suggesting we'd all be wise to have gold and/or oil in our portfolio.

The real gold debate comes with the question of how to own it. Among the choices:

- physical gold—bullion (bars or wafers) and coins (like the Maple Leaf and US Eagles, increasingly purchased from ScotiaBank);
- gold mining stocks or mutual funds (the TSX is a leading global exchange for this);
- gold exchange-traded funds (some buy and store physical gold, some trade in gold contracts, some offer leverage to long or short the metal);
- derivatives (you can buy or sell future contracts with no intention of taking delivery of the underlying gold and in the process dramatically leverage your position); or
- certificates (this way investors own gold but do not physically possess it).

Given the momentum precious metals have, a reasonable option for most investors is to go with gold exchange-traded funds, which have low management fees and spare investors the hassle of trying to store and protect the physical metal. You can also easily employ leverage with an ETF offering double market returns. As for how much of a portfolio to expose to the metal, it's hard to argue with 5% as a conservative position and 15% as aggressive. It makes entire sense to combine that with an equal exposure to oil—and in a similar way.

Portfolio mix and the wealthy contrarian

Given all the options, how do you possibly put together a port-folio that will achieve the goal of financial security? There's no one-size-fits-all model, of course. Some of us want fat gains, while others value security and safety above all. People at or nearing retirement crave income, while young couples need growth (and think they need granite counter tops). And lately almost every-one's been massively diverted and thrown off track by a global real estate fetish, which is coming to an abrupt and rocky end.

In deciding what's right for you, don't lose sight of the ten rules of contrarian investing.

10 RULES OF CONTRARIAN INVESTING

1. The focus of investing is not the present, but the future. Don't be swayed by what's hot and trendy. Most investors have no idea what they're doing.

2. There's a lot to be said for contrarian investing. The majority of people notice trends long after they've started, pile in late and fail to clue in as to when the party's ending. Again, real estate provides the best recent Canadian example. Betting against the herd usually works in the long run.

3. Diversification beats the pants off buy-and-hold in the environment that we'll be in for the next decade. Sadly most people think current conditions will last indefinitely instead of being a bridge to the next phase of the cycle.

4. Therefore asset allocation is critical. Divide what you have to invest among the three main asset classes, and don't get blown off course by a hot stock tip or a market swoon. Just recall how many people missed cashing in at the top of the tech boom in 1999–2000, or who stampeded out at the bottom of the crash in 2008–9. Contrarians buy low and sell high. The rest of us buy high and sell low.

5. Never invest in anything without knowing how you're going to pay tax on the proceeds—as income, capital gains or dividends. This can seriously alter how much you get to keep. Tax-smart investing is not even on the radar of most Canadian families. If it were, everyone of them would earn every nickel of interest inside a TFSA (tax-free savings account) or an RRSP.

6. Understand where we are in terms of economic and market cycles, or at least talk to somebody who knows this stuff. Today timing is far more critical than in the past as we enter a period of slow growth and range-bound markets. Remember that history shows us the moments of maximum despair are usually those of greatest upward opportunity, while the times when society's most confident and bullish are the days to reap profits and sit on the sidelines in cash.

7. Work back from your goal in order to set investing priorities. If you need $500,000 at age 60, and you're starting from scratch 20 years earlier, then GICs and bonds won't get you there. Find an asset allocation that does. Do not obsess about what little you have, but rather how much you will achieve.

8. Make the maximum use of tax avoidance, tax deferral and tax minimization. That means tax-deductible

investment loans, a tax-deductible mortgage, RRSPs and RRIFs (registered retirement income funds), strategies using the TFSA and also registered education savings plans (RESPs). Canada actually gives its citizens a lot of chances to avoid being taxed. (See Chapter Six for these strategies.)

9. When it comes to both equities and real estate, abide by the Rule of 100. Deduct your age from 100 to get a rule of thumb for exposure. One hundred minus your age will give you the percentage of your total net worth that a house should represent. Likewise, 100 minus your age should be the minimum equity share of your investible assets (net worth less your home). Most Canadians have four-fifths of their net worth in one asset, their homes, making them undiversified and leveraging the risk they face. Houses can turn illiquid in a hurry. Just ask people in the great suburbs of Phoenix or Miami.

10. Learn and do as much as you can, but never risk your security by trying to do everything. Most investors don't even come in contact with new bond offerings, superior ETF products or dividend issues. Today fee-based advisors will design a portfolio, build it, monitor it and worry about your returns and taxes for 1% of its value. You don't need this to succeed, but it lets you get on with the rest of your life. It's a lesson far too few have learned.

Of course, take care to match your investment choices with the times. Some stocks give superior returns in a rising market while others protect you when it falls. Good portfolios try to have companies in them that are negatively correlated—in other words, which move in opposite directions, so you never have too much exposure at any one time to a big change in the economy. That means instead of having two car manufacturing stocks that move together, pair Ford off with Proctor & Gamble, which makes products people buy whether the economy is soaring or crashing. (After all, how can anyone get by without Iams, Febreze, Clairol, Fixodent or Gillette Foamy?)

Cash-type investments (money market funds, for example, plus T-bills) have provided positive and steady returns, but have shrunk to historically low levels. Over the years, stock markets have been choppy but consistently given investors the best returns, followed by bonds which almost always start to rise in value in the business/equity cycle in advance of equities. By switching money between these asset classes, within your overall portfolio, it's possible to achieve superior returns—and to reduce risk at the same time. Finding the right mix and the right time to jump is the challenge. The key is to make the move in advance of cycle changes, not after they've already happened, as most Canadians do. A great example of that, as I mentioned, was the flood of money coming out of equity mutual funds at the height of the market dive in 2008–9—exactly when contrarian investors were pouring in.

Remember: the business and equity cycles move together, with the stock market in advance. Historically, stocks have started to jump higher several months before the economy picks up. That's especially true after recessions that cause a lot of unemployment. By the same token, markets tend to sell off sooner than the market declines, since they are affected by rising interest rates and falling corporate profits—and while most investors at the peak of the business cycle are busy buying hybrids and hot tubs.

So, in general, smart market timers:

- sell long-term bonds and buy stocks when the economy tanks;

- increase equity holdings as the business cycle picks up;
- move into short-term paper during boom times and rising rates; and
- then slide into long bonds as that boom turns into contraction and possibly recession when interest rates decline.

Each part of the cycle can take months, or a few years, and along the way there are often big bear market rallies or bull market dumps, usually due to interest rate moves, changes in taxation or uncontrollable events like Nine Eleven.

How to tell if a stock's worth buying

One tool portfolio managers use to pick stocks is called the Dividend Discount Model (DDM). This gives a formula for determining how an economic cycle influences the share price of companies that have stable growth and predictable dividend payments. The idea is that a stock needs to provide enough of a rate of return to justify the risk investors take in buying it. But how do you measure that, or determine what's a reasonable price to pay for, say, a share in the Royal Bank?

The formula is simple, stating that the best price paid is equal to the stock's annual dividend, divided by the rate of return the investor demands or expects, minus the historic annual growth rate in the dividend paid. This provides a roadmap of what new investors should hand over in return for getting an expected yield. So, if an investor needed a return of 8% and wanted to buy stock in RBC, which is paying $3 a year in dividends per share and has increased that payout an average of 3% a year, what should she pay? The DDM would give an answer of $61.08 (don't worry about the math, since it's the principle that counts here). If bank shares were trading below this level, the investor has a good indication they're a buy.

It's possible to use this formula to see how equity prices will be impacted, along with the price/earnings (P/E) ratios of companies, by each of those four stages of the equity market, since we can estimate how interest rates and corporate profits will react throughout the cycle. P/E ratios are widely used by investors to determine if a company is fairly priced—and, in general, the lower the number the more attractive the stock (although popular 'glamour' companies like Google or Apple, which are in hot demand, will trade for more—at a price 30 times earnings as I write this, compared to 13 times for the Royal Bank).

This model tells us most of what we need to know: Stock prices of big, stable companies will fall as recessions loom, since interest rates are rising and growth rates falling. This is exactly what the central bank is trying to do with a higher cost of money—cool things off. During a stock market trough, the DDM suggests that stocks will start to jump in value as interest rates fall a lot faster than profits decline. This reflects the Bank of Canada's move to reduce the cost of money and try to kickstart the economy. During the expansion that follows, the model suggests a brief drop in stock prices as interest rates rise to temper the gathering boom and to moderate inflation. Finally, at the market peak, prices will rise as companies rack up good profits even though interest rates have started to creep higher again.

That's the theory. And it works. But how do you know where to put your money and what companies to invest in, either directly through stocks or professionally-managed mutual funds?

Not so hard, either.

Big rule: never fight the economy

Here's what portfolio managers often do—look for turning points in the economic and equity cycles I've just mentioned, and adjust assets accordingly. That's the essence of industry rotation. In other words knowing when the heck to bail out of pricey airline stocks before passengers stay home in droves in a falling economy, and when to snap up cheap airline stocks just before an economic recovery starts to take hold. Or it could be car companies. Or home improvement chains.

Those are known as cyclicals—industry sectors and the companies within them that experience greater movement and volatility than the market as a whole. In good times, they exceed returns given by equities as a whole, and in lousy times, they tank more. For example, the TSX changes in value an average of 55% during an entire business cycle. But in that same period, cyclical stocks will vary in price by an average of 100%.

Given our goal of trying to get the maximum rate of return for an acceptable risk, it makes perfect sense to ride the winners on the way up, then jump off and stick with a less volatile company during the down times. That's all industry rotation is about, and if properly executed, an investor should see his or her portfolio outperform the market on a consistent basis.

An example would be the traditional action of investing in bank stocks during a recession, then switching to consumer stocks, then into manufacturing companies, then commodities (forestry or mining for example) as the economy moves into recovery and expansion. That just makes sense. I haven't yet met a miner from northern Ontario or a forestry worker from BC who doesn't know they're the first to be laid off and the last to resume working in a typical business cycle.

Defensive stocks (such as banks and utilities), as you can imagine, move in a different pattern from cyclicals, rising less in bull markets and falling more gradually and softly during the bears. In a business cycle when the market, as I said, might vary by 55%, the typical defensive company would only change by 30%. In all this, it's useful to remember that 60% of our entire economy is driven by consumer spending, which is reflected in the stock market—so timing a coming expansion correctly and flipping into consumer-driven cyclicals can yield great returns. By the same token, however, missing the right moment to exit can easily erase gains once consumer confidence dips and spending dries up.

Let's get back to contrarian theory for a moment. In addition to technical analysis (charting the market moves), fundamental analysis (tracking the economy), cycle analysis (watching the business and equity cycles) and paying heed to sector rotation (cyclical and defensive stocks), simply being aware of the patterns of people around you will reveal much about what to do next. Gold's an example. Houses are another. Both are investment assets which make people quite emotional and lead them into positions of investing excess.

Fig 3-3 *Snapshot of an overbought market?*

Rapidly rising prices and increasing volumes can warn a contrarian of an overbought market, like Vancouver real estate in late 2009. This chart suggests a top is forming.

Just before the 2010 Olympics in Vancouver the average price of a single-family detached house in Vancouver reached $913,000, which was more than ten times the average family income—twice the level regarded internationally as unaffordable (see Figure 3-3). No doubt this asset was reaching the point of collapse as foretold by indicators we often see in the stock market—rapidly rising prices on widespread bullish sentiment. The number of houses changing hands in October of 2009, for example, was 171.6% higher than in the same month a year earlier—which was in the midst of the credit crisis affecting the global economy, and when an average house in Vancouver was $100,000 less. So, affordability was eroding fast and yet demand was increasing. How was that so different from Nortel at $130 a share?

Ditto with gold once the metal broke through the $1,000-an-ounce mark in late 2009. Suddenly gold bug web sites were bombarded with hits and major bullion dealers like the Bank of Nova Scotia were busy dishing out Maple Leafs and little wafers sealed in plastic. Public fascination was fuelled when a car was stopped at the Canada-US border, and an emigrating American subsequently arrested. In his trunk was a strongbox inside a suitcase containing $800,000 in neat rolls of gold coins. Border officials thought he must be a terrorist or a criminal, but it turns out he was a guy who simply didn't trusts banks and wanted 'real' portable wealth. He was released, with envy.

As I said, there are definite reasons to have precious metals in your portfolio (just as there are to own a house or invest in oil), but when new legions of investors pile in after a significant price resistance level has been breached, it usually indicates an oversold market, ripe for correction. Rational investors whip out their cheque books only when greed withers.

Some further elements of contrarianism are found in the Traffic Signal on the next page.

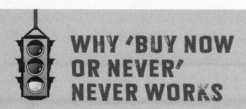

WHY 'BUY NOW OR NEVER' NEVER WORKS

■ When most investors think prices can only rise (the 'buy now or buy never' mentality), there's probably not enough investors left to keep prices rising.

■ Surveys of stock market investors have shown that if 80% of them are bulls, the market's likely overbought and will probably fall back. Just remember how everyone said 'it's different this time' when profitless dot-com companies were flying high. Of course it wasn't different at all—bulls make money, bears make money, pigs get slaughtered.

■ Conversely, when a small minority of people believe the market will rise, chances are that prices are oversold and won't stay so cheap for long.

■ There are statistical measures of this psychology, if you want to follow them. One is a gauge of how bearish, or negative, the public is feeling about investing, called the public short ratio. This indicates the relationship between the number of short sales (that's when a stock is borrowed from a broker and sold, in the hope of buying it back later at a cheaper price) made by average investors, compared to the short sales made by professional institutional traders. The assumption is that the little guy is a lousy trader, so trading opposite to what the public's doing is likely a profitable move. (Google this ratio to see what it currently indicates.)

An example of the public short ratio at work came in March of 2009, when global stock markets hit rock bottom after losing half their value in seven months. The ratio spiked higher, showing a large number were shorting stocks, convinced the market would continue to crash. They believed money could be made by selling stock at a higher price than it would be weeks or months later. Contrarians watched, then did the opposite, and cleaned up while the short sellers crashed and burned.

■ Another popular sentiment indicator measuring the number of bears and bulls among us contrasts the total of puts and calls purchased on the leading options exchange, the Chicago Board Options Exchange (CBOE). A call is a bet that a stock will rise in value, while a put is purchased by someone betting it will be worth less when the option expires (these are both called derivatives). Every day the CBOE adds up all the puts and calls on individual stocks as well as indices and publishes that information on its web site, free for you to track. When puts exceed calls, greed is in the air, and on days when the reverse is true, fear reigns. Once again, the logic is that most people get this wrong and when investors become too bearish, the market's ripe for a rally.

Finally, there are three other things I want to draw to your attention in deciding what kinds of assets to put into your portfolio in these times when asset selection is so critical. This can make the difference between sinking in a stagflated and swampy economy and achieving your goal of financial security. These considerations are made by any worthy portfolio manager with an aim to achieving the best possible returns with the least amount of risk—the holy grail of every investor.

1. Pick growth or pick value

2. Be active or passive
3. Company ratio analysis

Pick growth or pick value

Successful investing is all about timing. Growth managers get that. These stock-pickers seek companies with great rates of growth and market momentum, and jump on for the ride. Many successful equity mutual funds, for example, are managed by pros who are constantly looking for winners that will throw off a lot of profits, driving their share prices higher. This is called 'earnings momentum' and it commands a premium—growth managers will pay big bucks for corporations that are spinning higher (think Google) based on the potential for more growth as sector-leading companies.

Stocks like this typically have little payout in the way of dividends, since most of the cash they generate is sucked back into operations, which means capital gains are the goal for investors. You grab these stocks because they promise to outperform the market in the rising part of the cycle, and hopefully will survive the down times simply because they have momentum and the prospect of more growth to come. That means people who buy growth companies must be able to stomach greater risk for a larger potential return, because if these operations sputter, even for a few months, the market may punish them severely with a big price dump. Growth companies tend to be more volatile, with valuations swinging widely on a daily basis, and are inherently more vulnerable to market declines than blue chip stocks (banks, utilities, oil pipelines), which have stable and predictable earnings.

If you're aggressive, impatient, looking for superior returns over a shorter period, willing to time the market, thirst for capital gains more than income and the morning stock quotes won't ruin your breakfast, then growth stocks or a growth-oriented mutual fund might be for you. If not, there's always value investing.

Think of value managers as Saturn drivers as opposed to growth managers in their Camaros. These guys are bottom-up stock pickers who rely more on research than headlines and wait for the right moment to pounce on companies which have been overlooked, fallen into disfavour or are simply misunderstood and ignored because they lack growth and glamour. They spend a lot of time pouring over company financial statements (more on that in a minute), ferreting out intrinsic value, using ratios and formulas to measure debt and equity and operational performance. Based on all of that, they buy companies that they think the market has undervalued, and wait for that situation to be corrected.

Often value managers will snap up stocks in companies that are low risk and a lot less volatile than the market as a whole (that's known as the 'beta' of a stock—its relative variability compared to the benchmark of the market). They look for low prices, which means that, unlike growth companies, valuations have less chance of tumbling on a rogue headline or a market swing. Also unlike growth companies, value stocks usually pay high dividends, meaning investors get some regular income while they're waiting for their hoped-for capital gains.

But if this sounds boring, here's a surprise: History has shown that over the long haul, value investors get returns just as handsome as those achieved by growth managers, with two important advantages:

1. an income stream from dividends and
2. fewer ulcers, thanks to less volatility and fewer Cheerios-tossing daily price swings.

What style is right for you? If you're considering mutual funds as a core holding in your own portfolio (and that's a good decision, since funds give more diversification, vastly lowering market risk), this is an important question. Growth investing is higher-octane, higher-rewarding in the short term, more exciting and probably more crash-prone, while value investing suits people who want to gain more slowly, have less risk tolerance and more time to stay in the market. Value investors ignore bad days on the TSX or the Dow while growth investors are addicted to the ticker. Value investing has proven to be a great strategy in markets that are highly emotional, when fear is everywhere and good companies are pushed down in price along with the rotten. In contrast, growth investing can supply a seat on the rocket in early bull markets when new money is pouring in and the testosterone flows. Once again, success depends a lot on being able to understand how a market is moving, and reading the emotions behind it.

Be active or passive

Pick your style: Holiday Inn or hands-on

Recall what a good portfolio (apart from your residential real estate) should look like—the appropriate mix of three asset classes: cash, fixed income and equities. That mix will be determined by your age, how much risk you want to take and the rate of return you need or expect. It could also include a lot of things, from GICs and money market funds to government and corporate bonds, preferred shares, mutual funds holding bonds, mortgages or dividend-paying stocks, common shares in growth or value companies, equity, specialty or ethical mutual funds and derivatives like puts, calls and futures. The kind of bonds you buy can vary a great deal, with short or long terms and varying streams of income, just as your stocks or mutual funds can be in banks, oil companies, gold producers or companies making face cream. The choices are endless, which probably explains why a lot of people give up and just deal with the nice lady at the bank.

And here's another one for you: deciding if you want a portfolio which is actively managed, or if you're content just to invest along with the market itself.

Active management does what it suggests—a portfolio manager (it might be a financial advisor, a mutual fund, or it could be you) strikes an asset balance, and then constantly monitors it in a process known as strategic asset allocation. That's the task of maintaining the basic asset mix even as stock and bond markets, along with interest rates, bounce around. Every portfolio experiences drift as some assets rise and others fall, so it's important to stay on top of things and rebalance as necessary. Cash might build up too fast as dividends and bond interest income flows in, or a few stocks might explode in value, shooting your equity component too high. The idea then is to constantly sell off the assets in which you are overweight and buy more in the underweighted areas. That maintains the overall goals and intent of your portfolio, ensuring risk is kept in check through diversification.

This active sell-buying process to keep the mix in a narrow band is called dynamic asset allocation, and it's something you'd simply expect a financial advisor or a portfolio manager (if you have a million or so to invest) to do on a regular basis. That's what you pay them for—to set targets for various assets and then rebalance as necessary so you have consistent returns and a risk level you can stomach. This is a strategy popular with investors who want the Holiday Inn approach to their portfolio— no surprises.

Another technique used by some active managers is to deviate temporarily from the basic asset mix in order to seize opportunities that might come along—posed by a promising IPO (initial public offering of a new stock) or a pending plunge in interest rates making bonds irresistible. In that case the portfolio manager might load up on the IPO with the intent of selling for a quick capital gain, or buy bonds that will jump in value as yields go down and prices pop up. That's called tactical asset allocation and appeals to investors who believe, as I do, in the value of market timing.

It used to be said 'its not timing the market, but time in the market that counts.' These days that has changed.

As I said, most successful investors with a few hundred thousand to invest hire an advisor to set up and manage this kind of a balanced portfolio on an active basis—somebody who knows them intimately, will tailor the asset selection to their personal goals and understands the market well enough to buy stocks which complement each other and take advantage of the prevailing market sentiment, plus where we happen to be in the business cycle. As you can imagine, it's a big job, takes a ton of time, a lot of specialized knowledge and a passion to help the client. Or, you can try it yourself. Or, you can hand the job over to a professional mutual fund manager—a good solution for people who may not yet have enough money to justify a personal portfolio manager.

Lots of mutual funds will spread your money over a mix of assets, others will automatically rebalance, and still others will seek to take advantage of opportunities. One example is a Tactical Asset Allocation Fund run by a major bank. Its stated objective is to "obtain capital growth over the long term, while providing modest income. It invests primarily in a broad range of Canadian equity and fixed income securities and may invest around the world." This fund says it's ideal for people who want "medium risk" and has this asset allocation:

- **40% DEX Universe Bond Index** (an index comprised primarily of semi-annual pay fixed rate bonds issued domestically in Canada, with an investment grade rating and a remaining effective term to maturity of at least one year);

- **40% S&P/TSX Composite Index** (an index reflecting the performance of the biggest 60 companies trading on the Toronto stock market); and

- **20% MSCI World Index** (a stock market index of 1,500 world stocks).

Not a bad mix, obviously, and very reflective of a huge number of underlying assets. But it's a one-size-fits-all solution. And we don't all fit.

Index funds are a great idea. But not now.

At the other end of the spectrum is passive management of your money, based on the theory that it's probably a useless thing trying to beat the market itself. Many folks have come to this conclusion over the years, including a guy named William Sharpe who won the Nobel Prize in Economics in 1990 for being a genius (in his seventies, he's still packing lecture halls at Stanford University). Sharpe's insightful mathematical formulas and analysis of markets and equity prices led him to conclude that in the long run stocks are always fairly priced in respect to risk and return. Therefore it's not possible to outperform the market and paying for professional money management is itself a waste of money. That's called the efficient market hypothesis and while I don't agree with it, many people do. They are the ones who therefore believe in passive management.

Probably the most popular form of passive investing is to buy index funds—mutual funds that don't try to pick individual stocks, but simply invest in all the stocks represented in a market index. That way if the TSX, for example, rises by 100 points so will the index fund which mirrors it.

Investors like the simplicity of index funds, as well as the fact that they're generally cheaper to own. After all, nobody's steering the ship—actively picking stocks or switching between equities and bonds and cash—so it doesn't cost much to run them. According to Sharpe, this is the optimal way to invest in the market, and for those who want to take less risk, he thinks they should split their money between index products and Treasury bills, which are government-guaranteed and considered completely free of risk.

As appealing as this might be, however, a portfolio that gives you exactly what the market's returning is not a great idea when markets disappoint. In times when the business cycle dips or when there's a global financial meltdown, index funds will fall just as fast and hard as the market overall, and reflect the prevailing sentiment of most investors. That means you are as much a victim of fear and greed as the rest of the herd. There is simply no room for contrarian thought with an index fund that paces the market as a whole. Likewise, in a time when markets snake sideways—which appears to be our fate for many of the years immediately ahead—funds which mirror a broad stock market index will also drift, doing little to amass that pile of wealth we all want for retirement.

However, the story does not end there. Index funds are also available that will mirror just gold stocks, or energy stocks, health stocks, the bond index, international stocks and so on. Not only that, but there are bear index funds that will allow you to bet against the market as a whole, plus ETFs (exchange-traded funds), which trade just like stocks and can employ leverage to amplify gains (or losses). ETFs also mirror major market sectors, can focus on value or growth stocks, dividends or bonds, as well as various asset allocation models.

In Canada, Barclay's iShares dominate the ETF index fund category, led by the iShares CDN LargeCap 60 Index Fund (trading symbol XIU). It's set up to replicate the performance of the Toronto stock market index, with these top holdings as of the end of 2009:

- Royal Bank at 8.22%
- TD Bank at 5.79%
- Suncor at 5.76%
- Scotiabank at 5.00%
- Encana at 4.52%
- Barrick Gold at 4.41%
- Canadian Natural Resources at 3.82%
- Research in Motion at 3.38%
- Goldcorp at 3.37%
- Manulife Financial at 3.36%

ETFs and index funds proliferate in the US, and these are fully available to Canadian investors. Among the favourites are DIAMONDs (based on sectors of the Dow Jones Industrial Index), QUBEs (based on the tech-heavy NASDAQ) and SPDRs (which mirror the performance of various sectors of the S&P 500, the most broad-based American market).

For example, sector SPDRs (like the insects) divide the S&P 500 into nine sector index funds. Like other sector funds, they allow investors to pick and weight these sectors to try to achieve investment goals, based on the performance of large cap (capitalization—arrived at by multiplying the outstanding number of shares by the current share price) companies. Some categories offered are consumer staples, energy, financial, health, industrial, technology and utilities.

But, here's a problem. There are 346 fund companies in Canada, offering active funds, index funds, sector funds, asset allocation funds, ETFs and a huge variety in between. In fact, there are just over 24,000 choices and 11,000 distinct funds run by more than 1,500 portfolio managers. This is a mind-boggling offering. And while there's a ton of fund information available online and for free from places like Morningstar, The Fund Library and Globeinvestor, sifting through it and coming up with a selection that suits you is more than daunting. It's likely impossible. And that explains the popularity of funds that combine stocks and bonds together (called balanced funds), plus the index mutual funds and ETFs that mirror the market as a whole or one of the ten segments of it. Those kinds of fund choices take the thought out of the process for most people, especially do-it-yourself investors who (like William Sharpe) think it's a mug's game trying to outperform the market as a whole.

But it is possible. Without a doubt.

That's why the previous chapter walked you through technical and economic analysis; why I spent time describing the relationship of the equity and business cycles, along with the impact of fear and greed on asset values and the wisdom of contrarian thinking. Because of what lies ahead of us, as outlined in the first chapter—a unique combination of factors which will make the coming years a hell on wheels for most people—it's not going to be enough just to pace the market, because odds are that by 2015 it will be sitting at about the same position it sits in 2010. At the same time, however, various sectors will show solid gains, and many individual companies will excel in terms of profits and stock values. This is why everybody in a hurry to achieve personal financial security before things get even worse (thanks to peak oil, climate change, wealth imbalances and political upheaval—factors which await us within a decade) had better know what to do. This is the basis of my advice to determine a proper asset allocation of cash, fixed income and equities, and to make sure the growth component actually gives you lots of it.

The inescapable conclusion is that index funds won't cut it. Some sector funds and ETFs based on energy or financials or health care will outperform the market as a whole, for sure. And the most successful of investors could be those who find an advisor or manager with the knowledge and insight to build them a unique portfolio of companies with solid earnings, in the right place at the right time.

How's that possible?

Company ratio analysis

Diving in

One tool exceptional portfolio managers use is company analysis—a dive into a corporation's finances to see if it's being run properly, how much debt it's accumulated, its potential for growth based on past performance and the safety for investors of buying its stocks or bonds. Corporate analysis is a bottom-up approach, looking at the inherent worth of a company. It's a complicated and time-consuming process that requires a rudimentary understanding of accounting principles and the ability to read, often convoluted, financial statements.

As an involved and rational investor, you should know what your advisor is looking for, which includes a series of ratios assessing the company's performance in a number of key areas. Once these ratios are known, they give us a way of comparing corporations with each other, and with an industry benchmark. Here are some of the major ratios.

- **Current ratio.** Measures a company's working capital, or the difference between assets and liabilities. Ratio should be at least 2:1.

- **Asset Coverage.** Measures the extent to which a company can cover its debt obligations with assets after current liabilities have been paid. Ratio should be at least 2:1.

- **Debt to equity.** Measures how much debt the company has compared to how much capital investors have put in. It's a good measure of the risk a company's taken. Ratio should not exceed 0.5:1.

- **Interest coverage.** Measures the ability of the company to pay the interest on its debt, based on earnings. This is of key interest if you buy the company's bonds. Ratio should be at least 3:1.

- **Debt to capital structure.** Tells you how much debt there is relative to the company's whole structure. This should not exceed 33.3%.

- **Preferred dividend coverage.** Measures how safe the company's dividend-paying preferred shares might be based on how much money the company has. Ratio should be at least 3:1.

- **Price-earning (P/E).** One of the most common ratios, measuring the price of the company's stock against the earnings per share that it generates. There is no rule of thumb for this ratio, but in general stocks with low P/Es are considered to be value companies, and the better investment. However, when a stock's price is driven higher on the market based on investor demand because it's hot, the P/E can soar—which is often the case with companies in the technology sector, and others considered to be growth or glamour issues.

In addition, analysts look at gross, operating and net profit margins, the rate at which inventories are turned over, and the return a company generates on the equity that common shareholders have put in. Also, the quality of the management leading the company is examined; along with an analysis of the trend in earnings; and how liquid the shares are—whether or not the company's stock is easily moved on the markets by big orders from giants like pension funds. The more liquidity there is, the better protected little investors are from being sideswiped.

Okay, this is all heavy stuff, I realize. The chances of most people doing ratio analysis on companies whose stocks they want to buy is nil. Even learning to read financial statements is no picnic. But in this age of information overload, the kind of data in Figure 3-4 (this is for the Royal Bank) is available instantly, and free of charge.

Fig 3-4 *12 months data items—Royal Bank of Canada*

EBITDA Margin (Earnings Before Interest, Taxes, Depreciation, Amortization)	45.5%
Pre-Tax Profit Margin	14.5%
Interest Coverage	1.5
Leverage Ratio	21.4
Asset Turnover	0.1
Revenue to Assets	0.1
ROE from Total Operations	11.2%
Return on Invested Capital	8.2%
Return on Assets	0.5%
Debt/Common Equity Ratio	0.21
Price/Book Ratio (Price/Equity)	2.69
Book Value per Share	$20.17
Total Debt/Equity	0.21

Long-Term Debt to Total Capital	0.15
Cash Flow per Share	$2.14
Free Cash Flow per Share	$1.46
Tangible Book Value per Share	$13.39
Price/Cash Flow Ratio	25.3
Price/Free Cash Flow Ratio	37.2
Price/Tangible Book Ratio	4.05

Serious investors, as none who have gone before, now have the ability to drill into investments, to compare companies, gauge how corporations perform against the average of others in an industry, or the market as a whole—thanks to web sites that publish this stuff. For example, looking at the P/E ratio of a stock can help establish if it's at a reasonable price, given where we are in a business cycle. What investors seek is a company whose P/E stays reasonably constant over a number of years and cycles, even though it's normal for these ratios to rise and fall with the market itself. If you find similar companies in the same industry with comparable earnings, chances are the one with the lower P/E ratio is the best buy (although it might be out of favour with investors).

In fact, it makes far more sense to look at P/E ratios than it does the actual value of a company's shares on the market. What a P/E will tell you is how many years it takes to get your money back, based on recent earnings. For example, during the tech bubble of 2000, Nortel stock was trading at a P/E of more than 50, meaning investors were paying over $50 for every expected $1 in earnings. Worse still, when Calgary-based fraudster gold mining company Bre-X was a market darling, investors were rushing to buy in at a P/E of 1,000. Needless to say, this ended badly, as both companies disintegrated.

Figure 3-5 is an example of how P/E ratios can mean a lot more than the price of a stock.

Fig 3-5 *P/E ratios versus stock prices*

Company	ABC	DEF	GHI	JKL
Stock Price	.90	240.00	70.00	.60
Company Earnings per share	5.00	10.00	1.00	0.10
P/E ratio (price divided by earnings)	18	24	70	6

Looking at the simple chart in Figure 3-5 you can see that purely on the basis of corporate earnings, JKL is the best buy since investors stand a superior chance of getting their money back in a shorter period of time. And this is despite the company's shares being on a 'penny stock' basis. In contrast, GHI is trading at a huge multiple of earnings—70 times—so investors must be buying it for a reason that has little to do with how much money the company is making. That could well be if GHI was a glamour company generating headlines and media attention and attracting investor attention with its sexiness. If you remember the dot-com era, then you know how that's often a very dangerous kind of investment to make. So one conclusion here is that stocks with cheap prices are risky, or ones that cost a bundle are safe and stable. Instead, rustle up the P/E ratio and have a look for yourself.

It's very worthwhile knowing enough about company and ratio analysis to be able to ask your advisor exactly why he or she is selecting certain stocks for you, or to quickly scrutinize the holdings of a mutual fund company that's caught your eye. You can also research the P/E of a stock market itself—the TSX, Dow, S&P or NASDAQ, for example, to get some insight into whether a market is frothing along on a tide of investor greed, oversold in an atmosphere of mounting fear or whether it represents true value.

You are what you own

Much of the information above concentrated on the stock market. With good reason. Life expectancy in Canada is shooting higher, which has dramatically increased everybody's need for financial assets. By that I mean liquid assets—things that can be turned into cash and used to finance your life—as opposed to residential real estate that can be intensely illiquid (and soon could be again). The best source of growth is the equity market, which reflects the economy as a whole, the country's competitiveness, business conditions and the prospects going forward. Everybody should have some exposure to this, especially now that we face several years of relatively low and stable interest rates in which the return from GICs and other no-risk investments will be sub-par. Of the three asset class choices you have to choose from—cash, fixed-income or equities—this is the one task investors should spend the most time on. Understand the options. Explore many of those 24,000 mutual funds. Get the basics of technical, fundamental and company analysis—at least enough to answer the basic questions of where we are in the business and market cycle, and how greed and fear are influencing everyone else. Determine what parts of the economy will give the return you need, such as the banks, energy and oil, gold and mining, health care or technology.

You can choose to do this yourself or you can hire it out. But never abdicate all responsibility to understand what's going on. It's your money. It was tough earning it and the stuff deserves your care. But it also needs to grow. Especially now. At the same time, everyone's different. We all need to find our own balance of assets which gives us the rate of growth we'll need, along with safety of capital and income.

For example, what should the investment profile of Bart and Jean, a middle-class couple in their forties look like, assuming they already own a home? This would be a good start.

Total net worth = 100%

- **House.** This should account for no more than 40% of the couple's total net worth (and the equity in the home is net of any mortgage debt or line of credit pledged against it). Younger families will obviously have a larger proportion of their net worth tied up in a house, and Boomers today should be mortgage-free. If you're not, you're probably heading for trouble.
- **Investible assets.** This is the other 60% of net worth, and the amount that needs to grow steadily over the next 20 years in order to achieve the critical mass required for retirement. I'm assuming in this example that Bart and Jean don't have any corporate pensions (seven in ten of us do not), and have only CPP and OAS to look forward to in retirement. That maximum amount of $16,600 a year each (and it's all taxable) will need to be heavily supplemented in retirement by an orderly drawdown of their own savings.

Portfolio

- **Cash.** Maximim 5%, kept in interest-bearing, liquid securities. Best bet is a money market mutual fund.
- **Fixed income.** Between 30% and 40% in investment-grade short- and medium-term bonds, a mix of provincial and Government of Canada securities plus high-grade corporates and bank preferred shares.

- **Equities.** Minimum 65% in large-cap companies purchased for growth potential, stable earnings, sound ratios and in sectors appropriate for the business cycle. It could be a mix of financials, energy, technology and industrials, for example, combined with sector funds and a TSX S&P ETF.

In contrast, a retired, single woman who needs income and safety of capital above all would hold 10% cash, 75% or 80% fixed income (the majority of it in short-term bonds, which are less volatile, plus preferreds), and still have an equity component of 10–15%, put into blue chips such as bank shares. As for a young couple in their late twenties or early thirties, the best asset mix might be 5% cash, 15% fixed income and 80% equities, with a lot of that sheltered in the tax-free environment of an RRSP or a tax-free savings account. This is in stark contrast to the majority of young adults I run into who are incredibly risk-averse. Even inside their RRSPs (intended for long-term appreciation) they stick GICs and money market funds that are destined to seriously under-perform relative to their needs. This is a huge miscalculation of the nature of risk, setting these people up for a serious crash later.

Now, let's cash in those Canada Savings Bonds, and get back on the road.

Four

GETTING THERE

The greatest return for the least risk

'The wheels of the economy will fall off'

He grew up in an apartment over his parents' grocery store in Chicago and was addicted to *The Shadow* comic books. Harry played baseball in a vacant lot, turned into a violin-playing geek in high school and would change investing psychology after reading in a public library one afternoon. It was 1952 when the world first heard of this Harry Markowitz guy, and then, not too many listened. It took almost 40 more years for him to win a Nobel prize. Yet Markowitz is still an unknown. And it shows.

His conclusion was stark and simple: there's a way to measure risk and reward. Once you know it, you can be empowered. Investments can be put together to achieve your objective. Or as close to it as chance will allow.

I thought of Harry when I opened my blog one morning a year or so after the wheels came off the North American economy and saw these words. They were posted on a Saturday by a realtor in Kelowna, a Boomer I'd never met, but had come to know through his posts as an insightful, rational, hopeful person:

"The saddest thing is that I have completely lost interest in achieving financial growth," he wrote. "I just don't think it is worth it anymore. There is too much risk and even if you are successful it appears government is just going to piss it away through increased taxes and stricter regulation.

"Were I to do it all over again I might make only one, all-beit significant, change and that would be to have sought a secure government job. You know the 9:00 to 4:00 gig with benefits, no stress, weekends and evenings off, paid vacation and a retirement plan... Time has taught me that I am in no way unique. I suspect there are a lot like me. What is that going to do to the economy when those of entrepreneurial inclination lose it and simply stop? The wheels of the economy will fall off, that's what will happen."

He's right. Such a fatalistic attitude is shared by millions of people these days when they look out over the landscape of their lives. Repeatedly we've been told to invest in safe and secure assets, like houses and GICs and bank accounts, to eschew risk as represented by the stock market or small, start-up employers, to trust government, multinationals and an ever-expanding economy. The Holy Grail for most has been a career with a big corporation, then to enjoy paid-off real estate, grandchildren and an indexed company pension.

Yet the wheels did come off. Interest rates crumbled turning investments cold. Real estate values soared, so high that just hanging on squeezed out most other options. Big fancy companies run by CEOs making millions ended up being the first to throw employees overboard when the economy sputtered. And pension plans have continuously been biting the dust, or left underfunded by uncaring corporations.

Are these the new realities?

So, are these the inescapable realities of our age?

- It was a myth that progress and economic advance would lift us all.
- Seven in ten have no pension and inadequate savings.
- Millions have expensive homes, yet virtually no money.
- The Boomers feel jilted, while their adult kids resent the generation that stoked house prices and spends their inheritance.
- Wealth isn't being distributed, but accumulated.
- Average incomes are stilted while the ranks of millionaires and billionaires soar.
- Trying to get ahead, as the Kelowna real estate agent said, is just too risky.
- The middle class is kaput.

Easy to think such things. And you'll hear a lot more in the same vein as the next few years unfold, bringing with them more tax, tepid growth and structural unemployment. Many Boomers whose jobs and careers were chewed up in the global financial crunch—when big companies scrambled to lay off workers by the thousands—will never be employed again. Meanwhile the capitalist bastion of America will be in decline, weighed down by staggering debts, the deliberate outsourcing of jobs, its futile burden as the world's cop and a simple inability to compete.

Absolutely, this is a different age—a 'new normal' as the TD Bank economists pegged it in 2009, as they forecast what could be a lost decade ahead. Millions of people are learning now that the lessons of the past, the things they learned about risk and reward, didn't work. Period.

Obviously those lessons were flawed. If they weren't we wouldn't be on the cusp of history's greatest retirement crisis. However, risk can be contained, reduced and even harnessed. Investing is not a game of throwing darts at the financial pages full of stock quotes, but a discipline like everything else. There are principles to be aware of, tools to use and proven strategies to follow.

This is why I've presented technical and fundamental analysis in this book, the link between the equity and business cycles, company ratios and the tenets of contrarian investing. You certainly don't need to master this stuff, but it should show you why the people who work at investing usually don't worry about money. They never buy a house or a stock or a marketable bond and hope for the best. Instead each move is made in the context of the times, with some expectation of what comes next and in a way that mitigates risk instead of leveraging it higher. And you can do this too. Straight up.

Know the risk you can control

So, back to Harry.

Markowitz' big advance was the 'modern portfolio theory,' which is used by advisors and successful investors to achieve desirable returns, regardless of the financial weather. Harry determined that risk can be broken into two hunks—one, market risk (or 'systematic' risk), which you can't do anything about. That's Nine Eleven, a global credit crisis or a sudden move in interest rates. The other risk, unique risk (or 'unsystematic'), you can certainly reduce, if not control. So, the total risk of investing is the two of these things put together which is called the 'variability' or volatility of an investment.

There's a term for this total risk—'standard deviation'—which you'll run into when doing research on stocks or mutual funds.

The amount that any particular investment deviates from the movements of the market as a whole is called 'beta.' So, when you pull up info on a mutual fund, you might well see something like the table in Figure 4-1.

Fig 4-1 *What funds tell you about risk*

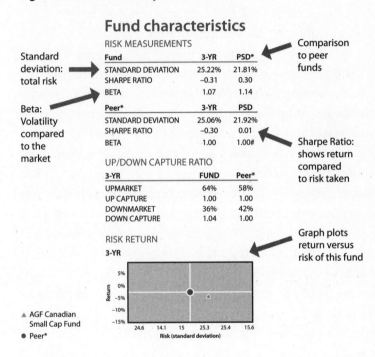

Fund characteristics

RISK MEASUREMENTS

Standard deviation: total risk ➡

Beta: Volatility compared to the market

Comparison to peer funds

Sharpe Ratio: shows return compared to risk taken

Graph plots return versus risk of this fund

Fund	3-YR	PSD*
STANDARD DEVIATION	25.22%	21.81%
SHARPE RATIO	–0.31	0.30
BETA	1.07	1.14

Peer*	3-YR	PSD
STANDARD DEVIATION	25.06%	21.92%
SHARPE RATIO	–0.30	0.01
BETA	1.00	1.00#

UP/DOWN CAPTURE RATIO

3-YR	FUND	Peer*
UPMARKET	64%	58%
UP CAPTURE	1.00	1.00
DOWNMARKET	36%	42%
DOWN CAPTURE	1.04	1.00

RISK RETURN
3-YR

▲ AGF Canadian Small Cap Fund
● Peer*

Here is some of what this AGF fund information tells you in Figure 4-1.

- With a beta of 1.07, this fund has a higher volatility than the market as a whole. (A beta of 1 equals the market, so this is 107% more volatile. If the market falls or rises 100 points, this will move by 107).
- The standard deviation is higher than similar funds in the same category (small cap companies), so there's

more risk involved in buying it than others—but possibly a greater rate of return.

■ The Sharpe Ratio tells you with a negative number that you can expect a hard time making money in the current market.

■ Which is borne out by the graph. This fund is past the centre point for risk (bottom scale), and yet below the breakeven point for return (left scale).

A rational investor would probably decide not to buy this fund in the environment of a volatile market when small cap companies are bouncing around in value. Instead, a conservative investor would seek a fund with a beta of less than 1.0 (which is more stable than the market), a lower standard deviation and a way more promising chart.

But while this fund is obviously a high-risk investment, you can expect it to outperform a rising market, just as it will tank more in a falling market—simply by knowing the mathematical measures of risk. In fact, that's just what happened. This mutual fund gave a whopping –47% loss in 2008 when the global financial system took a dive, and yet leapt by 33% in the following ten months alone.

Why buy this fund if it has increased risk?

Watch the fearful, and do the opposite

Well, if you were a contrarian and looked at all the fear washing over the market following the collapse of Wall Street; if you noted the plunging interest rates which would inevitably be positive for the next business cycle; and if you believed that massive government stimulus would do nothing but spur the coming equity cycle, then investing in a fund of this nature might have been a stroke of genius.

This also underscores another theme I've mentioned, which is that from here forward market timing is a superior strategy to buy-and-hold. An investor owning this small cap fund over the course of two years would have netted nothing, with a big loss offset by an equally large gain. But had the investor matched the potential return of this high-risk fund with the extreme point reached in the business and equity cycle when the global meltdown took place, then the reward would have been great.

The Traffic Signal below provides some things to remember about getting rid of risk when piecing together an investment portfolio.

SOME RULES OF PORTFOLIO RISK & RETURN

- The more securities you have in a portfolio, the more the risk falls. Buying one or two or five stocks is an inherently bad idea. Remember my friend Suk, the walking disaster with a few speculative companies? Don't be him.

- The ideal number of stocks has been mathematically determined as 32. More than that, and there's no further reduction in risk. This principle holds true for both stocks and bonds.

- Two stocks that move together (such as two banks, two car companies, two gold producers) increase risk, since this makes your portfolio more affected by market swings. All you're really doing is adding to the weight of one industry grouping, without any hope of really boosting the overall return.

- Two stocks that move in opposite directions (a gold producer and a utility, an airline and a train company) reduce risk since they will counterbalance each other during the business cycle. In fact, two stocks that are perfectly matched this way yield no overall risk.

- The intensity with which stocks move in relation to each other is called 'correlation.' Similar stocks are positively correlated, differing ones are negatively correlated. This is a principle worth remembering, since it applies to much. For example, gold and oil are positively correlated, since they generally rise and fall together. Most hedge funds are negatively correlated with stock markets (see Figure 4-2).

Fig 4-2 *Negatively-correlated stocks*

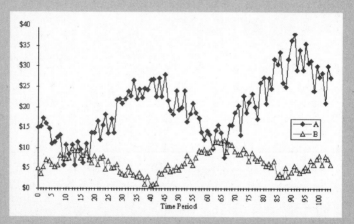

When two stocks move in the opposite direction to each other, like the ones above, they are 'negatively correlated.' It's a smart move to build this into a stock portfolio because a correlation such as this one can seriously reduce risk. Typically one of these stocks (B) might be a defensive company, like a utility, while the other (A) is a cyclical, like an airline. Volatility and returns are a lot less for the utility, while the airline throws off a high yield in good times, but crashes in a recession.

- In fact a lot of hedge funds depend on negative correlation, since they buy stocks that will outperform the market while shorting those that will likely fall more. This long/ short strategy is designed to give absolute year-over-year returns with a very low corresponding risk.

- If you have two stocks that give high returns, and they're negatively correlated (move opposite to each other), you will still have an overall high yield, but slice your risk.

- The biggest risk you take when buying stocks is not market risk (the things you cannot control) but unique risk, which you can reduce through diversification and correlation. The stock market overall will always recover from a dive, but individual companies can be wiped out.

- The risk (standard deviation) of a portfolio of stocks is always less than the standard deviation of the stocks it contains. That's what a portfolio manager or advisor does—picks companies which complement each other to achieve your goal.

- To assume more risk, and the potential for a greater return, all an investor needs to do is use leverage (borrowed money) to buy the securities.

- Higher risk (standard deviation) means higher potential return. The goal in putting together a portfolio is to work back from your goal (say, a 10% annual return over five years), selecting securities with a beta that will get you there, and a level of risk you can tolerate.

- I repeat: 90% of the variation in what portfolios yield is determined by asset allocation.

- Derivatives (such as futures and options on a stock index) can substantially reduce or virtually eliminate risk, even on a portfolio full of high-octane, volatile stocks. Many professional portfolio managers and advisors use this in a process called hedging.

- Any stock, or portfolio (like an index fund) that moves perfectly with the market has a beta of 1.0. A portfolio with a beta of 2.0 potentially doubles market volatility—and doubles the profits or losses.

- Cyclical companies (GM, United Airlines) have betas greater than the market. Defensive stocks (Enbridge, Bank of Montreal) have betas lower than the market.

- So, in a rising market it's obviously more profitable to have a portfolio with a high overall beta, and in a falling market you want defensive companies and a portfolio with a low beta to limit your losses. Or, better still, know when to get out.

- History shows when investors are trying to get the best portfolio return with acceptable risk, the most important decision is the balance of assets—between cash, fixed-income and equities. Focus on this instead of trying to outperform an index, average or benchmark return.

How to find the perfect portfolio

With tens of thousands of stocks, funds and bonds instantly available, in addition to banks peddling their products, guys who cruise into town selling their no-lose tax shelters, insurance sales types and mutual fund hawkers, plus the entire never-a-better-time-to-buy real estate industry screaming at you, how can anybody put together a perfect portfolio? Does one even exist?

Books and web sites galore are devoted to answering that question, and I hope you check them out. Mostly they're in the business of selling you "six exchange traded funds that cannot possibly lose!" or "we have found the best four markets in the world for the next seven years!" or "tap into history's eternal wellspring of wealth, investment real estate!" Yeah, right. Treat these lines with the scepticism they deserve, because there are no simple solutions. No perfect portfolio. There's not one single mutual fund that will give the best asset allocation for everyone, and no handful of stocks or collection of bonds that can protect you if interest rates go up and the US invades Iran at the same time. And given what lies ahead in the half-decade to come, I'm betting most people would be very wise to reduce their real estate exposure, not increase it.

But all this is not to say we can't close in on the best portfolio for you—given your age, level of income and assets, family obligations, tolerance for risk, temperament, health, confidence and, of course, your goals. Part of this is to be expected, since every 20-year-old or retiree shares some of the same characteristics. To that extent, maybe a book written by a US investment guru who talks to Oprah and does CNN can help you a lot. Some generic advice is amazingly useful. But investing is a personal experience, since it can make you face each day with certainty, or keep you in night sweats.

When I work on a plan with somebody, writing it starts only after we've spent hours together chatting about their life so far, their family (pets included), how they feel about giving up some control of the money they worked so hard for, where they live and why, whether they have goals we can actually achieve, what they want their money to accomplish now and after they pass on, and—most importantly—their comfort zone. That last factor always tops the list. I may like riding my motorcycle too fast, for example, but there's no way I'm going to be talked into skydiving.

Having said that, there are some principles we've covered in the book that should lead us to the following conclusions.

The bones of your own personal strategy

While a single one-fits-all portfolio does not exist, there are some basic principles—the specific details of which will be different for everyone—that make up the perfect portfolio.

- **Separate your residential real estate from your 'investible' assets.** A house is a place to live that costs money to buy, finance and operate—so it's an ongoing net drain of wealth, not a generator of it. If the house rises in value and provides a capital gain after all the land transfer taxes, commissions, interest payments and maintenance costs, well great. Bonus. But houses can be incredibly illiquid in a lousy real estate market, might be sold at a substantial loss or even turn into a wealth trap as happened to 16 million US families who sank into negative equity in 2010. Do not make the mistake millions of Canadians are, that their houses equal constant and accessible sources of wealth, relieving them of the problem of having an investment portfolio.

- **Have a portfolio with balance in it.** That means cash-type investments, as well as fixed income and equities. This will give you liquidity (the ability to turn assets into cash fast), as well as income and growth. There is nothing more crucial than asset allocation to achieve growth and protect what you've got.

- **How much of each is critical to the overall return your money will earn?** This is the key decision, so this is usually my suggestion:
  - Keep the cash portion around 5%, so if you've got $200,000 to invest right now, no more than $10,000 should be into a money market mutual fund, T-bills

or a short-term bond. All of those things will give you some income, and can be converted into spendable money within 24 hours.

– Now deduct your age from 100 if you're a guy and from 110 if a woman. So, a 40-year old male will come up with 60 and a woman with 70.

– That is the percentage of growth assets, namely equity-based mutual funds or stocks, which should be in this plan. The rest should be invested in fixed-income securities, like investment-grade bonds or preferred, dividend-paying preferreds.

– For a 40-year-old woman (who likely has 50 years to live, 25 of them without employment income), we then get this balance:
  · Cash: 5%
  · Fixed income: 35%
  · Growth assets: 65%

With a $200,000 portfolio, this means $10,000 in cash, $70,000 in government bonds and preferred shares and $120,000 in equity mutual funds, stocks, segregated funds, commodities, ETFs (exchange traded funds) or sector funds.

■ **The fixed-income portion is best made up of the highest quality bonds,** like those issued by the Government of Canada, Alberta or Ontario, which have AAA ratings (despite their mounting debts) and a zero chance of default since they possess the power to tax. The best kind are medium term (three to five years left to maturity), because you can always hang on to them and know exactly what they will pay you when they come to term, plus these bonds are less volatile than long-term ones. Every time interest rates change, the value of bonds also changes (although the income they pay you remains constant), which means the longer a bond has before it matures the greater the chance a big hike in rates would reduce its value if you had to sell it before maturity.

- **Adding some bank preferred shares to this fixed-income portfolio is almost always a great idea.** The dividend payments are usually higher than the yield on the bonds, and this money is taxed at a significantly lower rate, boosting the after-tax return even higher. Since our banks are large, stable and secure, this is a perfect place to look for both income and security.

So far, so good. That's 40% of your money invested in assets which pay you an income stream and have less risk involved than driving on the 401.

The growth component is the one that always takes the most work, since the object is to get the best possible return with the most acceptable level of risk.

As I've explained, there are mathematical ways to arrive at this, and sometimes theory does help in practical actions. This is why we need to consider the 'beta' of any stock or mutual fund—the way it moves relative to the market as a whole—plus the 'standard deviation'—which is the amount it varies over time and the volatility compared to similar kinds of assets. Likewise, we want assets in this part of the portfolio that are diversified from each other, giving us negative correlation (so some rise and some fall as the business cycle changes).

- **Match your risk tolerance to your portfolio.** I mentioned two Nobel Prize winners, William Sharpe and Harry Markowitz, who each had landmark ideas about putting a portfolio together. Markowitz believes every investor should go for the maximum return, while Sharpe thinks investors should never strive for any yield that is beyond their own tolerance for risk. And I'm with Sharpe. He actually devised a formula for determining this called the Capital Assets Portfolio Model. It says the return you can expect on an investment should equal the current T-bill rate (the 'risk-free' rate) plus the beta of that investment times the total market return less the T-bill rate, or...

$$R_p = R_f + \beta \, (R_m - R_f)$$

Don't let this daunt you. The good part of this process is that the risk factor for investments (the 'beta') is well known, so what an advisor must do is use some analysis and research to match up stocks, funds and other assets with the goal of the client, given where we are in the business and equity cycle and the obvious challenges ahead (as I described in the opening chapter).

- **Include cyclical and defensive stocks.** The result in this case is $120,000 in assets which include cyclical and defensive stocks with varying betas, some sector ETFs to take advantage of pending opportunities (say, with the price of gold or oil), blue chips (banks, utilities) plus proven growth companies (like some of the tech giants) and a small component of higher-risk and higher-return, like a bond bear fund going into a period of rising interest rates (like we now face).

- **Maximize investments/minimize taxes.** And this all has to be done in a way which will maximize investment returns while minimizing taxes. Obviously the less tax a

client pays on returns, the smaller the overall risk to
the portfolio. That's why the advisor has to curtail the
amount of interest income received, while boosting
dividends and capital gains. It also means putting the
appropriate amount of this portfolio inside an RRSP
(typically that would be the bond component), while
also sheltering gains inside the relatively new TFSA
(tax-free savings account—more on this in a subsequent
chapter).

So there you have an ideal portfolio. Or the bones of it. You'll
notice there's no 'four easy, sure-thing index funds' here. No
time-sharing condos. Nothing exotic to blow up. No investments
you can't understand. Nothing that can't be monitored, modified, changed or improved since these days every week brings a
new development. Just a solid machine taking you steadily down
the road. Wind in your hair, and at your back. Perfect.

The coolest thing to do with your money

In short, putting together a portfolio is about the coolest thing
you get to do in financial planning. It's creative, challenging
and unforgiving. Risk and return constantly play off each other.
The market and economic environments are steadily changing.
Future threats have to be factored in. Changes in interest rates
or tax policy can affect everything. And the plan can't be done
in isolation from those personal issues that make you and your
situation unique.

This has to meld in with the rest of your life, such as residential real estate, and the debts you might have. Or a desire to leave
money behind in an estate for family or a charity. For many people, entrepreneurs and professionals like lawyers and dentists,

there are business considerations too. Plus insurance looms large, since products like universal life combined with growth assets like equities can provide a life-long tax-free stream of retirement income, while segregated funds can lock in all stock market gains while locking out losses.

In fact, let's have a brief look at those stress-busters, then a few words on picking bonds.

Seg funds—cake, and eat it too

As I mentioned before, early in January of 2009 a financial advisor I'd know for some years asked me to come to his city and give a seminar for existing clients. And the guy, in business for years, had slews of them. At that time the stock market was crashing, governments were panicking, interest rates were tumbling, Wall Street was staggering, layoffs were cascading and it looked like the whole mess could roll off a cliff. But while other advisors and mutual fund companies were cancelling public events they'd scheduled months earlier, he was merrily putting one together. I was happy he'd asked me to come and speak, but I had to ask him, "So, how are your clients reacting to all this mess? Are you able to reassure them okay?"

He grinned. "What mess?" he asked, on a day when the TSX (Toronto stock exchange) plunged another 500 points. "They're happy. I got almost all of them into seg funds."

It was a message that resonated off the walls—in the middle of a generational financial panic.

You can buy some stocks or bonds or dividend-paying preferreds or bars of gold bullion or oil futures yourself, or you can join together with other people and buy a whole mess of them. Together you can even hire a snazzy person to run it. And then you'd have created a mutual fund. That's all it is—a pooled investment with others, which is managed by a person you hope is smarter than you.

As I told you, there are more than 20,000 funds available to Canadian investors, with more being created weekly. Some have been excellent long-term performers while others I would not touch with those blue rubber gloves they wear on *CSI*, plus a barge pole. Some are very conservative while others are extreme, leveraged and good for people who like cliffs and body kites. Mutual funds invest in riskless government securities, bonds, commodities, stocks (among other things) or a combination. Funds that are more restrictive, less regulated, intended for more sophisticated investors and employ tools like short-selling and lots of derivatives are called hedge funds. (Some of those achieved the best returns in the country in 2009, after some of the worst in 2008.)

There are two issues with mutual funds, of course. They charge management fees which eat into the returns investors get (a big range, but expect to pay about 2% for an actively-managed equity fund), and the returns are not guaranteed. There is no Canada Deposit Insurance Corporation standing behind mutual funds to hold your hand and give you a cheque and a tissue if you lose money. Like stocks, funds can make you a pot of profit some years and wipe it away in others. That's why I am an advocate in times like these of timing the market, making constant adjustments, and only staying in an investment if the foreseeable prospects are positive.

But there's another way of guaranteeing you never lose any of your invested money and at the same time get the ability to lock in gains that might accrue during good years, months or even days. That is the big idea behind segregated funds.

Seg funds, as they're called, were invented by insurance companies and are actually insurance products—a highly interesting twist on the idea of term life insurance. They are 'segregated' because the assets in these funds are held in separate accounts by the companies that created them. In fact, unlike mutual funds in which you buy units and actually share in the ownership of the assets, with seg funds you're only a 'notional' investor, which means you own a contract promising you certain things, and not a portion of the fund itself.

However, the outcome is clear.

How to escape the volatility around us

There are a number of reasons why seg funds are a home run with many investors who just don't want to put up with the volatility and uncertainty of our times.

- These funds offer maturity protection, which means at least 75% and often 100% of the money you invest is guaranteed to be returned to you after a minimum period of ten years.
- At the same time, the money you invest in the seg fund (and there are many different kinds, just like mutuals) is invested professionally in assets which are intended to grow, giving you the potential of returns equal to those of a mutual fund.
- And there's more. Because seg funds are insurance products, they offer a death benefit, so the guaranteed money in the fund will be paid to your beneficiary, free of tax. Any excess above that guarantee will be taxed as capital gains usually are.
- Also since this is an insurance gig, seg fund assets are immune from your creditors in the case of bankruptcy—which is a huge plus for entrepreneurs, business professionals and others who may face liabilities down the road. Having said that, seg funds cannot be used as a shield for an impending bankruptcy. If you're already

insolvent, buying one of them will not protect you from creditors.

- You can hold a seg fund as a separate investment, or stick it into an RRSP (registered retirement savings plan), RESP (registered education savings plan) or RRIF (retirement income fund). When inside an RRSP, however, the person named as the annuitant (the one whose life is insured) must be the same as the one who bought the plan. Outside an RRSP, there is no such restriction, which means a grandparent can buy one for a grandchild, or a company can insure the life of a key employee and invest at the same time.

- Seg funds all have one feature in common: by law they must give you a guarantee of at least 75% of the money you put in, but only if you leave it there for ten years. Less than that, and the guarantee falls (more on that in a minute).

So, does it make sense to lock into something for a decade? After all, don't stock markets and economies as a whole always go up over the course of ten years? Is it worth paying a higher management fee for a seg fund than a mutual fund (about double) to get this peace of mind?

Well, ten years ago I would have said (and told investors so) that it was probably not worth chunking over 5% a year in management fees for a typical equity-based seg fund, when you could buy an index fund that paced the market as a whole for a fee of about one-half of one per cent. But now I've changed my tune. The times have morphed considerably since the days of the tech bubble. Nine Eleven. Central banks turned into growth cheerleaders. The US housing bubble and its decimation of the middle class. Runaway public and private debt. Currency swings. Crude at $147. Demographics. Global financial panic. Peak Oil. Climate change. In the years immediately ahead of us how could an investment guarantee not be attractive to long-term investors who want to park their wealth and sleep at night? Especially when you can get this...

Lock in gains, and lock out losses

Resetting offers the opportunity to take advantage of rising markets and eliminates the impact of falling markets through seg funds.

- A reset is another unique feature of many segregated funds that allows you to lock in new gains on a regular basis. The reset turns the clock back and begins a new ten-year guarantee, locking in the current market value of a fund. This means in a rising market you may be able to continuously pull the trigger and capture the increased value of the fund, while in falling markets you have an assurance nothing will be lost. If only life worked this way.

- Some funds will reset values once a year, and some do it daily. So, if the guarantee on your fund was $10,000 on a Tuesday and a market rally raised the value on Wednesday by $100, the new guarantee would be $10,100—and the time you needed to wait to cash it in would also be extended by one day.

- Resetting a seg fund and locking in a gain is not what Canada Revenue Agency calls a 'taxable event.' It does not trigger any kind of an immediate tax bill.

- Investors should know that in the event you die before the fund matures, the death benefit payable to your beneficiary is for the guaranteed amount. If the seg fund has performed badly and does not contain enough money at the time of death, then the market value is supplemented by the insurance contract to bring it back to the full amount. Plus, the proceeds of a seg fund bypass the probate process and flow immediately free of any government interference to your beneficiary. No waiting. No disputes. They'll like you even more because of that.

- When a seg fund makes money on its investments, that capital is flowed through to investors in a process called allocation. Unlike mutual funds, which make distributions that are taxable, these stay untaxed until the end of the ten years. Plus, capital losses are passed to investors, which is not the case with mutuals.

- Commission charges to buy a seg fund (very similar to charges paid when buying a mutual fund), whether it's a front-end or back-end cost, can be claimed on your taxes in the year you paid them as a capital loss. You get no such deal with a mutual fund.

- When buying a seg fund, pay attention to the kind of guarantee you're receiving. A 'deposit-based' guarantee will increase with every payment you make into the plan, whereas a 'policy-based' guarantee won't.

- And age matters. If you're over 80, for example, many companies won't sell you a seg fund—or the ten-year guarantee feature might be reduced. Like they never heard of immortality. And if you have a fund inside an RRSP, remember that in the year in which you turn 71 it needs to be moved over into a RRIF to maintain its tax-free status.

So, this is obviously a serious and viable option for many investors who want to avoid market risk, still believe in holding growth assets, and who don't mind paying more in management fees and waiting ten years for their money. But what happens if you need to cash in a seg fund before the decade is up?

In that case, your guarantee is sliced. You can certainly redeem a seg fund at any time (just like a mutual), but whenever you do the maturity guarantee is nibbled away proportionally to the amount taken out. The formula for calculating this is straightforward: Determine the amount of your withdrawal as a percentage of the market value of your seg fund at the time of the withdrawal (so, if your fund is worth $50,000 and you take out $10,000, that's 20%). Now multiply the original guarantee when you bought the fund (or the last reset amount) by the percentage withdrawn, and that will yield the new guarantee.

In the example in Figure 4-3, the fund was bought for $40,000 with a 100% maturity guarantee. After five years, it was worth $50,000 and you took out $10,000 to renovate your kitchen.

Fig 4-3 *Calculating seg fund guarantee*

Amount invested:	$40,000
Guarantee at maturity:	100%
Market Value after 5 years:	$50,000
Amount withdrawn:	$10,000 (20% of market value)
New guarantee:	$32,000 (80% of original guarantee)

In the example, if the seg fund had a daily reset feature, then the original guarantee of $40,000 would have grown to equal the market value in five years of $50,000 (assuming the investor did not stop the clock and the ten-year maturity period began). In that case the 20% withdrawal would have taken the guarantee down to $40,000.

As mentioned, the amount a seg fund makes you over and above the guaranteed amount is taxed as a capital gain (outside of an RRSP—inside, no tax). So if your $200,000 seg fund with a 100% guarantee grows to $300,000 in ten years, then the $100,000 earned will end up adding $50,000 to your taxable income (the other half is free). If your seg fund chokes, however, and the market value after ten years is less than the guarantee, then the funds the insurance company pays you to make up the difference is not taxable. If you reset the seg fund after five years, locking in a new guarantee of $250,000 and it's worth $300,000 at maturity, the taxable amount is still $100,000, adding $50,000 to your income.

And what happens in the event your life insurance company goes belly up before your seg fund matures? Actually, this has never happened. But if it did, an outfit called Assuris, which is funded by the industry, would cough up 85% of your guaranteed amount.

Funds which come with a no-losses guarantee

Finally, seg funds themselves have spawned a stable of innovative new fund products that investors should be aware of, some of which combine the best features of both insurance products and mutual funds.

- **Guaranteed investment funds.** Seg funds based on mutual funds. This fund-on-fund approach gives you name-brand mutual fund managers and a deposit guarantee.

- **Protected funds.** These mutual funds are quite common now, offering a ten-year maturity guarantee and reset features, but no creditor protection or death benefit. Unlike segregated funds, which can only be sold by people licensed to offer insurance products, these are available from most advisors.

- **Portfolio funds.** If you want a diversified portfolio of seg funds, this is a good option since these invest in a portfolio of funds. Sometimes called 'seg fund wraps' they can also give you more asset allocation and active management than many traditional segregated funds.

Are you a seg fund kind of person? Many investors are. In fact, like the clients of the advisor I spoke for in the middle of the 2009 financial storm, there were a whole lot of people deliriously happy they'd paid the higher management fees for a portfolio of segregated funds, even if it meant they were locked in for years in order to trigger their full guarantee. If you're risk adverse, hate the idea of losing money even temporarily, but understand that with today's interest rates you need growth assets like equities, this could be a solution, as are bonds, in which an investor can be absolutely sure what the future holds.

Bonds—the power & the glory

With his southern drawl, flip irreverence and gnarly obnoxiousness, I never thought I'd admire James Carville that much, even if he did rise to become a chief advisor to US President Bill Clinton. But when Carville said this, my attitude changed. "I used to think that if there was reincarnation, I wanted to come back as the president or the pope or as a .400 baseball hitter. But now I would like to come back as the bond market. You can intimidate everybody."

What Carville understands perfectly is when it comes to the modern world, debt speaks louder than equity. Governments like those in Washington and Ottawa and major corporations everywhere voraciously consume borrowed money. So, the bond market keeps expanding—now more than ever. Already the Canadian bond market's 14 times bigger than the TSX and growing by leaps and bounds. Between just the feds and the province of

Ontario, $300 billion in new bonds will be issued and bought by 2015. Meanwhile the world is being flooded with US Treasury issues, Eurobonds, corporate bonds and bonds and debentures from Crown corporations, agencies, states and municipalities.

All these entities cannot function without a diet of debt. This is one reason I'm convinced the coming years will bring higher taxes and slower growth—since billions more in interest will need to be paid. But this tidal wave of new borrowing also opens up more dynamic opportunities for investors who buy a chunk of this to stash away in their portfolio. Meanwhile the very existence of all this debt pretty much ensures interest rates themselves will be rising, as the competition for money ratchets higher. The debt market is where mortgage rates are set, so what happens there affects homeowners everywhere, as real estate values react to financing costs. The debt market holds governments ransom, dictating what rates their new debt must carry in order to find buyers. Bond traders react to government tax policy, budgets and currency moves, jacking up yields and forcing prices down when inflation spikes, for example. Intimidating everyone.

But not us. Not investors.

The triple-play advantage of bonds

Instead, bonds can (and should) form a part of almost everyone's portfolio because they're unique and powerful assets. Bonds are, as I said, debt. They make a promise to repay funds at a certain point in the future (called the maturity date) and, until that time, provide investors with a pre-determined stream of interest (based on the coupon rate). But that's not all.

The value of bonds is determined by market interest rates, so when rates rise, bonds fall in price, since existing bonds become less valuable. Conversely, when rates fall, bonds become worth more. In a falling rate environment, investors will pay more for bonds since they guarantee a stream of interest at a fixed rate into the future. If you happen to own a bond when that happens, your asset increases in value and you can sell it for a capital gain. So, bonds give you a triple play:

- a guarantee of repayment on a certain day in the future;
- an income stream based on an interest rate that will not change; and
- the potential of a capital gain.

What's more, bonds (at least 'investment grade' corporate bonds and government issues) are among the safest places in the world to put your money, and they're absolutely liquid— which means your piece of a bond can be bought or sold in a flash on the market, with the money in your bank account within three days. In addition, bonds come in lots of flavours. Some have an option allowing the owner to trade it in for common stock or preferred shares (called a 'convertible' bond), while others give an investor the option of extending the maturity date into the future ('extendible' bonds) or cashing it in early for full value ('retractable' bonds)—actions you can take as the interest rate environment at the time suits you.

You can also buy bonds that have had all interest payments removed, which means you purchase the principal amount only, paying face value (also called 'par value') at maturity. Typically you'd buy this kind of a bond, called a 'strip' bond, or 'zero coupon' bond, at a discount to face value—say $85 for each $100 of face value, payable in five years. So, rather than providing you with interest, the security simply matures at a higher price than that which you paid—guaranteed. Also, if interest rates drop while you own it, the strip can be sold to someone else at a higher price, since it's just become more valuable.

So, without a doubt, marketable bonds beat the pants off Canada Savings Bonds. Remember, CSBs are non-transferrable, which means you can't sell them to anyone else. They never rise in value if prevailing interest rates drop. The interest they pay is usually far below that of marketable bonds. There are no sweeteners, like the ability to convert to other securities or change the maturity date, and CSBs are not a whit more secure than the short-, medium- or long-term securities issued in the bond market by the same Government of Canada. In short, there's no reason to buy a CSB unless: you have only a small amount of money to invest and cannot afford a marketable bond; you really like the nice lady at the bank; or you never read this paragraph.

Bond investing, step-by-step

Below are some facts and guidelines about bond investment.

- A bond is a long-term debt obligation that guarantees repayment at a certain date and interest payments in the meantime that (in the case of corporations who issue them) is backed by physical assets.

- A government bond is not backed by assets, but rather by the power of that government to tax. That, by the way, is the ultimate economic force.

- A debenture is just like a bond but is usually secured not by specific assets but a general claim on a company's assets. Also called an 'unsecured' bond.

- The maturity date is the expiry of a bond, the day on which a lender is repaid in full.

- Face value, or par value, is the worth of the bond. For simplicity's sake, all bonds are referred to in terms of $100 of face value. So when you see in the newspaper a bond price is quoted at $99.20—that's how much you have to pay now to get a bond paying you $100 at maturity.

- The coupon rate is the interest rate attached to the bond, which never changes. So, a Telus 6% five-year bond will pay you 6% of the amount you buy every year until it matures in five years, usually in two payments annually.

- Yield is not the same as coupon rate. The yield of a bond does change, as market interest rates affect the price of the bond, making it more or less valuable. If rates rise, the bond price (per $100 of face value) declines, and the yield goes up, since new investors demand a competitive return. If you know the bond price and the coupon rate, you can calculate the yield simply.

    The formula is *Yield = Income / Price*

    So if that Telus 6% five-year bond was selling today for $93, the effective annual yield would be:

$$\frac{.06}{93} = 6.45\%$$

- Bonds that are priced at less than $100 are said to be trading at a 'discount' and those with prices above $100 are trading at a 'premium.' These days, after interest rates were at an historic low point and have only one direction in which to travel, pretty much all older bonds are on the market for more than face value, which is the pricing mechanism that keeps them consistent in a low rate environment. (You can see with the Telus example above that although the bond has a coupon rate of 6%, it pays an investor more because of its discounted price.) Bonds that trade at exactly $100 are said to be at 'par.'

■ You don't need a fortune to buy marketable bonds. They are usually available in denominations of $1,000 or $10,000.

■ The largest issuer of bonds in this country is the federal government, and these federal securities have the highest possible rating—which also means they can pay the lowest going rate of interest, compared to bonds issued by, for example, Suncor or the Royal Bank, which are still highly-rated and called investment grade.

■ Short-term bond-type obligations are called Treasury bills, or T-bills, and are a very popular place to stash money for short periods of time. They come in hunks from $1,000 to a million, with yields that rival or exceed that of CSBs, and are 100% safe and instantly liquid. T-bills (like strip bonds) don't pay interest, but are purchased at a discount to face value and come with three maturities—91 days, 181 days and 365 days. T-bills are issued by the feds, plus some provinces and other government bodies, with Ottawa being the biggest provider—selling a mess of them every two weeks through the Bank of Canada.

■ How do you know what a fair price for a T-bill is? Well, like everything to do with bonds, there's a formula for that, too.

$$\text{Yield} = \frac{\text{Face Value} - \text{Price}}{\text{Price}} \times \frac{365}{\text{Days to Maturity}} \times 100$$

So, a 181-day T-bill bought for $97 would have this yield:

$$\frac{100 - 97}{97} \times \frac{365}{181} \times 100 = 6.23\%$$

- Corporate bonds can be a great investment, since the rate of return is higher. But be careful to choose an issuer with a good credit rating ('BBB' or above), since the greatest risk here is that of default. Many corporations issue 'mortgage' bonds that are backed by physical real estate the company owns, but you can also buy collateral bonds that are issued by outfits, like holding companies, which do not have land or buildings to pledge.

- And there are bonds denominated in Canadian dollars or other currencies. For example, you can get a US-pay bond issued by a Canadian bank that pays you in American currency and is payable in greenbacks upon maturity.

- How do you know what a trustworthy bond is? That's the job of credit rating agencies—DBRS (Dominion Bond Rating Service), Moody's Canada and Standard & Poor's. They assign letters from AAA (highest) to CC (very speculative) to D (in default). Bonds with a 'C' rating are also known as 'junk bonds'—usually the securities of distressed companies—which pay the greatest amount of interest, since that's required to attract investors.

- And here is how bond quotes look in the financial pages, for example that Telus bond:

Issue	Coupon	Maturity	Bid	Ask	Yield
Telus	6.0%	Jan 15/15	92.65	93	6.45%

This tells you what the bond pays, when it matures and what it's currently priced at in the marketplace. The 'ask' price is what the bondholder wants for the security and what it can be bought for, and the 'bid' price is the latest offering price, or what it can be sold for. The yield is the effective rate of return based on the current 'ask' price.

The awesome power of income plus growth

The reality is most people have absolutely no idea how bonds are priced, or the way in which they can add capital gains plus income and a payment guarantee to individual portfolios. But I hope you can see now what an awesome combination it is to have some secure bonds churning out a steady stream of interest and giving you a future guarantee of payment; while equities harness shorter-term moves in the economy, the market and the business cycle, throwing off capital gains; and some preferred shares are generating tax-advantaged dividend income. That's the power of diversification, and by adjusting the mix of equities, bonds and cash, you can tailor risk and return to your stage of life and your position on the money road.

So, how do you choose which bonds to invest in? Long or short, government or corporate, convertible or not? The best idea is to work with an advisor who does this stuff all day, and who has the online data service alerting him or her to new bond issues, changes in pricing and availability. By the time many retail investors determine what a good debt security might be, there's just no guarantee it'll still be there to buy.

How to pick bonds that suit you

Here are some of the factors that should play a role in picking bonds that are right for your portfolio.

Credit Quality

Bonds you never have to worry about going into default come from government, most particularly the Government of Canada, although a provincial government bond isn't going to fail, either, nor is a security issued by a governmental body like the Export Development Corporation or a utility. However, don't assume a bond pays peanuts just because it comes from government. For example while five-year GIC rates were 2%, 100% secure provincial bonds in my portfolio were paying in excess of 4.5%.

These triple-A issues are rock solid, but don't throw off the highest rates of interest. So if yield is what you are after, then an investment grade corporate bond is perfectly acceptable. Large corporations such as Bell, Rogers or Enbridge might fit the bill, giving you an enhanced yield and tons of security. For example, in Figure 4-4 are some corporate bonds on the market at the end of 2009, most of them medium term.

Fig 4-4 *Corporate bond yields and prices*

Issuer	Coupon Rate	Maturity	Price
Bank of Montreal	7.92	2012	100.00
Bank of Nova Scotia	4.8	2012	99.65
Bell Canada	8.88	2026	106.02
Cambridge Shopping	10.79	2012	116.95
Canadian Natural Resources	4.95	2015	103.84
Canadian Tire	4.95	2015	104.39
Canadian Utilities	6.14	2012	110.74
Enbridge Consumers Gas	10.6	2012	101.67
Encana	4.3	2012	105.05
Farm Credit Corp.	4.3	2020	103.63
Hydro One	5.77	2012	109.93
Loblaws	5.4	2013	107.36
Manulife Insurance	4.67	2013	105.04
OMERS Realty	4.09	2013	104.43

Coupon rate

It's clear to see on the list of corporate bonds in Figure 4-4 that a range of coupon rates is available, largely depending on the credit rating of the issuer. The price of the bonds is arrived at in the marketplace, and the fact most of these were selling at a premium (more than the par value of $100) is a reflection of the low-rate environment in place at the end of 2009, which made these bonds more valuable because of their higher yields. To an investor it means this: If you bought $1,000 worth of the five-year Canadian Tire bond it would yield $49.50 in interest and $1,000 at maturity. The yield would be 4.74%. That is a return 125% higher than you'd get from a five-year GIC at one of the major banks (they were paying 2.1% in the fourth quarter of 2009). So why would any rational, conservative and income-oriented investor put money into a bank, instead of buying a bond issued by a bank, or other major Canadian corporation?

But as the list shows you, various issuers with less strong credit ratings are forced to offer higher rates of return—and many of these bonds could be ideal for your portfolio, since it's highly unlikely outfits of the quality named above will be going belly-up.

Once interest rates start to rise, bonds like these fall in price, which automatically boosts the yield for new investors. As a rule of thumb, the lower the credit rating of the issuing company, the higher the yield. By the way, you can follow bond pricing online at a slew of web sites, free of charge.

When you buy a bond (or your advisor does it for you), you'll know the face value, the coupon rate, the price paid per $100, the bond's current yield (such as the 4.74% yield on the Canadian Tire issue), and you'll also be given a 'yield to maturity.' The yield to maturity is an important number, since it's the total return the bond would pay if you bought it now at the market price and held it until maturity, reinvesting the interest at the same rate. With the example of the Canadian Tire bond, this YTM would equal 3.99% —which amounted to a 90% interest premium over a five-year bank GIC.

Maturity

The length of time outstanding on the bond is its maturity. In general, short-term bonds are three years or less until maturity, medium bonds are up to five years and long bonds are ten years or more. Bonds issued in the past continue to trade right up until they expire, and the price keeps changing according to the number of years or months left of interest payments, the original coupon rate and current market interest rates.

So, a 15-year government bond issued with a 6% coupon rate ten years ago would today be a five-year bond, still with a 6% rate. If prevailing interest rates are higher when you come to buy it, the bond will probably sell at a discount to face value, and if rates are low, then it will come at a premium.

This illustrates an important point for investors: The bonds with the greatest volatility in their pricing are the longest ones. That's because interest rates have a lot more opportunity to bounce around in an unforeseen fashion over 10 or 20 years than they do over two or three years. Another tip: bonds with lower coupon rates are more volatile than ones with higher rates, since a relatively small change in market interest rates will affect the price of the lower-coupon bond more dramatically. Bottom line: Short-term bonds (five years or less) with the highest coupon rate available will probably give you the fewest surprises.

Duration

This is a term that relates to a bond's volatility, or the extent to which the value of it will bounce around as interest rates change. The definition is the rate of change in the price of the bond for every 1% move in market rates. But you don't need to figure this out, since the duration number is already calculated for all market bonds—which means you can compare them easily. This is a good thing, since contrasting bonds with varying maturities and coupon rates would otherwise be too daunting for most of us.

The bigger the duration number of the bond you are considering, the more its value will change along with rates. That means if you expect interest rates to plunge, buying a bond with a high duration would give you a hefty capital gain when and if it happened. By the same token (and more appropriate for the road ahead), if you believe interest rates have nowhere to go but up, and the Bank of Canada will be moving its key rate higher over the coming years, the best way to protect your bond values is to buy securities with a low duration. They will be impacted less by the rate jump and hang on to more of their capital worth.

Canada or foreign

There are tons of Canadian bonds that will pay you in foreign currencies, such as US or Australian dollars. The advantage is you diversify out of Canadian currency, which has been bouncing around dramatically over the last few years, but the disadvantage is you have to buy the securities in the same currency, and timing foreign exchange conversions is a crap shoot on most days. However, this is a good option for those people who might earn offshore income in the form of a pension, or who get an inheritance from another country they'd like to keep in that currency.

For years I have maintained a US dollar portion of my own investment portfolio, just to hedge against fluctuations in the value of the loonie. US-pay bonds from trusted Canadian companies have proven to be a very satisfactory way of managing that money.

Care for a sweetener?

Bonds are not always just bonds, since many come with what are called 'sweeteners' or inducements for investors. The four you should be most interested in are:

- **convertible** bonds, which give you the option to convert the bond into common or preferred shares in a company at a set price. The option to convert is usually yours, so you don't have to do it, but if the value of the shares rises above the value of the bond, then a smart investor has the chance to convert, sell the shares, and pocket the profit.

- **retractable** bonds give investors the ability to cash in their securities years before the maturity date. Why would you do this? Well, if interest rates started surging and the value of your bond dropped below par, you could always cash it in early for full value.

- **extendible** bonds are the opposite—and the investor is given the right on a short-term bond to trade the debt for an equal amount of new debt with a longer maturity. So, a five-year bond could be turned into a ten-year one. Why would you want to do this? If you had a bond with a great coupon rate and prevailing interest rates took a dive, this is a certain way of keeping the party going.

- **step-up** bonds offer a feature you often see with various kinds of bonds (even Canada Savings Bonds), where an investor gets a guarantee that if the security is not cashed in, the rate of interest paid will step higher each year for a set period of time. This helps protect the borrower from having to replace a lot of debt if market rates start escalating.

Coupons or strip

Several years before her death, and during a time of relatively high interest rates, my smart mother (with the help of her crafty son) decided to set aside some cash for her grandchildren. She dispatched me to buy two strip bonds, for which she paid less than $2,000 each, that had maturities of a decade. When the time came to carry out her wishes, those strips had matured and were worth more than $5,000 a piece, which meant she'd tripled the value of the gift.

Regular garden-variety bonds pay you interest twice a year. As mentioned, sometimes bonds are 'stripped' of their interest-bearing coupons (long ago bonds came as fancy documents with coupons attached, each one representing an interest payment), and sold as the principal amount only, called the 'residual.' So, this pays you no interest, and as a result, the bond is purchased at a discount to face value. The bigger the discount, the more of an effective rate of return you get on your money—but you have to wait until you cash it in to realize that gain. (By the way, you can also buy one or more of the stripped coupons, which trade separately.)

Why would you want a strip bond? Mostly because what you see is what you get. Doesn't matter if market rates rise or fall, since what you paid, what you get and the return are all known, and will not change. If you don't hold the strip to maturity, however, its value in the marketplace will actually be affected more than that of a regular bond (which has an income stream), which could mean a bigger capital gain or loss. Also a bummer is the fact that the money the strip is earning you (the annualized return between the purchase price and face value) is considered by Ottawa to be earned income, so it's taxed annually even though you get none of it. A solution to that: stash the strip inside your RRSP, your tax-free savings account or your RRIF.

As you might imagine, there's a lot more to bond investing than I've presented here, but these are the basics we all need to understand—because we should all own bonds. How many and how much of your total net worth depends on your risk tolerance, age, circumstances, objectives and the need you have for income as opposed to growth. Bonds are anything but boring. Suspender-snapping bond traders have been financial market gods for decades, and there's even a believable case to be made that the bond market has substantially altered the course of history (read Niall Ferguson's *The Ascent of Money* for dramatic proof).

Given what lies ahead, as debt-drenched countries increasingly lean on the bond market, affecting interest rates and competing for capital, we should all be watching carefully. These are the days to be a lender, not a borrower. Watch what government does. Do the opposite.

A few words on a dirty word

When the American and global financial systems came to the brink of collapse in the winter of 2008–9 there was no shortage of blame to go around. American homeowners had been rash in bidding up the price of homes to an unsustainable level and taking on trillions in new debt. Mortgage lenders had reduced standards, created subprime loans and shovelled money over to anyone able to fog a mirror. The US Fed, America's central bank, had dropped interest rates to a level that stayed too low for too long. Wall Street bankers were rapacious, greedy pirates. Politicians were totally asleep at the switch.

But special disgust was saved for the investment banking industry, which gave us words like securitization, collateralized debt obligations, asset-backed commercial paper, risk arbitrage, hedging and, most famously, derivatives. God-fearing, normal people discovered with awe that Wall Street types making millions a year had packaged together twitchy mortgages into new debt instruments, secured triple-A ratings on them, and then sold these in 'tranches' (or slices) to unsuspecting buyers around the world. Even more fantastic was that reputable organizations like AIG, the planet's biggest insurance company, would have entered into a series of bets with hedge funds and other shadowy players on the creditworthiness of the very assets changing hands—bets worth trillions of dollars, many of which went horribly wrong and imperilled the world.

This, sadly, is how most people found out about hedge funds and derivatives—both of which many Canadians should consider for their investment portfolios. And you don't need red suspenders or a Lear jet to do so. In fact, using derivatives like options (puts and calls) or hedge funds (using long/short strategies) can reduce the level of risk and augment returns most effectively.

Derivatives: how to make a lot of a little

Derivative is the term applied to something that derives its value from something else, called an underlying asset. That could be a stock, a stock market index, a commodity like gold or cattle or currency. People trade derivatives instead of the real thing, because it allows the use of leverage, since the underlying asset is seldom actually bought or sold in a way that necessitates physical delivery and because it's a cheap form of insurance against unexpected market moves in an uncertain world.

I won't dive into all the complexities of this, but there are some tools you need to know about—like options. These are contracts between a buyer and a seller based on an underlying asset, for example 100 shares of the Royal Bank. With a 'call' one side purchases the right (but not the obligation) to buy the shares, and is called the 'holder.' The other side agrees to sell 100 bank shares (if called upon to do so), and is known as the 'writer.' The contract has a price to it, which the holder pays to the writer, and the deal also places a future value on the underlying asset, in this case the shares.

So, I might buy a call on 100 Royal shares at $60 each for delivery in February, and for that I might pay $4 a share, or $400. I'd do this expecting Royal shares, then trading at $60, to be worth $70 by the time the option expires. If so, I would then own and sell 100 shares, worth $7,000, for which I spent $6,400 (the purchase price of $6,000 plus the premium of $400). That means I'd have a profit of $600, which cost me $400, for a return of 50% on my money in a few weeks.

In comparison, if I had bought 100 shares of Royal Bank at $60 (and spent $6,000) selling them later for $7,000, my profit would be $1,000, for a return of 16% on the $6,000 invested. That, in a nutshell, is why people use options to make money on all kinds of things—putting up a relatively small portion of the value on the expectation of future price changes.

But what if Royal Bank shares tanked, and slid from $60 to $50 by the time the option expired? Then as the holder of the call, I'd be 'out of the money,' and refuse to close the deal. My loss would be the premium that I paid for the contract—$400—which is less than the $1,000 loss I would have experienced buying the actual 100 shares that later dropped by ten bucks a piece.

The $400 premium belongs then to the person on the other side of the deal, called the writer. So why would someone want to be in that position? First, for income, since the writer gets to keep the premium, whatever happens. Second, the writer might believe Royal Bank shares are overvalued and will fall in price, so there's little risk to taking this contract on. Or the call writer might own Royal Bank shares already and is looking for a way to reduce the risk of owning the stock. So, if it falls in value below the $60 deal price (called the 'strike' price) and the contract expires, the $400 premium received mitigates the decline in Royal Bank shares by $4 a piece.

The same logic can be used with 'puts' which are the flip side of calls. Here the holder buys a put on a stock (or a stock index, or a bond, or 100 ounces of gold, etc.) that he or she thinks will cost less at a fixed point in the future. That means for the cost of the premium paid—$400 for those 100 RBC shares trading at $60 with a put contract for $50—the put holder is hoping the stock falls to $50. Then the contract will be exercised, the writer hands over 100 bank shares in return for $5,000, which the holder can sell for $6,000, making a profit of $600 ($1,000 less the premium paid). Again, that's a 50% return on the $400 spent.

The writer on the other side of the put contract is making an opposite bet, assuming the underlying asset will rise in value. In that case, the contract will expire and he gets to keep the four hundred bucks. But if the stock does drop and the contract is exercised, he has to buy the shares. This might not be such a bad idea if the writer was planning on buying 100 shares of RBC stock anyway—because the price is now $4 a share cheaper (using the money the put holder paid as the premium).

Two faces of options: speculate and protect

As you can see, there are several possible outcomes with puts and calls, since any investor can be a holder or a writer in either case. Strategies abound.

- Buy a call to speculate, and to leverage your money for a far greater potential return. For example, in the bank shares in the example above, you'll earn a much better return through an options contract than simply buying a stock that goes up in price.

- Buy a call to lock in the future price of something you wish to buy. For example, you could enter into a contract to buy gold at $1,200 an ounce. If the price rises above that, you make a profit exercising the contract, and if gold is less, you let the contract expire and buy the gold at its lower price. This way you have bought protection against a price increase.
- Buy a call option to purchase a stock that you have shorted in the market. (Sounds complicated, but this is just a way to almost eliminate the risk involved in selling stock short—shares you borrow from a broker then sell on the expectation they will fall in value. If they don't, a call option gets you off the hook.)
- Buy a put to speculate that an asset will fall in value, but with a small risk to you if it does not. You might bet that silver will fall by July and enter into a put for a few hundred dollars on silver worth thousands. If you bet wrong, you lose the premium—and are not forced to buy the metal. If you bet right, you exercise the contract, or sell it on the options market for a higher price than the premium you paid—again, without needing to take delivery of the actual underlying asset.
- Buy a put to protect something you own by setting a floor price for it. You might buy a put-option for 500 shares of Bank of Montreal at $40, when you already own the stock. That way you know you've got a guarantee of selling the shares for forty bucks until the contract expires, so if the stock tumbles to $30, that was cheap insurance.

As well as options, investors should also know about futures. Thankfully, they are simpler, since instead of writers and holders of puts and calls, here you only have to choose between going

long or short on a futures contract. You buy a contract to speculate that the value of an asset will increase, or to hedge and lock
in a future purchase price.

As with options, most traders never actually take delivery
of, or have to unload, the asset the contract is based on. So, if
you bought a contract for 100 ounces of gold for delivery in the
future at $1,200 an ounce and the metal hit $1,500, the contract
itself would rise substantially in value since it represented real
intrinsic value (whoever owns it can buy $150,000 worth of gold
for just $120,000). Instead of buying and selling the physical
metal, you would unload the contract, and pocket the profit.
This is an example of going long.

As with any investments that involve leverage, futures can
pose significant risk to an investor as well as the potential to
exaggerate profits. They are exchange-traded forward contracts
that can be based on stock market indexes, precious metals,
currency values or bond prices. The person going long agrees to
buy something at a set price on a specific day, and the party
going short agrees to sell it. Unlike with options, no upfront premium changes hands. Also unlike premiums, if you agree to buy
something in a long position, you cannot let the contract expire
and walk away. Instead, you have to accept delivery or buy an
offsetting short position to cover yourself—which is what most
investors do.

The greatest risk for the least return

We all face a mountain of risk in the years ahead, speeding down
this road. It's inevitable—higher taxes, indebted governments,
more interest charges, a wave of senior citizens, homeowners
borrowed up to their lobes, a retirement and pension crisis, market volatility and the near-certainty of a real estate thud. I just

can't see how any of those threats can be avoided, which means risk is inescapable. So how do we cope, and keep moving ahead?

It sure won't be by taking on any additional risk that does not bring with it an equal or greater reward. That means not investing is a risk. Investing too timidly is a risk. Investing for too small a return is a risk. Trying to avoid risk may well bring you the greatest risk, since we enter this time of uncertainty with too little wealth and long, long lives stretching ahead.

The point of investing now is not to avoid risk. It's too late for that. Just sitting on your money in cash or GICs or savings bonds, or buying a house and hoping for the best are not viable options. The odds are you'll simply run out of cash, especially in the world of higher taxes, stiffer prices and rising interest rates I see ahead of us. That's why we all have to be far better educated and then systematically use this knowledge to beat the odds. The happy news is that it absolutely can be done. Never before have so many excellent assets and strategies been available to the average investor, or so much in-depth information yours for the downloading.

Understanding how a modern diversified portfolio is put together, with correlated investments and calculated risk is empowering. So is knowing how seg funds and mutual funds work, how to do your own market and company analysis, how to pick bonds or use derivatives to hedge risk and safely leverage. One book won't equip you to conquer these things, but I hope it sheds some light on what options you have, and highlights strategies that excite or intrigue.

The next step is yours. Take it.

Five

ROAD BLOCK

How our houses led us astray

We've never gambled so much on one asset

The sharpest financial jolt you'll ever know may come from the thing you worry about least. And when it does, there will be lots of blame to spread around.

Residential real estate represents the single greatest potential danger to your financial well-being. But that's just the start. A housing decline—even a modest one—is the nightmare that keeps the federal finance minister tossing at night. And the governor of the Bank of Canada. And the bank economists, along with the behemoths they work for. It's the sword hanging over the entire economy, 20% of which is made up directly of spending on real estate, and 60% from spending by consumers who own houses.

Real estate has ballooned past all measures of importance to the economy as a whole. Mortgage debt technically enslaves the population. Vast amounts of family net worth are buried in it. Housing's bubbles have crushed economic activity in the past, and the next one seems destined to have more destructive impact than all previous busted booms put together.

Never before have Canadian families gambled so much on one asset. Never have so many people gorged on debt to buy something at epic prices. And absolutely never—not even with tech darling Nortel or dream merchant Bre-X—have we seen emotion play a larger role in devastating investment decisions. As if they'd learned nothing about what caused the global financial crisis of 2008-9, or never heard of the housing collapse that decimated the American middle class, Canadians enter into the next tumultuous years at risk as never before. This will not end well.

If you're reading this while the market is still in a frenzy, complete with bidding wars, shooting prices and a 'buy now, or buy never' mentality—especially among first time purchasers—then count yourself lucky. You have adequate time to get out, short the market, diversify or hunker down for the inevitable changes to come. The real estate boom, which developed in 2009, quickly took on the classic aspects of an asset bubble, fuelled by direct government manipulation of the market and central bank actions that may well cause irreparable damage.

But the most potent impact will be on those who, in the last few years, bought into housing believing it to be a long-term storehouse of wealth, a worthy and easier alternative to stocks or bonds and threw all their money at a down payment or a renovation. They will be paying a big price for not diversifying, and not looking south at what a potent destroyer of money a home can be.

Real estate values in Canada will tumble. Exactly when this happens will depend on how soon energy-induced inflation rolls over us, how fast and far interest rates rise, how profound our structural unemployment is, how much the Boomers panic and how soon millions of recent homeowners realize what a mistake they've made. This will result in large numbers of families slipping into negative equity, a wave of foreclosures and power of sale actions and a slide in housing prices that will wipe out billions of dollars in middle class wealth, especially in Vancouver, Calgary, Victoria, Edmonton and Toronto.

The bidding wars and over-paying will end. The surge of new listings will swamp the dwindling number of new buyers. Sales volumes will retreat from record highs to record lows. Those young couples who emptied their RRSPs and borrowed from aging parents to make down payments will feel deceived, and homeowners who did not sell at the top, reaping a once-only capital gains bonanza may regret it for years.

Who will buy unaffordable houses?

Across most of the developed world, in America, Britain, France, Spain and elsewhere, families with too much debt and too much real estate have experienced the same heartache. They've learned the same lesson—that buying houses at ever greater prices with ever more leverage always ends the same way. Values collapse. Debt does not.

How will this happen?

If history is any guide, it will not be swift or dramatic, as many people anticipate. Rather, a slow but steady stream of events will inevitably tip the scales of market balance. There are ten major reasons this will occur (see Traffic Signal).

The generation of the house is over

None of these factors should surprise. In isolation, most would not be enough to prick an asset bubble on their own. But I'm sure the road ahead guarantees we'll see a large number of them

TEN REASONS REAL ESTATE VALUES WILL FALL

1. Rising energy prices and personal taxes eating into disposable income.

2. Hikes in sales taxes, such as the HST, or an increase in the GST increasing the costs of home ownership.

3. Incremental moves up in interest rates.

4. More plant closures and unemployment.

5. Stagnant family incomes and the looming reality of mortgage renewals in 2014 or 2015 at far higher rates.

6. An increase in houses coming to market as aging Boomers realize this is their last chance to cash out.

7. Underfunded corporate pension plans and a retirement crisis.

8. Dismayed urban homeowners fleeing surging property taxes imposed by cash-strapped cities.

9. A financial crisis as the US dollar slides, debt soars and the 2012 presidential election is fought over protectionism, which could be devastating to Canada.

10. And above all, a plateau of unaffordability as the cost of the average house exceeds the ability of the average family to buy it.

happen in quick succession, or even concurrently. How could it be otherwise? We know, for example, interest rates have nowhere to go but up. We know governments are hopelessly mired in debt and will have to find new revenues. We know the Boomers have most of their wealth in houses, and are now into their sixties. We know that in markets like Vancouver, where the average single-family home in 2009 took nine times the average income to buy it, housing is beyond the reach of most families. Therefore it seems assured that the next few years will bring a confluence of events and trends which guarantee the *generation of the house* is over.

How could it be otherwise?

And how will it end? As I said, history suggests it could be a long, sliding process in which homeowners see equity drained away on a weekly basis over the course of years. Those who detect the early signs (we are already surrounded by them) and make their move can escape with their wealth largely intact. Those who wait, hoping an initial decline in sales volumes will reverse in a few months, can be quickly trapped in a spiral. Most will get it wrong.

Looking south, for example, Canadians believed the American housing market collapsed completely within a few months— an event that our 'prudent banks' and 'stable lending practices' make impossible here. In reality, the US crumble took years to unfold, despite Herculean efforts by Washington and billions of dollars in public money to slow or reverse the bleeding. Also a myth is that Canada is any different, as I will discuss in a moment.

The housing market in the United States had its apex in the autumn of 2005, as interest rates started to increase and the prices of homes reached a point of impossibility. Shortly afterwards came the inevitable results of relaxed lending standards, as defaults climbed and foreclosures turned from a problem into a crisis. Despite that, more than four years later—well into 2010—the housing market was still on its knees and sinking fast.

In late 2009, for example, one in seven mortgages was in default or foreclosure, one in four families slated to lose their homes and one in three was in negative equity. With millions of credit-worthy borrowers facing the real prospect of losing their homes in 2010 and 2011, house prices in most major markets were still in decline. The only real buying activity was that of vultures, snapping up the cheapest of foreclosed homes—feasting on the carrion of a dying market.

Incidentally, there will be plenty for Canadian vultures to snack on.

A potent symbol of the decimation of real estate as the iconic American commodity came on November 18, 2009, when the 80,300-seat Pontiac Silverdome football arena outside Detroit, built for $55.7 million, was sold to a Toronto firm for just $583,000—about 1% of its value and less money than a two-bedroom standard condo cost on the north shore of Lake Ontario. This is what happens to property values when a community loses too many jobs. The unemployment rate in the Detroit area at the time was 35%—higher than during the Great Depression.

Do such things happen only in America?

Hardly.

In the Toronto area in 1989, the price of an average home hit more than $261,000, which was a staggering increase of 250% from the level of 1980. A real estate boom fuelled by moderate inflation had turned into a classic asset bubble. New condo buildings sprang up from every vacant lot. Young couples sucked on coffees and slept overnight in lawn chairs outside new home sales centres, waiting their turn to go in and buy unbuilt houses. Multiple offers, bidding wars and offers for more than the listed price were everywhere. Houses were flipped after just weeks or days of ownership. In fact, some homes closed multiple times on the same day as buyers sold their accepted offers to new purchasers. Overall, there was a sense that anyone who did not take the plunge and jump into the market would be priced out forever.

Classic bubble behaviour

Greed and fear joined hands to propel rash buying decisions.
People lined up to grab an asset when it was at the absolute top of
the price curve—as they were doing again in Toronto, Vancouver
and Edmonton in 2009. (See Figure 5-1 for a graphic represen-
tation of the long-term increase and decrease in the home prices
of one US city.)

And then it was over. In slow-mo.

Fig 5-1 *Housing's long descent*

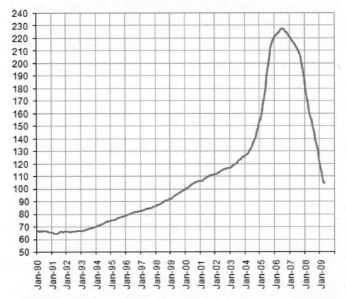

Case-Shiller Home Price Index for Phoenix, Arizona
January 1990 through April 2009
Index Value of 100 = January 2000

*The collapse in American real estate values took years, not months, as this tracing
of home prices in Phoenix, Arizona shows. Most US cities recorded their highest
real estate values in 2005, and by early 2010, the grinding retreat was still in
effect, as a third of all homeowners faced the prospect of their homes being
worth less than their mortgages. This is an experience Canadians should study.
We are not immune.*

As in the US, and as is almost always the case with housing values, the collapse in Toronto prices in the late eighties and early nineties took years to find a bottom. By 1993 the average price settled at $189,000, for a 27.5% plunge from the peak. Sales volumes collapsed. Thousands of licensed real estate agents left the business, and untold numbers of condo units giving negative monthly cash flow were the legacy for 'investors' who bought the wrong property at the wrong time, in the wrong way.

It took until the beginning of 2002—a staggering 13 years after the high-water mark in 1989—for housing prices to recover. But even then, homeowners who hung on had received no compensation for more than a decade of inflation and ownership costs, and were thrust into new losses after paying real estate commissions to get out. All around, it was an unmitigated disaster for real estate investors—a lost decade during which the Toronto stock market had doubled in value, despite the tech bubble meltdown of 1999–2000.

As is always the case, bubbles cause blindness.

Real estate is finished. Equity markets are not.

This is the pattern you should expect over the next decade. Real estate as a slam dunk investment is finished. Equity markets will advance, despite stagflation and sideways momentum. Thanks to the ten reasons I detailed in the earlier Traffic Signal, it will be virtually impossible for the average homeowner to make money on their property, and only the wildly fortunate will break even. Most who bought in 2008 or 2009 or 2010, especially with little down and long amortizations, risk being wiped out.

The mantra of 'buy now, or buy never' will be proven to be as false and immature as it always has been. Demand for Canadian real estate was drawn forward by extreme and foolhardy government measures, and there is now no doubt of the outcome.

If you are reading this while a bubble still exists in your community, there is still time. In a few pages, I will show you how to prepare.

So much for the 'ownership society'

At the beginning of the second decade in this century, America's been shredded by its former fetish with housing. It is unclear if it will ever recover in our time or that of the next few generations. Only the foolish among us would see no link between what happened there and what is destined to take place here. Canada remains utterly dependent for a great portion of its national wealth on the US, and for a large proportion of our jobs. Like the Americans, we have allowed our economy to deindustrialize, sending tens of thousands of positions to places like India and China. Instead of earning wealth by producing things, we do it now more and more by selling each other services and by exporting raw product—the bulk of which are natural resources—to the south.

This has a dramatic impact on real estate.

Like the Americans, we've presided over the shuttering of factories and the export of both equipment and skilled jobs. Manufacturing now accounts for just 12% of the US economy while in Canada it has shrunk to 15%. In contrast, the financial services sector has swollen to 22% of all economic activity, while both countries are utterly dependent on consumer spending. In Canada, six of every ten dollars spent are related to consumers, while in America it is seven dollars.

At the heart of the consumer society is real estate. According to a CIBC study, 40% of all national personal net worth is in real estate, while other studies find 80% of the net worth of home-owning families is tied up in their houses. This makes them utterly undiversified and hugely at risk. With the rapid escalation in house prices that took place after the 2008–9 global financial collapse—defying the experience of all other western countries, save Australia—Canadian families are more real estate dependent than ever. It does not bode well.

The importance of real estate to the viability of both economies was shown dramatically in 2009 as Ottawa and Washington primed the pump. The effort was aimed at one thing—encouraging more borrowing, more debt, more loan risk even at a time when the economy was fragile and contracting. In Canada, this led to a frenzy and a bubble eerily similar to that which erupted in California, Florida, Arizona and Nevada four years earlier. In the States, the massive stimulus failed to ignite in a society where millions of people had just learned what a punch granite countertops and stainless appliances can deliver.

"It will be a long time before people think of owning a home as a good investment again," Tuck School of Business professor John Vogel told Bloomberg News in late 2009 as President Obama poured more billions into the real estate market. "A lot of what drives housing is psychological, and right now there's a distinct lack of confidence in real estate."

House prices between 2005 and 2009 across America were the most unpredictable and volatile ever. From double-digit annual increases in every market in 2005, they plunged into double-digit nationwide losses in both 2008 and 2009. The first decade of the new century had been consumed with bricks and mortar, especially after the terrorist attacks of Nine Eleven, when the Fed made the momentous decision to crash interest rates to then historic lows. That opened the floodgates for cheap mortgages, a movement embraced and promoted by Washington and the president, George W. Bush, who openly celebrated an 'ownership society.' "We're creating... an ownership society in this country, where more Americans than ever will be able to open up their door where they live and say, welcome to my house, welcome to my piece of property." (George W. Bush, October 2004.)

Across the country, house values jumped more than 80%, while in New York and San Francisco it was more like 150%. In Los Angeles, prices doubled. In response to vaulting costs, at a time when family incomes were static, mortgage lenders reduced standards, leading eventually to the widespread use of subprime loans and a host of new borrowing products. Loans with teaser rates appeared, giving ultra-low payments for a defined period of time before market rates kicked in. Banks did a brisk business in interest-only mortgages, or negative amortization loans where payments did not cover interest charges, so the shortfall was automatically added to the principal. There were also so-called 'liar loans' based on the self-reported or unverified income of the borrowers, plus 'Ninja' mortgages, given to people with ostensibly 'no income, no jobs and no assets.'

Behind the financing excesses was a Wall Street industry that bought loans, bundled them together and sold them to unwary investors across the world. Meanwhile government-sponsored mortgage giants Fannie Mae and Freddie Mac also absorbed billions in loans, removing the risk from lenders and transferring it to the taxpayers. The conditions, and the psychology, were perfect for market excess.

The outcome should have been obvious, but to most it was not. Writing in 2006, US investment advisor and author Peter Schiff issued this largely unheeded warning: "If the dot-com mania was the warm-up, the main act is the real estate bubble. Stock market collapses are bloody, but their damage is pretty well limited to those who bought overvalued stocks. Real estate, though, is all about leverage, and that debacle, already well under way, is going to affect virtually every American."

By the middle of 2006, real estate values were falling fast after average prices reached a level that was four times the typical

American family income. (By 2010, the average Toronto home cost 5.8 times income and in Vancouver it was nine times.) Across the country, houses would fall by a third, and in cities like Miami, Las Vegas and Phoenix by half. Communities in southern California saw declines of up to 70%, a disease which soon spread to the former manufacturing states of Michigan, Ohio, Pennsylvania and South Carolina as unemployment rates skyrocketed.

Nothing like this had happened since the 1930s

As house prices collapsed, homeownership fell into disfavour. By 2009 the number of people owning their homes had dropped to a ten-year low. Falling values had wiped out trillions in equity, and plunged 16 million families into negative equity—many of them with decent incomes, good credit ratings, and who'd had absolutely nothing to do with subprime mortgages. The lesson was that in a society that had allowed its national wealth to be wrapped up in the emotionalism and subjectivity of real estate, and willingly shed so many goods-producing jobs to create so many lenders and realtors, a crisis of confidence could become an economic one. And it did. America choked. The world gagged.

Not since the 1930s, when real estate values dropped 39%, had anything like this happened. But in the thirties, 65% of all profits, and jobs, came from manufacturing. In 2008, it was just 7%. The timing of the real estate collapse could hardly have been worse.

In Canada, people watched it unfold with detached fascination, amid assurances from the housing industry, bank economists and politicians that things were different here. Days before the 2008 federal election the prime minister said Canada would not enter into recession or run a deficit. Ten months later the country was mired in negative growth and plunging into new debt at the rate of more than $1 billion a week.

On the streets of the major cities, however, reality was still distant. An unrenovated home in Vancouver listed at $749,000 sold for $1,033,000 in late 2009 after 18 offers were submitted. A young couple in Toronto shot a video of their baby 'signing' an offer to try to persuade the vendors of a home to choose them. (They lost.) In the midst of a recession, house sales across Canada lurched ahead 74% while prices surged 20%.

It suddenly smelled a lot like Phoenix, circa 2006.

Why it isn't any different in Canada

At the heart of the Canadian denial was the oft-repeated mantra that we're somehow morally and fiscally superior to the Americans; that our financial institutions are more guarded and buttoned-down; that we are less of a risk-taking people with a history of personal prudence and caution. Facts, however, say otherwise.

If the American housing market flew too close to the sun because of speculative price increases and lax lending standards, ours was flapping right behind. Between 2000 and the end of 2009, the average Canadian house increased in value by 106%, eclipsing the ten-year America-wide jump which ended in the fizzle of 2006. In Vancouver the average single-family detached home travelled from $400,000 to more than $931,000, while in Toronto the average sale value for all resale homes went from $220,000 as the decade began to over $450,000 by 2010—rivalling the experience of the 1980s that ended in a 27.5%, 13-year-long rout (see Figure 5-2).

Here we go again.

Fig 5-2 *Will this bubble end the same way?*

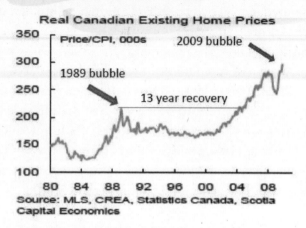

The last time Canada had a housing bubble, fuelled by a sense that buyers had to take action or forever be priced out of the market, was in 1989. What followed the burst was a 13-year wait for those who bought in at the peak to simply break even. The odds of this happening again? Given what lies down the road, it's all but assured.

In other words, Canadians were as completely speculative with residential real estate values as Americans. More so, in fact. And in both countries, while real estate was soaring in price, median family incomes through the period barely moved. The inevitable result was a surge in household debt, particularly mortgage loans. By December of 2009 the average household debt to income ratio had hit an historic high of 145%, slightly greater than the debt load being shouldered by Americans. The month before the federal Office of the Superintendent of Bankruptcies reported a 36.4% increase in personal failures.

But an appetite for expensive homes and fat mortgages were not the only ties that bound real estate-manic Americans and Canadians, or the lenders that fed them. While northerners clucked in derision over Ninja mortgages and subprime horror stories, Canadian mortgage lending standards were also taking a dive. The first disaster was Ottawa's 2006 decision to amend legislation governing the mortgage business and allow 0% down mortgages and those with 40-year amortizations to be eligible for government-backed insurance. In a flash, major banks were issuing loans to people without savings, and new US-based mortgage entrants were clamouring to enter the Canadian market.

Why would the federal government change the rules, opening up homeownership to people without money? Were the politicians not aware of what was then unfolding south of the border?

The short answer is the migration of George Bush's 'ownership society' to Canada, and its enthusiastic embrace by the country's Conservative government. This was evidence of a conviction that citizens who move into houses and mortgages are the natural engine of economic growth and more likely to support right-of-centre policies. However, it took less than a year for it to become obvious the decision was feeding an asset bubble, creating over-valuations and ultimately pricing average families out of the market. Finally Ottawa relented, partly after my tirades in parliament and my book *Greater Fool*, and in late 2008 recanted the change. The minimum down payment became 5%, and the maximum amortization period 35 years. The change did virtually nothing, however, to dampen a frenzied market, with 5/35 mortgages the standard choice of young and first-time buyers. (In December 2009, the federal finance minister warned rules could be tightened again to address the growing bubble.)

But this relaxing of mortgage lending standards was just one example of a trend towards the most accommodative housing financing in Canada's history. At the same time in 2008, major banks were approving mortgages on homes nobody had appraised, but which fit into accepted postal code designations.

Canada even got (and still has) its own version of 'liar loans' as banks like CIBC removed a condition for self-employed workers to prove their incomes. For example, the bank's Self-Employed Recognition Mortgage is described this way:

> "This mortgage makes it easier for you to buy a home if you're self-employed. Our simplified approval process is designed specifically to meet the unique needs of entrepreneurs. You'll benefit from a range of mortgage products with built-in flexible options and less paperwork. We recognize that the self-employed have traditionally faced greater scrutiny in qualifying for mortgage financing. That's why CIBC has streamlined the mortgage approval process to ensure our self-employed customers receive the respect and credit they deserve when applying for a mortgage. Approval is based on your self-declared income, strong equity and excellent personal credit history. Best of all, you don't need to prove your income. If you're self-employed, and you have 35% equity (or 5% equity for a high-ratio mortgage), this mortgage can provide an ideal solution for your home financing needs."

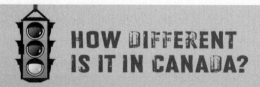

HOW DIFFERENT IS IT IN CANADA?

- Americans let their real estate market become a hotbed of speculative excess. So did we.

- Americans let mortgage lenders finance houses for buyers with no savings. So did we.

- Americans encouraged homeowner debt. So did we.

- Americans embraced the ownership society. So did we.

- Americans adopted fiscal and monetary policy designed to keep the fires burning. So did we.

And in so doing, we both laid the foundations for disaster.

A bubble the government wanted

Make no mistake, the government wants you to buy a house. An expensive one. The bigger the mortgage the better. In fact, consumers were the essence of Canada's Economic Action Plan, that multi-billion-dollar catch-all designed to rescue our society from the jaws of deflation and the kind of decline which gripped and ripped the American middle class. Recognizing that we have created an economy in which consumer spending—especially on housing—is far more potent than manufacturing cars or digging up potash, Ottawa pulled out all the stops to encourage the formation of an inflationary asset bubble.

The commitment to real estate was embedded in the government's philosophy, as witnessed by the zero-down payment, 40-year amortization debacle early in its mandate. But once the financial meltdown hit, house pumping became a central plank of public policy. And that's a key reason why Mark Carney, former Wall Street investment maven and Department of Finance insider, was encouraged as the new Bank of Canada governor to plunge interest rates to unheard-of levels in early 2009. The central bank's overnight rate hit 0.25% for the first time in history, followed by a melt in the chartered banks' prime to 2.25%, and heralded an age when mortgages could be had for as little as 1.5%.

Incredibly, that rate allowed a couple to carry a $500,000 mortgage with a 35-year amortization for just $1,500 a month, requiring an income of only $54,000. A year earlier, borrowers were happy to lock into a fixed rate home loan at 5.35%, which meant only those with an income of $94,000—35% higher than the typical family—could carry it.

In a matter of weeks, Carney had changed the landscape so families with incomes 25% less than the median could buy homes costing 80% above the national average. And in doing so, Ottawa got the irresponsible, out-of-control result it apparently craved.

The response was immediate and electric. House prices started to soar even as unemployment mounted, factories closed, retail sales dwindled, exports slid and federal finances fell off a cliff. Suddenly hundreds of thousands of young couples who lacked savings and had been shut out of real estate ownership by market mortgage rates and their incomes could afford to jump in. Their salvation came in the form of government-insured mortgages giving them 95% leverage, banks being encouraged to lend freely, variable-rate loans barely higher than the prevailing rate of inflation, 35-year amortizations which were the equivalent of rent and a purposefully blind eye turned by those whose job it was to police against market excess.

Sales and prices surged. The question realtors were asked changed from, "How much does it cost?" to "How much does it cost a month?"

With 2% mortgage money driving demand, and house valuations climbing weekly, the direction we were headed in was clear: over a cliff. After all, when Americans allowed house prices to inflate while dropping the bar for homeownership and openly encouraging runaway household debt, the outcome was inevitable. How could Canadians follow the same path, and expect a new destination? I asked that question in my 2008 and 2009 books, and daily on my blog.

Tales from the street: 'Frightening how ridiculous it seems'

Some of the tales from the street, snippets of life never making it into the mainstream media, were telling:

"I have been keenly observing the real estate market especially in the core, ranging from Roncesvalles to Danforth," wrote a thirtysomething from Toronto. "In fact this wkend, I visited a few open houses in Roncesvalles, all in the same neighbourhood. It was like Halloween, but with adults walking in large groups down one street and up the next, running into each other again and again, giddy about their possible new purchases. All the realtors were very flippant, casually remarking they're taking offers on Tuesday and are expecting their respective house to go for nothing less than 80–100k over asking."

And this, from a husband and father in Thornhill, Ontario, a suburban hub north of the GTA:

"Past month. Our neighbourhood, 3 houses sold for approx. 10% over asking price. We're talking about 25 year old modestly upgraded homes that are going for 650–800K.

We looked at a house yesterday that was listed last week. Entertaining offers tomorrow. listed at 740K, will bet my right nut it's gonna go over 800K. Sorry, no home inspection allowed. What would an inspector find anyway? Wife wants the house, I want a drink. Current residence is paid off and at todays 'take what you want' rates were good for a 1.5M house. Wow, I'm rich. Wife doesn't understand why I'm hesitant over a possible 50K mortgage. Honey, I've spent more time inspecting a $5000 used car than this three quarters of a million dollar house. What part of this process seems normal to you?

Plan a—Want to sell and go rent for a while. Darling wife/3 kiddies aint gonna let that happen.

Plan b—there's a raging inferno out there, where's the fire department. Isn't somebody responsible for putting this out of control mess out? What? the fire dept. is pouring more gas on the fire? clean up in aisle 8, calling mark carney. that was so sweet of him to 'remind' everybody that they're responsible for their debts. how did that work out for greenspan/ bernanke? what? you can't just walk away from a house in Canada? hello debt slave lifer.

Plan c—wait until our house hits 1M, sometime next year I guess. Sell, buy an entire neighbourhood in Florida, California (hate having neighbours that I can see/hear) and invest the rest in Goldman Sachs. I hear they're taking over the U.S treasury dept and the federal reserve. Oh wait, they already own both. my bad.

Plan d—sit back, relax, and suffer a bit more in your 2100sq/ ft house and move up another 1000 sq/ft when things calm down (when it crashes and burns?). oh the horror, how will we make do in our 25 year old, paid off, 2100 sq/ft house before we can really live it up in our new, 25 yr old, 3000+ sq/ft house?

Frightening how ridiculous it all seems when you actually read it back to yourself."

By the way, the home mentioned above listed at $740,000, sold for $818,000 after multiple bids were presented on the day offers were accepted. About this time, on the streets of Toronto, more scenes suggesting the end stages of the bubble market were quickly approaching. As a new, unbuilt, mid-town condominium project was released for pre-sales, a skirmish broke out among dozens of people who had lined up—some of them for days—in the cold November rain and fog.

When morning sales began, November 25th, this is how *The Toronto Star* described the scene:

"Competing lines of real estate agents waiting to buy new luxury condos turned ugly on Bloor St. this morning with jabbing, shouts, threats and accusations of queue-jumping. Some of the agents, who lined both sides of Bloor at Bedford Ave., had been waiting for more than a week to buy units in the X2 development at Jarvis and Charles Sts. Others arrived last night.

By this morning, there were three separate lines of potential buyers, each claiming the right to have first crack at the condos. Around 8 a.m., a representative for builder Great Gulf Homes threw two of the three warring lineups into a fury by declaring their long waits and place-holding invalid. Chanting "X2—Unfair," shouting and holding up freshly made signs with the word "unfair" on them, the agents who had waited the longest protested the decision.

The 30 north side real estate agents started arriving Tuesday night around 11, according to accounts from both sides, usurping the priority once held by another 40 agents who turned up 10 days ago and stretched along the south side of Bloor St. As dawn broke over Bloor, the two outside lines started to realize there was another group of realtors inside the Intercontinental Hotel on the north side, who had been there since Nov. 22, with instructions that "first come, first served" sales would begin in the second-floor Willard Room.

Kevin Killackey, a Remax agent on the north side, said, 'There was no actual procedure set up. Those people over there figured they'd start their own system and go across the street.' Last night, he said, 'people were jabbing each other. Police had to break it up.'"

A market destroyed: paying people to buy

Meanwhile Barack Obama, watching the US dollar fall as public debt mushroomed, was desperately trying to blow air back into the housing bubble that had deflated and shellacked the US economy in a patina of debt. Over $20 billion was allocated to a rebate of $8,000 being handed over to every real estate buyer who had not been in the market for three years, and then extended to include a $6,500 gift to anyone who had owned a home for at least five of the previous eight years, and wanted to move up. And this was no gift to the economically disadvantaged, but an outright subsidy to the middle class—those who had always put too much of their net worth in a house. The credit was available to single buyers with an income of up to $125,000, or married couples earning as much as $225,000.

As it had paid people to buy cars, so governments now paid and subsidized them to buy houses. In doing so, it replaced the laws of supply and demand, distorted the market and inflated the price of real estate. Most damaging, it actively encouraged more private, household and personal debt, in the wake of a global crisis that had been caused by excess credit.

The wise among us did not forget, however, that no nation can borrow its way to health.

This will not end well

How could it? Market forces have been banished. When the Bank of Canada dishes out what is almost free money, income's no longer an issue when buying real estate. There is no brake on housing prices, opening the door for speculative excess taking valuations to a pinnacle from which they risk collapse. If history is a guide and experience after the last bubble tells us anything,

35-year-old buyers in 2010 could be 50-year-olds before they can sell to break even. A new lost decade of feeding a mortgage at steadily increasing costs to support a home in which equity gains are zero.

What a potentially horrible wrong turn to take on the money road, while investors who diversify their wealth in equities, bonds, preferreds and cash—as well as real estate—travel headlong towards financial security.

CANADA'S OWN SUBPRIMES

Ottawa's decision to drop interest rates to the lowest point in history, while maintaining government-sponsored insurance for high-ratio, high-risk loans (through Canada Mortgage and Housing Corporation) profoundly affected the market. A real estate correction in late 2008, blowing off price excesses, was turned overnight into an asset bubble, pushing sales volumes and valuations to unheard-of levels, in the midst of a recession.

With the certainty that interest rates would rise in the coming years as the economy recovered from its near-death experience, mortgages in the 2-3% range became Canadian subprimes. Just as American lenders had entrapped borrowers into massive loans and expensive home purchases with low introductory 'teaser' rates, destined to be replaced in a few years by much higher market rates, so Canadian banks and brokers did the same. Some consequences were immediate. Others we will live with for a long time.

What the Bank of Canada did along with the banks' compliance was effectively duplicate the subprime situation in the US (see the Traffic Signal). The *costs* would be felt by everyone.

- **Low rates encourage excess borrowing.** Purchasers hot to buy houses in a rising market tend to think that existing mortgage rates will remain at that level for the foreseeable future, especially first-time buyers who've never faced a renewal. Rock-bottom lending rates mean people with below-average incomes qualify for loans they'd simply not be able to service in normal times. This time bomb was the height of irresponsibility by policy-makers.

- **Low rates spawn bidding wars and recklessness.** When money's so cheap and measured in monthly payments rather than overall debt, frenzied and inexperienced buyers in a competitive situation (often created by realtors promoting an auction environment) are willing to pay tens or hundreds of thousand extra to 'win' the competition. Realtors call such a tactic a 'bully offer'— blasting through a bidding war with an extreme offer. In November 2009, *Toronto Life* carried a story of the bidding war experiences of a young couple keen to buy a Toronto house listed at $529,000. They immediately offered $46,000 over asking, and an hour later agreed to the seller's demand for another $10,000. Their initial price range was $350,000 to $450,000. Final amount spent: $585,000.

- **Low rates making houses more expensive.** Obviously. By massively increasing the amount of money people can borrow on the same level of income, they flood the market with liquidity, allowing sellers to raise prices and establishing new levels of expectations of all home-owners. And while market rates will eventually turn the market cold and dampen valuations, affordability for everyone has been dealt a blow.

- **Government policies remove lender risk, encouraging less prudent lending.** In Canada, CMHC (Canada Mortgage and Housing Corporation), a federal agency, insures all mortgages in deals where buyers put down less than 20% of the price—which lately has been the majority of new borrowers. By removing the risk from lenders who don't need to worry so much about repayment or the credit-worthiness of the borrower, this practice is akin to that in the US when government-sponsored entities Freddie Mac and Fannie Mae backed loans, and along with Wall Street investment banks securitized them. Quietly in 2009, Ottawa allowed CMHC's insurable loan limit to rise to $600 billion—larger than the national debt and an increase of almost 200% from just two years earlier. The government was clearly in the bubble business.

- **These policies skew the market for risk and responsibility.** With CMHC standing behind all high-ratio loans and banks off the hook for default, lenders don't need to charge a risk premium on loans to dodgy borrowers. That means a young couple with no savings and just 5% down can borrow money as cheaply as the move-up buyer with 80% equity. So much for caution.

- **Artificially low rates destroy housing affordability for most families.** Perhaps for an entire generation. At the average mortgage rate for the past 20 years, just over 8%, the average family could afford to carry a $250,000 mortgage. Yet to buy the average home in Toronto required cash for a down payment and closing costs of over $200,000—in 2010, the equivalent of almost three years of pre-tax income. In Vancouver, the cash needed surpassed $500,000, or seven years of pre-tax income. The legacy of such a bubble is a real estate drought, the consequences of which will be long lasting and profound.

- **Low rates encourage and facilitate debt.** By every measure, consumer debt raced ahead after the Bank of Canada dropped its key lending rate. Household indebtedness increased by 9% during 2009, and mortgage debt hit an historic high. This indebtedness will have to be paid off at far higher future costs.

- **This sets us up for a massive drop in disposable income.** Interest rates will increase as inflation becomes a destructive force, as the US tries to support its faltering dollar, as new issues flood the bond market and as central governments move to contain and limit the damage they have caused. As the cost of money increases, so will the debt servicing charges faced by millions of families carrying bigger mortgages, lines of credit and consumer loans encouraged by rock-bottom rates. This drop in disposable income is one of the reasons we are entering into a long period of stagnant growth every investor must prepare for.

- **All this guarantees real estate is a non-starter.** Relatively speaking, for years to come. The cheapest mortgage rates in history, combined with government incentives to splurge, such as the Home Renovation Tax Credit, made us spenders when we should have been savers, and brought housing demand forward. After every asset bubble, people always reconsider what they have done and this one will be no different. The legacy this time was a raft of equityless and indebted owners, unaffordable houses, a badly distorted marketplace and the potential for a lifeless economy.

And how is that so different from the mess Americans face? The question now is what we do about it.

Step One: Get out while you can

The residential real estate market in Canada will not continue to rise without end. Houses will not appreciate without sustained demand. Since interest rates will inevitably increase, that demand will only come if the economy grows, unemployment melts off, new investment pours in, personal incomes improve and consumer confidence jumps enough to compensate for the higher cost of money.

The odds of this happening in the next five years I would put at zero. In fact, there's every reason—as I detailed in the opening pages of this book—to expect from now to 2015 and beyond to be a time of tepid growth, volatile markets, rising taxes, increased costs and reduced incomes. It will not be without massive opportunity for those who understand where energy, commodity, precious metal and equity markets are going, but for homeowners there's only pain ahead. There is no payoff coming, no assured equity growth and fewer and fewer greater fools to sell to. I hope you are reading this book when there is still time to exit because the window is closing.

Canadians are about to suffer the most significant potential wealth erosion in living memory. The impact of a residential real estate decline will eclipse losses experienced when Nortel imploded, stock markets tanked in the winter of 2008-9 or dot-coms turned into dot-bombs. The best strategy many people can follow, especially those who have little skin in the game and bought in 2007 or 2008 or 2009 with close to nothing down, is to get out. Sell. While you still can. While fools still abound.

The biggest threat now is negative equity
Here is your plan of action.

- List your home and do it in a reasonable, goal-oriented fashion. Soon hundreds of thousands of other people will be coming to the same conclusion, so the point here is to quickly extract your equity and, above all, pay off your debt.

- Do this by seeking the agent in your area with the best success rate and the biggest marketing budget. Set your price slightly below the market value of the home. Do what you must to ensure first impressions are flawless (outside paint, manicured walkways, perfect lawns and gardens, sealed driveway) and that prospective buyers feel they can immediately move in. Commission a home inspection (typically $500 to $1,000) and have the report available so that condition can be eliminated before an offer is written.

- If the market in your area is still hot, fall to your knees in thanks, then get with the program. Call for offers at a certain time to engender maximum investor interest. Host an open house for other agents.

- Stage the home for maximum impact and attractiveness. Today's buyer is all about fluff and appearances, and by spending a few hundred or a few thousand (costs range from about $200 to $4,000), you may be able to realize a

sizeable return on investment. Staging involves declutter-
ing, rearranging furniture, maximizing room views and
curb appeal, plus renting furniture and storing pieces
which detract. If you happen to be selling a vacant
property, never list without doing this first.

- After staging and redecorating, take pictures, write a
  feature sheet and work with your agent on creating
  a professional, full-colour brochure. Make a pdf and
  email it to everyone on your contact list. Register your
  street address as a domain name and throw together a
  simple web site for your home. Email that link everywhere and go on community blogs and sites to post it
  in comments. Hit Craiglist.

- In other words, do everything you possibly can to get
  action, and as soon as possible. This is a race against the
  inevitable.

If you read this after the bidding wars have already ended,
property values are falling, mortgage rates rising and the buyer
delusion has faded, then you obviously need to be even more
aggressive. If you have the bulk of your net worth tied up in a
single property, and simply cannot afford to see it drop by a quarter, a third or more, then do not delay. This is especially critical
for homeowners with little equity who bought with 5% down or
35-year amortizations, which do nothing on a monthly basis to
reduce the mortgage principal.

The greatest danger you face is negative equity—when a
declining housing market brings the value of your home below
the amount of your mortgage. In the middle of 2009, the number of American families in that predicament had soared to
10.2 million, on its way to 16 million. That equalled an astonish-

ing one in four, while in some states (Michigan, Nevada, Arizona, Florida) up to 50% of all homeowners with a mortgage were under water.

In Canada, with the bulk of new buyers in 2009 doing so with 5/35 mortgages amid the froth of a bubble market, thousands were at risk of negative equity with a price decline of even 10%. More likely, of course, the market could fall by twice that, and even more in areas like the Lower Mainland and portions of the GTA. The trouble with negative equity, as millions of Americans have found, is that it turns a home into a trap, making a sale virtually impossible.

For example, a home in Mississauga, Ontario, bought in a bubble market for $528,000 with a 5/35 mortgage and then sold after a modest 15% market correction would have a balance sheet similar to the one below.

Purchase price	**528,000**
Closing costs	11,035
CHMC insurance	13,800
5% down payment	26,400
Total cash in	51,235
Mortgage debt	501,600
Selling price (15% decline)	**448,800**
Commission (5%)	22,440
Net proceeds	426,360
Less mortgage penalty (3 mo)	(7,200)
Less mortgage principal	(501,600)
Less cash in	(51,235)
Net loss	133,675
Loss as % of cash invested	260%
Cheque required to close sale	**$82,440**

Now, imagine if there were a decline such as experienced after the 1989 bubble—27.5%. Or if certain Canadian markets repeated the experience of places like Stockton, California (a San Francisco commuter community not unlike Mississauga) and executive-style, two-storey homes with designer kitchens dropped in value by half. The results would be devastating.

Even in this example, with a modest 15% market correction, the buyer's loss is 260% of the money invested—showing what real estate leverage can do. Worse, the home   be sold without a cheque for $82,400 on the day of closing, payable from the seller to the mortgage company—on top of two years, or $56,700, in monthly payments (at a 3% rate).

And what happens if a young couple could not raise $82,400 to get out of the deal, fearing a 15% drop could deepen their negative equity and destroy their financial future? Not much. Default is no solution, since the homeowners are on the hook for every penny of mortgage money borrowed and will be sued (and lose) if they walk. The property cannot be sold or the title transferred until the loan is discharged. So the single escape route might be personal bankruptcy, which is drastic enough to be a career-stopper in many corporations and professions. But, I am sure, this will be far more common in the years ahead, for exactly these reasons.

Step Two: If you must stay, lock in

I've already given you the reasons why interest rates must inevitably rise. The timing is unclear, as is always the case, but the outcome is not. Lending rates have been kept at an artificially low level since the global financial panic as a desperate measure to induce borrowing and spending, to manufacture economic demand and blow air into the housing bubble. In the US, this effort largely failed since it came too late in the decline phase.

What it did do was fuel a bubble in financial markets, where stocks roared higher even on tepid earnings and rising unemployment. It also helped establish the mother of all carry trades, as investors borrowed billions at next to nothing in the US, then invested the money in the bustling economies and frothy markets of other countries—like China.

In Canada, rock-bottom rates did come in time to reflate the declining real estate sector, spurring a tidal wave of new borrowing, sending house prices soaring and creating the bubble I have described in these pages. But that will end with the inevitable jump in mortgage rates. The return of inflation, the move to higher rates in the US to rescue the greenback, the crowding out effect of new government issues in the bond market—all of this will lead to hikes by central banks, rising bond yields and rapid, painful jumps in mortgages.

How high? How fast?

We can only conjecture. But credible economists have said they feel once the Fed and the Bank of Canada get serious about restoring sound monetary policy they think key lending levels will rise two or three times a year, by as much as a half or full point, depending on the ability of the economy to swallow them. That means someone with a 3% variable rate mortgage who ignores things for a few months could wake up one day and realize his mortgage interest is being increased to 5%, adding to the size of the debt each and every day. Worse, he will face a mortgage renewal in 2012 or 2014 or 2015 at market rates—as opposed to emergency rates—which could restore the normal 8% level for home loans.

Many might not afford the next mortgage renewal

Could you live with that? Consider what this would mean for the average Vancouver single-family home bought at the time of the 2010 Olympics with a super-sized 20% down payment.

Purchase price (average SFH)*	$931,000
Down payment (20%)	186,200
Mortgage	744,800
Payments at 3%	3,524
Income required to service	127,000
Renew mortgage at 8%	
Payments	5,684
Income required to service	204,624

Single family home

While Vancouver may be an extreme case, just run the numbers with your own mortgage, realizing that the interest rates offered in the two years following the collapse of Wall Street and the global credit crisis were total aberrations. If they allowed you to grab a house with all-time low financing, great. If you loaded up on cheap debt and then used every trick in the book—weekly payments, doubled-up payments, truncated amortization—to get the thing paid down as fast as possible, then you indeed used these emergency rates to build some equity.

But most people, at least the bulk of new, first-time buyers who propelled the market, did the polar opposite. They borrowed the maximum amount (or close to it) that emergency rates would allow, then leveraged up their real estate purchase by using a low down payment and a maximum insurable amortization of 35 years. The result was impressive—a piece of real estate they would never be able to own under normal circumstances, and perhaps 20 years earlier in their lives.

However, as with a leveraged stock market move, there can be a vicious potential recoil.

For example...

- if you try to sell your home, and cannot,
- if you're living where you want to stay, and for personal or family reasons find it impossible to move, or
- if you need to buy some protection now from an inevitable renewal at market rates which you may not even qualify for,

...you should lock in.

Turn the variable rate loan into a fixed-term mortgage for at least five years. Depending on the lender and when you read this, a seven- or ten-year term might even be advisable.

I know that in other books, in media columns and seminars, I have preached the desirability and wisdom of borrowing short and variable, since study after study has shown that doing so saves money. But these are not normal times. Rates will never in your lifetime replicate those decreed by central bank emergency policies. There is only one path ahead, and only one way—other than bailing out of your real estate and debt obligation—to buy some time. Lock in now.

Step Three: Diversify while you're still able

Never make the mistake of viewing real estate in isolation from the rest of your assets. But, trouble is, most do. They pay too much for a home based on emotion, appetite, peer pressure or a spouse who wants to nest. Then they justify it as an investment, retirement nest egg, storehouse of value or source of stored wealth. Bad idea. Houses are horribly illiquid in down markets, very expensive to both buy and sell and will soon cost much more to carry. Even if you have a paid-off home, it represents a large quantity of cash that is yielding no income, and costing money to maintain. Thus, only by realizing sizeable capital gains is there any cause to confuse it with an 'investment.'

Worse, just as the Americans did, we've allowed residential real estate to get so expensive that by the time we finish acquiring it, most of our net worth is tied up inside. That wasn't a big problem for those who owned houses in the seventies or the eighties, when double-digit inflation promised healthy price hikes regardless of demand, but that world's gone. The years ahead will have inflation, alright, but in the single-digits only, while consumer incomes are under assault from all those things I have catalogued—higher taxes, runaway energy costs and increased interest charges. Oh yes, and a whack of Boomer listings flooding the market. In short, you do not want to have almost everything you have worked so hard for stuck in one asset that has a grand chance of falling in value.

This is why borrowing against equity is smart, but not as many Americans did during their own bubble—to finance purchases of boats, vacations and hi-def TVs. Instead of using your new found equity as an ATM, use it as an investment bank, accomplishing two very distinct yet crucial goals:

- lower risk through diversification and
- reduced taxable income.

For example, if you own a two-storey in Winnipeg, which you bought in 2005 for $300,000 and it's grown to be worth $450,000, with $220,000 left on the mortgage, you obviously have $230,000 in equity. However if mortgage rates rise at your next renewal, which will cause the housing market to decline, that equity could diminish fast. A 15% market drop would reduce the home's value to $382,000 and your equity to $162,000. That's not a 15% decline in your equity, but rather a 29% dump. Ouch. Wouldn't it have been nice to get that extra $67,500 out of the bricks and mortgage before the market took it away? And would you not have been further ahead to invest it in some good, solid growth assets—meaning all your eggs were not in the same basket, subject to the vagaries of househunters in The Peg?

Of course. And that's what an equity take-out loan is all about, also called a HELOC (home equity line of credit). You borrow against your equity to remove the money and put it in the kinds of investment grade securities I have already discussed. That seriously reduces your risk by broadening your investments from only one asset (the house) to many (in the balanced portfolio).

At the same time, the interest on the loan is fully deductible from your taxable income because the proceeds are being used for investment purposes. So at the end of the year, just add up the interest paid and deduct it on your tax return. That's sweet. A further bonus, if you are reading this while emergency rates continue to be in effect, is the ultra-low cost of borrowing, since home equity loans usually come at the best rate—prime. Beyond that, interest rate increases are not a worry, since all interest charges can be written off your tax bill and virtually all lenders are happy if you just repay the interest, not the principal.

What's the downside? You have a new debt, of course, equal to the funds borrowed. If that bothers you, don't do it. But a rational investor understands that tax-deductible borrowing is a significant tool, especially when the funds are used to generate investment income or capital gains and to achieve diversification and lower overall risk.

In the case above, you can kiss $67,500 goodbye and still have a house. Or you can have the house, a $67,500 investment portfolio throwing off income and growth and tax-deductible borrowing.

Is that a choice?

Step Four: Consider a safe haven—renting

The safest place to be with regard to housing over the next few years is probably out of the market. Yes, opportunities to buy at a deep discount to bubble prices will materialize and when that happens, you will know about it from the wailing over the water cooler or across the table at Tim's. But for now, my advice is to either get out completely or lock in long-term financing immediately if you choose to stay, and move equity into safer places with more assured growth and fewer histrionics.

Or, you can do as many smart and wealthy people do, and rent. Since a basic rule in successful financial lives is to buy what appreciates and rent what doesn't, leasing accommodations—especially from hapless owners who cannot sell—could be a very smart move until the volatile, predictable and dangerous years ahead of us are passed. I have no doubt that investing in a balanced portfolio, of the kind I described previously in Chapter Four, will bring you more financial security than trying to ride out a housing market which has been skewed and skewered by government intervention.

Some will argue that renting is (as some realtors love to phrase it) 'throwing away money' that could be used to pay off a mortgage. However, in the days when too many real estate professionals have been the biggest pumpers of 35-year amortizations, that statement is utterly hypocritical. Virtually no principal is paid off in the first third of a long mortgage, the homeowner is actually just renting money, not repaying it. Therefore after years of owning rather than renting, the owner is no better off. Cash flow devoted to putting a roof over your head is likely similar in both cases, but the owner is responsible for a big and untouched debt, while the mortgage-free renter moves on.

Moreover, if I am right about the inevitability of a correction taking real estate prices lower, why not get equity out now and lease somebody else's problem? Recall that after the last (1989) bubble burst, housing prices took 13 long years to recover—plenty of time for those who sold out at the right moment to buy their old home back at a fraction of the bubble price.

In Chapter Three we talked about a ratio (the price equity, or P/E, ratio) to determine if a stock is worth buying, based on its price and the earnings the company produced. If the price is expensive and the earnings low, then the P/E is high—not a good thing for short-term capital gains, and often indicative of a 'hot' stock investors have bid high and probably wise to avoid. The same principle can be used to gauge whether a house is a reasonable price to buy, or a much better deal to rent.

The Price-to-Rent ratio is one tool to determine if a piece of real estate is fairly valued relative to its ability to earn income in the marketplace. If the asking price or current market valuation bears an unrealistic relationship to what it can be rented for, it's probably not worth what the vendor is asking, but it might be worth renting. Here's how to determine that.

Take the annual rental income and divide it into the property's price tag, and then measure it against an historic norm. One good benchmark is a P/R of 16—which is a long-term average. So, for example, a three-bedroom, two-and-a-half bath, five-year-old townhome in Milton, Ontario with a double car garage, and on the market for $309,000, could be rented (as I wrote this) for $1,250, or $15,000 a year. The P/R ratio is just over 20.

To buy the same home with a 3% mortgage would require one year's worth of rent ($15,000) as a 5% down payment, and then $1,400 a month to carry, plus property taxes and the upfront cost of land transfer tax. Doubtless a realtor would tell you to buy, since other than the down payment, the carrying costs are similar. But this doesn't factor into the equation the certainty of higher interest rates (the monthly goes to $2,300 with an 8% mortgage) or the most important consideration: a market correction. In that case, a mere 10% price plop would value this unit at $278,000, which is $15,000 less than the mortgage, putting the owner in negative equity. Add in the down payment and a 5% commission to sell, and the 'investment' will result in a loss of more than $45,000, or a negative return of 300% on the money used to buy the place.

Now, tell me why owning is better than renting.

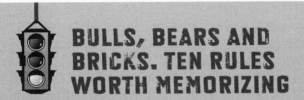

BULLS, BEARS AND BRICKS. TEN RULES WORTH MEMORIZING

Bob Farrell was a famous market analyst with Merrill Lynch, whose Ten Rules for Investing have been widely admired—and with good reason. Farrell distilled the impact of emotions and momentum on investments and his words stand as a reminder that people (not markets) make prices, and people, almost always, don't change. They overbuy, then oversell, rinse and repeat. I include these rules because there's basically not much different between buying and selling a house or some shares in the TD Bank.

My comments specifically related to real estate are in italics.

1. **Markets return to the mean over time.**

   When the price of financial assets goes too far in one direction, it always comes back. Euphoria and pessimism both cloud people's heads.

   This is far more pronounced with residential real estate than with stocks or mutual funds stuck inside an RRSP, since we have allowed houses to 'define' us in terms of

*social status. This emotional aspect magnifies the finan-
cial impact of real estate, and the bad decisions made,
causing most people to vastly over-value or under-value
housing. Thus, a crappy bungalow in Vancouver can sell
for $900,000, and a McMansion in Windsor, Ontario, for
$200,000.*

2. **Excesses in one direction lead to an opposite excess in
the other direction.**

   Any action too far in one direction not only brings you
   back to the baseline, but leads to an overshoot in the
   opposite direction.

   *Our tendency to invest by extremes lies at the heart of a
   recurring boom-bust cycle in real estate. Being a 'social'
   commodity, housing attracts massive interest and investment (greed) on the way up, then is shunned (fear) and
   devalued on the way down, inevitably with supply over-
   whelming demand.*

3. **There are no new eras—excesses are never permanent.**

   Whatever the latest hot sector is, eventually it overheats,
   the mean reverts, and then overshoots. As the fever
   builds, a chorus of "this time it's different" will be heard,
   even if those exact words are never used. And of course,
   'it'—human nature—is never different.

   *I'd say this was a lesson appropriate for much of BC, in
   the wake of the 2010 Olympics, or the rest of Canada as
   emergency interest rates phased out.*

4. **Exponential rapidly rising or falling markets usually
   go further than you think.**

   They do not correct by going sideways. Regardless of
   how hot a sector is, don't expect a plateau to work off

the excesses. Profits are locked in by selling, and that invariably leads to a significant correction—eventually.

I cannot foresee a soft landing for the residential housing market in Canada—as there was none in the US—in the wake of the 2009–10 real estate bubble although the process will take years. This brought future demand forward, took prices to an unsustainable level and swelled household debt to historic levels.

5. **The public buys the most at the top and the least at the bottom.**

   That's why contrarian-minded investors can make good money if they follow the sentiment indicators and have good timing.

   When housing markets boom, demand trumps supply and available listings drop, causing prices to rise and erasing value from the market. In times of bust, listings flood in, prices drop, sales plunge and value returns. Contrarians win.

6. **Fear and greed are stronger than long-term resolve.**

   Investors can be their own worst enemies, particularly when emotions take hold. Gains make us exuberant, enhance well-being and promote optimism. Losses bring sadness, disgust, fear, regret. Fear increases the sense of risk.

   As the most visible of personal investment assets, real estate is also the most emotional. A rising market creates an illusionary 'wealth effect' that causes homeowners to spend large, while a falling market quickly instils a profound fear of personal financial failure and has an immediate impact on consumer expenditures and the wider economy.

7. **Markets are strongest when they are broad and weakest when they narrow.**

   Hence, why breadth and volume are so important. Think of it as strength in numbers. Broad momentum is hard to stop. Watch for when momentum channels into a small number of stocks, or an increasingly exclusive component of real estate buyers, such as first timers.

   An example in real estate is the phenomenon of a strong but narrow housing boom caused by first-time buyers gorging on cheap mortgage rates and ultra-long amortizations. Average prices can shoot higher as a result of their activity, but market momentum stays fragile with the potential to be dashed as rates return to normal levels.

8. **Bear markets have three stages.**

   Sharp down, reflexive rebound and a drawn-out fundamental downtrend.

   Study the last burst bubble in Canadian markets in the late 1980s, and the 13-year period it took for prices to recover.

9. **When all the experts and forecasts agree—something entirely different is going to happen.**

   If everybody's optimistic, who is left to buy? If everybody's pessimistic, who's left to sell?

   Asset bubbles, in houses as in stocks, create their own demand and rising momentum. Supported by a media that has a vested interest in perpetual economic growth, the investing public is rarely given any perspective.

10. **Bull markets are more fun than bear markets.**

Step Five: Short the housing market

Investors in equities and bonds sure know how to make money when the market rises—or falls. In fact, in wild and volatile times the opportunities for aggressive or active moves increase dramatically. In Chapter Four I gave some examples of how investing in derivatives, like options (puts and calls), allows you to make low-risk, high-octane bets about where markets, stocks or commodities are headed. A slew of hedge funds you would be wise to learn about put such strategies to practical use. And then there's short selling.

Here's how this time-honoured move works: If you think Barrick shares will decline when the price of gold falls on a US Fed rate hike next month, then you can borrow some of the stock from a broker and sell it. The money goes into your brokerage account, then a portion of it is used to buy back Barrick stock in a month when it's hopefully cheaper. You give the stock back to your broker and keep the difference—that's your profit from the short sale. As I explained, the same thing can be done with leverage using options. Buy a put on Barrick stock for pennies on the dollar, then sell your contract for a profit if the stock takes a dive.

Simple enough (and an example of why equity investing is far more dynamic and less cumbersome than slogging through real estate transactions). In contrast, most Canadians have the bulk of their net worth tied up in residential real estate, on which they can make money only if the market advances and prices shoot higher. Not just slightly higher, but dramatically higher— since the cost of buying and selling houses is extreme compared with stock commissions or mutual fund fees.

But while it's yet impossible to short houses the way you can short a stock, there are some techniques worth using in a hot, frothy, bubblicious real estate market that is destined to cool.

Note: Some readers may consider the following strategies to be harsh and even heartless. But this book is about getting you to the destination of financial security, and emotionalism over real estate is the greatest road block most of us face.

Bubble buster # 1

Unloading real estate you own at the top of the market is obviously a way to realize tax-free capital gains on a principal residence. One way to 'short' the market would be through buying back later, at a lower price. In fact, if you were to sell in a bidding war you'd be able to get pretty much any closing date you wanted in an unconditional deal with a serious non-refundable deposit of at least 15% of the purchase price (simply make that a condition of the sale).

Demand a long closing of at least three months or, even better, six.

One of two things will likely happen: the market will have crested by the time the deal closes, giving you top-of-the-froth sale proceeds with which to buy a new house. Or, the buyers will realize they made a horrible mistake and paid far too much in the middle of a bubble, get cold feet and refuse to close the deal. Not a problem. Then you get to keep both the house and the serious deposit. In effect, you have removed that 15% of your bubble-time equity, converted it into cash, and done so without any corresponding debt on the other side of your personal balance sheet.

Now, take that money and use it to plump up your non-real estate investment portfolio, achieving diversification and lessening your risk. Save enough, though, for a few congratulatory beers.

Bubble buster # 2

Alternatively, you could sell a property at the top of the curve, get a guaranteed tax-free high yield on your sale proceeds, and quite possibly reclaim the asset, along with pocketing opportunity money at the same time. This is feasible because in the environment of an asset bubble, most people's emotions run roughshod over their intellect. A technical analyst, as I explained in Chapter Two, would call this a head-and-shoulders moment.

Let's say you have a mortgage-free property that could fetch $400,000—again, likely in a bidding war. Being a seller's market, you're clearly in the driver's seat and can insist on a large deposit which is non-refundable. (By the way, the real estate agent will fight you on this since it is non-traditional, but you have every right to amend the agreement of purchase and sale to tip it into your favour.)

Now, offer the buyer an attractive vendor take-back mortgage—five-year term, completely open, at less than bank rates. In fact, following the global credit crunch and the advent of emergency interest rates, many banks stopped offering flexible long-term, open loans. So this can be a great deal for the purchaser.

Insist on 15–20% down, and with the vendor take-back mortgage you will have not only a whack of cash on closing, but an annual income flowing from the proceeds of your principle residence. In other words, you've taken your over-valued property, put tens of thousands into your pocket and likely created enough cash flow to rent a similar home—secure in the knowledge that you'll still get your principal back in (at the most) five years. When you do, it will also be tax-free since it came from the sale of your home.

But what happens if the housing market collapses and your buyers find themselves underwater, with a house worth less than they paid? What if they walk or default on payments?

Whatever the outcome, you win. Put the house under power of sale or foreclosure. You retain the option of selling it again in the open market (and keeping the cash you've already collected), or putting it back into your own name after a process that will last some months—unless the owners succumb and sign it over to escape debt and litigation. Plus, if they don't capitulate, you always have the right to sue them for missed mortgage payments, legal costs and any shortfall that might occur between the mortgage amount and a sale amount—no matter how distressed the market might be.

Getting a judgment would be virtually automatic, or just regain title and move back in. And you'd be wealthier than you were before by the amount of the sale deposit, without having had to invest any money.

Bubble buster # 3

Yet another 'short'-selling strategy is to list a home during bubbly times when more speculative investors abound, complete with a tenant in place willing to pay a substantial market rent. This makes the property very attractive since the buyer will start receiving income from the real estate asset immediately upon closing, helping to finance the mortgage payments and significantly lessening the burden of ownership.

In fact, by selling with a quality tenant and cash flow in place, you may be able to ask, and receive, a premium price in a hot market. But how do you win, other than selling for top dollar? Simple: you be the tenant.

That way you:

- stay in your own home and avoid the cost and bother of moving,
- avoid having to go out and buy another home in a hot, overpriced market,
- no longer need to worry about maintenance costs or property taxes on the home,
- can cash out your tax-free capital gains at the top of the curve and
- will likely receive enough of a price premium for having a tenant in place to pay for your rent for a couple of

years, meaning you get your cash, stay in your home, and live for free.

Then, assuming the market has returned to a state of sanity, you can go out and buy another home at a reasonable cost. Or maybe buy the old one back at a discount to previous value.

Bubble buster # 4

Finally, a simple and effective way to avoid the potential train wreck of the Canadian housing market, and achieve the one thing this book stresses—diversification—is to bail out, invest and rent. This means getting out of real estate now, and staying out for a few years until a semblance of normality resumes. The good news is you can sell this asset for an historically high price (should you be reading this book while the bubble continues in some form) and realize what could be the greatest tax-free capital gain of your life. Then do something constructive and stabilizing with the proceeds.

For example, if you sold an upscale suburban home in Calgary for $700,000 with a $300,000 mortgage on it, you have four hundred thousand in proceeds. Instead of sticking it in a 'high yield' bank account or a low-paying GIC, why not spread it among the preferred shares of some blue-chip utility and bank stocks? The average recent dividend yield of 5.1% for utilities and 4% for banks (and insurance companies), produced a blended yield of 4.55%.

That would give you an income of $18,200 a year in tax-advantaged income (more on the advantage of dividends in the next chapter), or in excess of $1,500 a month to put toward rent, which is enough to secure a four-bedroom home in the burbs. To those who argue rent is a waste of cash, I say again there is essentially no difference between payments on a mortgage amortized over 35 years and leasing a home—especially when you are relieved of property taxes, insurance bills and maintenance costs, not to mention the burden of buying (land transfer tax, legals, etc.) and selling (commission).

Let your investment portfolio take care of your housing costs, until such time as value returns (and the pendulum will probably swing enough to create a real estate buying opportunity), and then reassess. In the meantime, your dividend-paying preferred shares are churning out income and perhaps even rising in value to yield a capital gain. They are 100% liquid, unlike real estate, and also have a history of adding stability to a stock portfolio due to their relatively low volatility (as the chart in Figure 5-3 from CIBC World Markets, issued in November 2009, shows).

Fig 5-3 *Letting dividend income pay your rent*

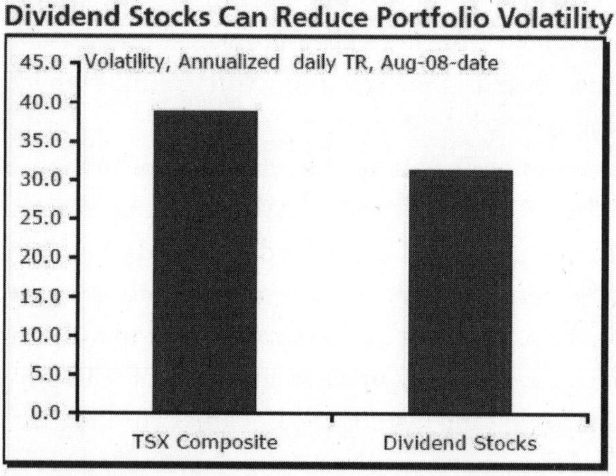

Dividend Stocks Can Reduce Portfolio Volatility

Bubble buster # 5

For many Canadians, being a vulture in the decimated US housing market seems irresistible, and a way to find value even when things in Canada are out of control. After all, consider the confluence of events—crashed housing prices, the lowest mortgage rates in a lifetime and a Canadian dollar bobbing at times near

100 cents US. Homes in Reno or Phoenix that were selling for $300,000 in 2005 could be scooped three or four years later for $130,000 to $150,000. In early 2010, there are almost 1,000 houses in hot, sunny (and dry) Phoenix for sale for less than $50,000.

So, why not buy? States like Arizona and Nevada have growing populations and housing markets that appear to be close to hitting the bottom. In fact, as Canadian property values hit new highs, investors flocked to downtown hotels in Calgary, Vancouver, Edmonton and Toronto to hear real estate gurus give them the skinny on how to profit from the misfortune of the American middle class. Without a doubt, there are strong arguments to buy property at the bottom of the curve—especially with more potent Canadian dollars. This could well be the vulture opportunity of the century. Here are a few points to remember.

- It's still no picnic getting a mortgage in the States, especially if you are a non-American. The best bet is to use a US subsidiary of a Canadian bank. Better still, borrow your money here and use cash.
- When you do borrow and close the deal, be prepared for extra costs. US mortgages come with 'points' which are unavoidable closing fees. In addition, you'll have to hire a local title insurance company as well as a lawyer.
- If you secure a tenant to help cover financing costs or as an investment property, you must pay US tax on the income. That means filling out a tax form showing the rent collected and all allowable expenses in order to determine the taxable profit.
- Selling is not as simple as finding a buyer (itself a huge challenge). More forms must be completed by your lawyer and a 10% federal withholding tax on the proceeds stays in the hands of the buyer. You can get a clearance certificate for sales under $300,000, but that takes more paper, and a few months.

- Many individual States also have withholding taxes on the money your sale nets.
- If you die while owning a piece of US property, there are special non-resident estate taxes to pay on anything valued at more than $60,000, although if you have a tax lawyer or accountant familiar in cross-border investing, your heirs might wiggle out of that one.
- And speaking of your spouse, make sure any property you buy in the US is registered properly. In Canada you can change the name on a deed easily. In America, you might face a gift tax as high as 40% of the property's value, simply to transfer title.
- And be wary of property taxes. Some States, notoriously Florida, cap residents' taxes while raising them without limit or recourse on rich foreigners like us.

Do these factors outweigh opportunity? Absolutely not. In fact, a very wise Canadian might be one who understands the nature of something called 'arbitrage' in the securities business. That is the simultaneous buying and selling of an asset or commodity in different markets in order to realize a riskless profit. In the case of real estate in these two countries, a rare situation exists when there is a bubble in Canada that cannot last and a bust in the States that is overdone. As both of those markets move to a more normalized situation in the coming years, it's hard to see how a seller in one who buys in the other will not gain.

Will it ever be Canadian vulture time?

Looking over the rubble of the American housing market, many Canadians find it inconceivable that a similar condition could develop here. Perhaps it is. The perfect five-year storm that blew through that country starting in the fall of 2005 came about from the confluence of a number of factors, some of which—subprime mortgages, collateralized debt obligations and a lack of regulatory oversight—may not be seen again for a long time, if ever.

But as this book strives to underscore, we have our own set of dangers which cannot and should not be ignored. The national finances are in as bad shape as household balance sheets, while the population ages and emergency rates prove temporary. That's enough to worry about on its own, and more than enough to tip the housing market off its public pedestal.

In my 2009 book, *After the Crash*, written during the darkest days of the global financial meltdown, I speculated on housing's decline. At that time the real estate market was in fact suffering the falling prices I had earlier predicted, but this was reversed months later when the Bank of Canada dropped interest rates to an all-time low and borrowers piled in. Frankly, I did not expect Canadians to have such a bottomless appetite for new debt, especially at a time when layoffs and plant closures dominated the headlines, nor that they'd end up duking it out in Vancouver bidding wars or throwing elbows desperately trying to buy unbuilt condos in Toronto. This wave of speculation swept the market to a new high—and a new level of danger.

No asset rises endlessly. All booms end badly. This should be self-evident, but every generation seems destined to make the same profound discoveries. As Bob Farrell said, it's always different this time. And it never is.

No doubt in my mind, then, that the pendulum will swing in the other direction for reasons articulated here. No doubt houses will go from being over-valued to under-valued. No doubt the days will come when buyers fade, the number of listings explodes, sales volumes tumble, the ranks of real estate agents thin again and prices drop below the intrinsic value of the assets themselves. It happens with all markets, and that's when the vultures circle.

Here are some guidelines on how to successfully vultch.

- **Offer what you're willing to pay, not what the vendor asks.** When listings pop and sales fizzle, every offer must be taken seriously. Only an offer will get you a sign-back showing the true level of desperation you're dealing with.

- **Always submit the offer with a deposit cheque,** which focusses buyer attention. However, the offer must stipulate the cheque is not cashable until a firm and binding agreement is reached.

- **Whatever the listing agent says, throw in all the conditions you want.** This will create an offer that's completely tailored to your needs and wants while providing elements you can remove in order to gain things you really desire. In a normal market a rational buyer always protects him- or herself with clauses allowing home inspection and time to arrange financing.

- **In fact, insist on a home inspection.** This condition should give you five business days to complete the process, and is normally done at the purchaser's expense. Almost all properties need some kind of work done in order to make them perfect, and when you get the inspector's report you have important leverage to help drive down the price in final negotiations. Get an estimate of the cost of the repairs and demand the deal to be rewritten with the price reduced by that amount.

- **The closing date is also an important poker chip to play.** Have your agent find out what the vendor wants, and then use that to help leverage the price down. Additionally, you can throw any assets you see around the property into your offer—power tools, appliances, lawn tractor, Harley-Davidson, whatever. The more you put in, the more clutter there is for the vendor to wade through, and the better chance you have of securing the best deal.

- **Consider making two offers at the same time on two competing properties,** and then let that fact be known (through your agent) to the vendor. That will add even more pressure to the homeowner, as he tries to figure out what he must do to save the deal, and give you what you want. This is payback for all those multiple-offer situations greedy vendors placed buyers in during the bubble years.

- **You can always make a low-ball offer, get a sign-back, and then just let the thing die.** Wait a week and go back in with another one, for the same low price. Odds are you will not get the same response this time. The stressed-out vendor may hate you, but he'll close.

Don't buy a house you can't sell later

Finally, always buy what you'll be able to sell, hopefully to a greater fool. This solves one of the greatest drawbacks of residential real estate—a lack of liquidity. In anything other than a bull housing market, properties can take months or years to unload, with the priciest of listings traditionally requiring the longest time. In a depressed economy this translates into one price reduction after another, the risk of the listing going stale and a sense that you're truly trapped inside a diminishing asset.

If I'm right, that's the kind of real estate market that will exist in almost all Canadian cities for most of the next few years. As mortgage rates rise, the economy sputters along amid higher taxes and persistent unemployment, and the housing buzz fades away, it will once again be buyers in the driver's seat, which means falling valuations and no more auction-type environments. Expect to see more distressed sales, especially in the suburbs surrounding major cities like Toronto, with the inevitable effect on adjacent property values.

Also ahead of us are the implications of peak oil, demographics and climate change. All will come to influence real estate deeply.

Higher energy costs will be one of the major stories of the next ten years—great news for investors with shares in integrated oil companies, exploration firms or energy mutual funds and sector ETFs—and this will change consumer tastes in housing. Energy efficiency will be a prerequisite for getting the best resale price. The impact of higher energy costs on real estate preferences will be similar to that of an aging population, as smaller homes replace two decades of wasteful mini-mansions. It's not hard to see a great future for tight, affordable, manageable bungalows and townhouses in good urban neighbourhoods with access to public transit. That may end up being real estate's holy grail. At the other end of the desirability scale will be sprawling suburban houses in distant former farmer's fields, with natural gas-guzzling pool heaters, unwanted hot tubs, too many bedrooms and the need to burn a litre of gasoline in the minivan to pick up a litre of milk. Also relatively unloved will be cottages, chalets and other secondary properties people have traditionally financed with equity taken from urban homes.

If you're serious about staying on the money road, remember where it ends. Financial security, peace and independence are the goals. A house may be part of that. But only part. Too many have lost their way thinking the path ended at their front door.

Six

TOLL ROAD

Why tax avoidance is legal

There's a tax storm coming

Four well-dressed men walked into my Bay Street office one day with a rich offer. They'd pay me big bucks to visit eight Canadian cities and give public seminars on tax planning. What's the deal, I asked?

"We're promoting literacy," one of them quickly said. "And it's a great opportunity for people to slash their tax bill." As it turned out, the promoters had bought skids of surplus, unread comic books they planned on shipping to developing countries as 'reading materials.' They were selling the scheme as a tax shelter for investors who could then write off their charitable contribution against taxable income. I threw them out.

They later found another guy to do the speaking. Thousands of people signed up, and in a few years Canada Revenue Agency disallowed all the deductions, sending out large tax bills. That should have surprised nobody. But I think it shocked everybody. Except the promoters. They split.

Tax evasion is illegal. Tax avoidance is not. Trying to hide money seldom works. Moving it offshore is a recipe for being hunted down. Buying something only to get a tax break is dangerous—and absolutely not worth it. Treat everyone with a tax-saving scam the way I did the comic book guys.

Having said that and given what the next five years will bring, avoiding taxes is now essential. In the next few pages you'll find a number of strategies that are quick, effective and totally legal. I strongly urge you to join me and others, and let those Canadians not paying attention hand over more than their fair share. After all, we know what's coming.

Canada is in a debt and deficit crisis following the global financial meltdown. In every year between 2010 and 2015 Ottawa will spend tens of billions more than it gathers in taxes (see Figure 6-1). The federal debt has again surpassed a half-trillion dollars and the feds set a record with that 2009–10 deficit of $56 billion. Meanwhile the independent Parliamentary Budget Officer estimates that by the middle of this decade we will still be bleeding red—and that is without any more crises popping up.

Fig 6-1 *Ottawa's fast-flowing river of red ink*

	2008-09	2009-10	2010-11	2011-12	2012-13	2013-14
			($ billions)			
Budgetary balance	-5.8	-54.2	-43.1	-27.9	-23.2	-19.0
Federal debt	463.7	517.9	561.0	588.9	612.2	631.2

Source: Parliamentary Budget Officer, Ottawa

But, let's face it, the odds of things not working out exactly as planned are huge. The US is in rough shape with its housing market unlikely to even hit bottom before 2012. At the beginning of 2010 there were more than 500 American banks on the watch list, on top of the almost 130 that failed in 2009. There's every reason to believe the greenback will continue to lose value, and equal reason to think interest rates will be rising, further slowing growth. Countries from Japan to Dubai to Britain have amassed unrepayable debts and the economic recovery every politician dreams of has proven elusive and expensive.

For example, look at Figure 6-2 to see how indebted the Americans were to the rest of the world by the beginning of 2010. Now tell me they don't also have a tax storm coming.

Fig 6-2 *America's massive foreign-debt hangover*

Federal Debt Held by Foreign & International Investors

www.businessinsider.com/clusterstock

In Canada, as Figure 6-1 shows, the feds will spend at least $170 billion more than will be raised in taxes between just 2010 and 2015—unless, of course, taxes increase. This is a national disaster on its own, but as interest rates increase so will charges on the accumulated debt, making things worse. Corporate taxes collapsed following the global financial crisis as profits vanished and at the same time a spike in unemployment meant a crash in income taxes paid while jobless benefits spiked. It's what economists call a vicious circle.

Yet this is only part of the story. Every major Canadian province is in deficit. Cities are in budget crisis. User fees are exploding, along with new pressure on property taxes and sales taxes. The 2010 introduction of the HST in British Columbia and Ontario was a taste of what's to come, while Toronto charges its citizens a new tax to buy a house, own a car or put out an extra bag of garbage.

The last time Canada faced a federal financing problem this big, we got the GST. But this time the problem's far more acute (and the GST is still in place). The national tax shortfall is greater. Every level of government is in hock. Our major trading partner is on its knees. Trillions have been spent trying to bail out corporations and banks. Emergency interest rates are as low as they can get. And still we're staring at years of red ink, reduced services, mounting debts and—without a doubt—yes, higher taxes.

How the Boomer bust will make this worse

By the way, I didn't even mention something the independent budget office in Ottawa is rightfully obsessed with—the impact of the Boomers, that I outlined in Chapter One. Almost 70% of this crowd have no corporate pensions. Half have no RRSPs, and as many have no retirement savings whatsoever. While the majority own real estate, they seem destined to start unloading it about the same time, when the market is exhausted and prone to be pushed down by a surfeit of new listings. Not only will this not solve their retirement income problems, it will depress the market for everyone else, costing a lot of equity. Most importantly for government, by 2015 we will have 9,000,000 newly-minted public pensioners also reaching the age when they become major health care users.

This, then, is the cause of a structural deficit in Canada, estimated to be $15 billion a year by 2015, which you can add to the deficit left as the hangover of our tough economic times. While the economy will eventually adjust, none of the Boomers will get younger or dial the clock back and start saving for retirement. There is no escaping the demographic wave hitting us— when real estate is an endangered commodity and the world floats on debt (see Figure 6-3).

Fig 6-3 *Our newly-indebted world*

2010 debt as % of GDP

Canada	**80%**
Britain	82
Germany	84
France	85
India	86
US	94
Italy	120
Japan	227
China	22

Source: International Monetary Fund

Are you depressed yet? Hopefully not, because there are a host of things you can do to escape the inevitable tax storm that's coming. While higher taxes are hardly a solution to the problems countries face, debt can't be amassed forever without leading to unimaginables such as hyper-inflation and the destruction of currencies. The strategy at this stage on the money road, when the dangers ahead are so clearly visible, is to invest with balance and purpose, avoid assets destined to take a hit and be absolutely aggressive about minimizing the tax you have to pay.

Lucky for us, it's not hard.

Tax avoidance

As I said, tax avoidance is legal. (Tax evasion is not.) What does that mean?

- You can (and must) chase after every legitimate deduction.
- You can ensure that loans—or even your mortgage—have tax-deductible interest payments.
- You can shelter investments in RRSPs, tax-free savings accounts, RRIFs or registered education savings plans (as well as inside segregated funds and universal life policies).
- You can use assets you already own to make contributions to those shelters, and get government rebates for doing so.
- You can use leverage to remove money, tax free, from an RRSP or a RRIF.
- You can cut your current income taxes by deferring taxation or splitting income with your spouse or kids.
- You can change how you make money to reduce the tax you pay.

What is not tax avoidance is, for example, opening an offshore bank account, moving income elsewhere and thinking you have nothing to pay. That's evasion, and the odds of you being found out by the CRA (Canada Revenue Agency, formerly Revenue Canada) are shockingly high. Canadian residents are required to pay tax on their world income, no matter if the money you own lives in a foreign bank account and pays you in another currency.

So, forget that. Not worth the effort. Besides, if you live in this country, drive on its roads and use its health care system, you should pay tax. How is that not your responsibility? However, you also have the legal right to pay the minimum amount of tax—and that's why tax avoidance is legal and these days completely necessary.

Change the way you earn your income

First, change how you make money. When it comes to investments, all returns are not created equal. Some are sitting ducks for over-taxation while others offer a huge incentive. There are three forms of income—interest or salary income, capital gains and dividends from Canadian companies—and three different tax treatments.

The worst way to earn money is in the form of *interest or salary income*. This includes:

- bank accounts—savings, daily interest chequing, high-yield, etc.;
- Guaranteed Investment Certificates (GIC);
- T-bills;
- savings bonds;
- interest payments from marketable bonds; and
- strip bonds.

It doesn't matter if the interest you earn is not actually paid to you, as with savings bonds that accrue interest or T-bills bought at a discount to face value. Regardless, Ottawa considers this regular income and you'll be dinged annually for money you didn't get.

That's bad enough, but the worst news is that this form of investment income, like the salary or wages you get on the job, is fully taxed—100% of it is added to your taxable income, which is then subject to your marginal tax rate.

> *Example:* $5,000 in interest income earned on savings accounts and CSBs for someone in the 22% federal tax bracket (income to $75,000—and remember that provincial taxes are added to this) would attract $1,100 in federal tax.
>
> $5,000 (interest income) x 22% (tax rate) = $1,100 tax

A much better way to earn investment income is in the form of *capital gains*. A gain of this nature is realized when you buy something, then sell it for a profit. It could be a stock or an apartment building, a mutual fund, rental condominium or a marketable bond.

Capital gains taxes were first brought in 40 years ago, cranked up to a bizarre level, and then scaled back when it was realized investment dollars were simply migrating to other places (like the US) where tax treatment was more humane. So today this is a vastly better way to earn income because one-half of your capital gain is completely tax exempt. The other half is added to your taxable income and whacked at your marginal rate. That means the maximum amount of tax a capital gain can attract is approximately 25%, which is half the top marginal rate.

Example: $5,000 earned by buying 1,000 units of an equity mutual fund at $50 and selling them at $55 by a person in the 22% bracket would mean a tax bill of just $550 (since only half the gain is taxable). Obviously you are better off by 50% to have earned that amount of income as capital gains rather than interest—a lesson GIC savers seldom take into account.

$$\frac{\$5{,}000}{\text{(capital gain)}} \quad \text{x} \quad \frac{50\%}{\text{(exempted)}} \quad = \quad \frac{\$2{,}500}{\text{taxable income}}$$

$$\$2{,}500 \text{ x } 22\% \text{ (tax rate)} = \$550 \text{ tax}$$

For most taxpayers, though, there's an even better way to get that income—in the form of *dividends from Canadian companies.* This is usually achieved by buying preferred shares of companies with a solid record of paying dividends, such as banks and utilities. Not only will you save a bunch of money on taxes, but the yields paid by these kinds of corporations are vastly higher than GIC or savings account rates.

Tax law gives dividends a break since they flow from the profits of companies that have already been taxed, so this is a way of avoiding double taxation. Since nothing is ever simple, the law requires you to 'gross up' the amount of dividend income you receive, and then apply a generous tax credit to reach the final amount. But it's worth the effort.

The gross-up multiple is 45%, and then the tax credit is 19%, so the simple way of doing the math is to (a) multiply the dividend income by 1.45 then (b) deduct 19 from your marginal tax rate and multiply the 'grossed up' dividend amount by that to get the tax.

Example: $5,000 earned in dividends, multiplied by 1.45 equals $7,250. For the taxpayer in the 22% bracket, subtract 19 from 22 to get 3%. Multiply $7,250 by .03 for the final tax of $217.50.

$5,000   x 1.45 = $7,250
(dividend income)   ('grossed-up' income)

$7,250 x (22% - 19%) 3% = $217.50 tax

So, the same $5,000 earned as investment income in three forms yields three very different results (see Figure 6-4).

Fig 6-4 *Tax payable on $5,000 earned, in 22% fed tax bracket*

Interest income	Capital gains	Dividend income
$1,100	$550	$217.50

The numbers in Figure 6-4 speak for themselves, don't they? Outside of a shelter like an RRSP or a TFSA (tax-free savings account), the tax implications of every investment must be weighed equally with the return you expect to earn. For example, a GIC earning 3% when inflation is 1.5% and a taxpayer in the 40% tax bracket (federal and provincial) is actually yielding a real return (the nominal after-tax return less inflation) of just three-tenths of one per cent. So, in an era of historically low interest rates and increasing levels of personal taxation, it's hard to understand why anyone would want to have significant amounts of money in 'safe' investments such as this. The small additional risk of a dividend-paying bank or utility stock—with twice the yield and 80% less tax is one that any rational investor would take.

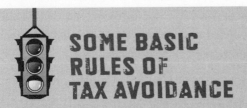

SOME BASIC RULES OF TAX AVOIDANCE

As you can see, earning interest income puts an investor at an immediate tax disadvantage, unless those investments are, as I have stressed, in a shelter such an RRSP or a TSFA. So the primary rule of taxation is:

- The first assets to go into a tax shelter are those that earn interest, such as bonds and GICs.

   Here are a few more rules to remember when deciding on asset allocation and the critical after-tax return on your money.

- In three of the four tax brackets we all fall into (incomes up to $123,000), the least amount of tax you will pay is on Canadian dividends.

- In the top tax bracket (incomes in excess of $123,000), investments paying you dividends or capital gains are equally attractive.

- It is possible to earn up to $35,000 a year in dividend income from Canadian corporations, and legitimately pay not a cent in income tax. That is true because the 19% dividend tax credit is higher than the 15% tax bracket itself, which covers income earned up to about $37,000.

- However, if you have a plan that automatically reinvests stock dividends in more stock, then the value of that will be included in your annual taxable income. Later you can deduct this when you calculate your capital gain upon selling.

- For tax purposes, whatever the investment, don't forget to deduct your legitimate costs, which include

  - interest charges on money borrowed to invest (more on this later);
  - fees paid to an advisor or counsellor;
  - charges for a safety deposit box;
  - costs of storing your investments, such as safekeeping for gold; and
  - accountants' fees.

- Finally, reducing your tax bill is the most effective way of increasing your income—a lesson that millions of GIC, CSB and online 'high-yield' savings account investors have yet to learn.

By low, sell high and pay less

If you follow the rules of asset allocation in Chapter Four, then a large amount of your income will be in the form of capital gains. That's how stocks, mutual funds, seg funds and non-residential real estate pay you. The object is to buy low and sell high. The difference is a capital gain and only half of that amount attracts tax. That's why this is such a better deal than chasing after interest income in a low-rate world.

And here's another: when calculating a capital gain, commissions are a write-off. So, commissions paid to buy a stock or a mutual fund are added to the cost of the stock, and that means they increase the 'adjusted cost base.' This simply equals less tax. The same principle applies to commission paid when a stock or fund is sold.

Example: Buy 100 BMO shares at $30 and sell them at $40. The commission on the buy side is $200 and the sell side is $220.

Cost of the stock, 100 @ 30 =	$3,000
Plus commission	200
Adjusted cost base (ACB)	$3,200
Sell the stock, 100 @ 40 =	$4,000
Less commission	(220)
Net sale proceeds	$3,780
Capital gain	580
(Sale proceeds less the ACB)	
Taxable capital gains (50%)	290
Tax payable in 29% bracket	$84.10

Tip: Add commissions together (on the purchase and sale of securities) and the total is the amount by which the overall capital gain will be reduced.

With capital gains taxes, also be aware if you lose money on a stock or a mutual fund, that loss can be deducted from a gain, to reduce taxable income. The 'capital loss' (as it's called) can be carried back to rejig tax bills three years into the past, or carried forward to reduce future taxes indefinitely. Capital losses can only be deducted from capital gains, unless you own a stock which has become worthless (Nortel again springs to mind), in which case CRA has a form for you to fill out.

Two other points to bear in mind when it comes to losses:

- If you want to dump a dog stock that has no prospects of reversing its losing way, then doing so near the end of the year will let you claim that loss against capital gains income in the same year. Just ensure you sell it in time for the transaction to clear by December 31st. That requires a sale at least three business days earlier.

- And if you dump a stock, but buy it back within a month, the CRA will disallow the loss, calling it 'superficial.' This is to prevent sales solely in order to claim a capital loss. Be warned this rule also applies to securities owned by your spouse or any company you might control.

The best amount of tax to avoid paying is all of it. While that's not possible on income from salary or wages, for many people it is achievable by using a tax shelter. The best ones are the RRSP—registered retirement savings account—and the TFSA—tax-free savings account. Both could be named better, since retirement or saving may be secondary to the primary goal of amassing enough wealth to be financially secure and independent.

RRSPs are badly understood, which is a surprise since we've had them for so long. The deal is a great one: you can stuff up to 18% of your annual earned income (or a maximum of $21,000 a year) into a vehicle in which no tax will ever be levied on the money your money earns. Not only that, but you can deduct the contribution you make from your regular taxable income. This is an unbelievably good deal, especially when you consider the points below.

- You can carry forward any unused contributions forever.

- You can borrow money at the prime rate to make up those missed payments, deduct all this from your taxable income, then get a cheque back from the government for up to half the loan amount. Use that to pay the loan down—and the feds just paid for 50% of your debt while you get to keep 100% of the asset inside your RRSP.

- You can transfer assets you already own (a GIC, mutual fund, seg fund, stock, etc.) into your plan—called a 'contribution in kind'—and for doing so, Ottawa will send you a cheque for up to half the value of them. That means you will be paid money for selling yourself assets you already owned.

This is partially why an RRSP is a dream vehicle—especially when you can get money out of it whenever you want without paying tax (more on that shortly). In concert with a TFSA, this allows a couple with a decent income to shelter more than $50,000 per year, the bulk of which can be written off from taxable income, resulting in a further tax saving of up to $20,000. The combination is stunning. Hook that up with a non-registered (outside of a tax shelter) portfolio giving you tax-preferred dividend and capital gains income, and you can see why affluent people with professional advisors stay that way.

But there's lots more.

Put your mortgage inside your RRSP

I was walking through the lobby of the Empress Hotel, in Victoria, one rainy afternoon (is there any other kind in BC?) when a well-dressed, middle-aged couple approached. The guy took my hand and pumped it. "We just want to thank you," he said. "Ten years ago we read your strategy for an RRSP mortgage, and it's made our lives incredibly better—even if the bank hates us." And off they went, heading to a restaurant where a cup of tea costs five bucks.

And he was right. I first publicized the RRSP mortgage years ago as an example of how incredibly flexible this tax shelter can be. I mean, imagine the power of putting your home loan inside your own retirement plan, making mortgage payments to yourself instead of the bank and accruing wealth in a virtually risk-free way? It's not for everyone, since it takes a bit of work and money—and in a low-rate environment like the one we've lived through, it's not as sexy as riding equity markets or precious metals, but it works.

How does this happen? Simple. Here's what you need:

- a self-directed RRSP (the kind you can put virtually any asset inside, with which you make the decisions, and which costs a few bucks a year to maintain);
- cash or cashable investments within your RRSP equal to your mortgage, or a good chunk of it; and
- the willingness to set this up through a financial advisor, a third-party financial institution (like a trust company) and a few thousand in fees to get it ignited.

Your RRSP is allowed to hold a mortgage on any Canadian real estate—residential or commercial—owned by you or by an immediate relative, such as a parent or daughter. This means existing cash can be withdrawn from an RRSP and then loaned out as a home loan, with the conditions that:

- regular mortgage payments must be made back into your RRSP and
- those payments must be at 'market' interest rates.

As you might imagine, a mortgage is an ideal investment for an RRSP to hold, simply because of the awesome way a home loan throws off money. In the early years, almost all of the monthly payments are interest due to the amortization of the loan, which means over the course of a typical 25-year payback period, roughly three times the original borrowed amount is taken from the mortgagee. When you are both the lender and the borrower, that's a good deal.

And while all this cash is being paid into the RRSP, the money can be used within the tax-free environment of your savings plan to invest in growth securities, such as well managed equity mutual funds, stocks themselves or a host of other great stuff. In addition, once an RRSP mortgage is set up, you are obligated to make payments into your plan to service it—which does not affect your ability to make new annual contributions. In reality then, you have just found a way to seriously fast-track the journey to retirement independence, and to exceed legislated contribution limits.

Also be aware that unlike a traditional mortgage paid in after-tax dollars to a lender, this is one you're paying to yourself. So, instead of a low rate and a short payback period, you want the opposite.

- Set up the loan with a long amortization—35 years or the longest term currently available—which means far more interest will be paid into your RRSP than with a conventional 25-year payback period.
- Since the RRSP mortgage rates must be comparable to market rates, shop around for the highest commercial rate and match it.
- If interest rates look like they'll be steadily rising, then you might be wise to consider giving yourself a variable rate loan that can be jacked up every time the prime pops.
- Make the loan an open one, repayable at any time. While you have no intention of doing so, this gives you the highest possible interest rate, plus a convenient way to wrap things up if you sell your property.

- You can also make this a second mortgage on your property, which will allow you to establish a substantially higher interest rate. It will require more mortgage insurance, by the way, since all RRSP mortgages must be insured through CMHC (which forms the bulk of the set-up costs I referred to above).
- And construct your RRSP mortgage in a traditional way without any fast-pay techniques you'd normally use as a homeowner, like weekly payments, prepayments or shortened amortization. The idea is to shovel as much money as possible into your RRSP, so stick with a monthly payment.

An RRSP mortgage acts like a conventional one, so you can choose any term you'd like, or even have an interest-only payment. If you default, your RRSP gains ownership of your home—which will be a mess to sort out. While an RRSP can own a mortgage, it can't own a house, meaning a forced sale would occur. However, if you do default, the mortgage insurance is there to reimburse your RRSP for the amount of the loan. And there are costs involved:

- the mortgage insurance fee (add this to the mortgage principal, because it is to your advantage);
- an appraisal, legals and set-up charges for the financial institution administering the loan (this is required, since you cannot run your own mortgage); and
- your annual self-directed RRSP fee.

The most common complaint I hear from people is the trouble they have in finding help to set up an RRSP mortgage, since they typically start by talking to their bank about the plan. Understandably, banks are in the business of making mortgage loans, not having you pay one off with your RRSP. So, the best first stop is a financial advisor who can get this all done for a modest cost and the least amount of hassle. (If you'd like help finding an advisor, email me at *garth@garth.ca*.)

Feeling aggressive?

Then combine the RRSP mortgage with a home equity loan to (1) find more investment cash, (2) get a tax-deductible borrowing, (3) exceed RRSP limits and (4) create a way of streaming income into your retirement plan. This plan might be of interest to somebody with a paid-off house, and a whack of cash or cashable investments already in their RRSP. It's also for investors who are aggressive, impatient to build wealth and understand that in a low-rate environment such as the one we've had for years, money borrowed cheap to invest for a higher return is smart money. In high finance, it's called a positive carry trade—and this is what hedge funds do to earn billions.

So if you have a good monthly cash flow from your employment income, you might consider this strategy.

- Take an equity loan against your paid-off principal residence. For argument's sake, a loan of $100,000 on a $400,000 residence is a conservative equity take-out of 25%. This HELOC can be had anywhere around the prime rate, which has hovered at generationally low levels for a long time.

- Invest the proceeds in your non-registered portfolio, which after reading this book, will include a small amount of cash, a modest fixed-income portfolio and a sizeable chunk of growth assets well correlated and timed to the business cycle, yielding capital gains and dividend income.

- Now you have a tax-deductible loan, because the proceeds were used to buy securities. If you set up payments as interest only, it means 100% of this cost is deductible from your taxable income.

- Finally, you can take $100,000 in cash from your RRSP, set up an RRSP mortgage and use this to retire the home equity loan at your convenience. Again, the main cost of doing this is purchasing mortgage insurance, which might cost up to $3,000. Is that worth the expense?

Well, look at it this way. By employing this strategy you have taken $100,000 in equity from your real estate and put it to work. That money is now in your possession in the form of growth assets inside your investment portfolio. The debt that you incurred from the bank to achieve those assets is now a debt you owe to yourself—in the form of a mortgage payable to your RRSP.

In other words you have created two pools of assets—the investments in your portfolio and the mortgage inside your RRSP), each worth $100,000. The cost of that was a $100,000 mortgage on your home (payable to yourself, plus the fees), and $100,000 less in your RRSP, which will be repaid at least three times over. Hard to see how that isn't a winner—especially over the coming years when interest rates rise and the mortgage throws off even more interest.

By the way, an RRSP can hold a mortgage on your own home, as described above, or on a property owned by anyone, in an arms-length transaction. In fact, there are brokers widely available who will put your retirement savings cash to work doing so in a fairly simple and quick process. All you need do is roll funds into a self-directed account, find a borrower (that's where a broker will assist), instruct your RRSP institution to release funds to your lawyer in return for a mortgage deed and then facilitate the payments into your account.

This is a great strategy when interest rates are high, or rising. Not so great when they are low. When market mortgage rates are at 3%, for example, and equity markets are returning 7% a year, your RRSP will obviously grow faster with a balanced portfolio of stocks than GICs or an RRSP mortgage. The tradeoff for cautious and conservative investors is that an RRSP mortgage on your own property will come clear of any risk (since you are the borrower and the loan is insured), and have a predictable steady stream of contributed income.

How to split income and goose your down payment

Here are some other RRSP strategies worth pursuing.

- If you make more than your spouse does, then income-split with a spousal plan. You're allowed to contribute up to your own limit in any one year to your spouse's RRSP. You keep the tax deduction while she or he gets the money to invest. After two years the money is considered their property, so if your sweetie is in a low tax bracket, it can be removed with a minimal amount withheld and no tax consequences to you. Any money taken out within the two years is attributed back to you.

    By the way, the existence of a spousal plan does not impact on the ability of your spouse to make full RRSP contributions to his or her own plan, to the maximum allowable limit.

- Borrow to catch up on missed contributions. The interest is not tax-deductible, but you can sure take the tax refund cheque and use it to pay down the loan.

■ If you're thinking about buying a house, remember that $25,000 per person can be taken from an RRSP (that's $50,000 for a couple) for a down payment. No tax will be deducted, and you have 15 years to repay it.

■ If you have cash for a down payment but no RRSP, then open one, dump the cash in and wait for your refund cheque. After the RRSP has been in place for 90 days you can take the $50,000 out and buy your house without any withholding tax being deducted—then use the refund cheque to reduce the mortgage or buy that heart-shaped hot tub for two.

■ Make your RRSP contribution in January for the current year, not for last year—the way most people do. By getting the money in early, you gain compounding—enough to give you $50,000 more at an average of 7% over three decades. That's money for doing nothing other than changing when you contribute, not how much.

■ As mentioned above, the 'contributions in kind' rule allows you to take assets you own outside an RRSP and transfer them into your plan. To do this you will need to have a self-directed plan. Once the transfer is made, this is considered to be a 'deemed disposition' that is a taxable event—so if there is a stock or mutual fund on which you've made money, capital gains tax will be triggered at the time of transfer. But if the asset is a strip bond or a GIC, for example, there's nothing to pay. The great news is that in return for making this transfer, you will receive a tax break just as if the contribution had been in the form of cash. Therefore you can actually profit by selling yourself existing assets, and shelter any income or gains they make in future from tax.

Get a raise without getting a raise

Here's another creative use of your RRSP—increasing the amount of money in your paycheque. This not only helps cash flow, but solves that annual problem of discovering each January or February that you don't have enough extra money to make the maximum annual RRSP contribution (remember, it's 18% of income or a max of $22,000 in 2010, thereafter indexed to inflation).

- Set up a monthly contribution plan with your advisor or your bank so money is transferred automatically to your RRSP.

- Go to the CRA web site (*www.cra.gc.ca*), click on 'Forms and publications' then download Form T1213, 'Request to reduce tax deductions at source.'

  Fill it out and submit it to the 'Client Services Division' of your local tax office. Once approved, you'll be notified and so will your employer, who can then reduce the amount of tax being sucked off each paycheque to reflect the RRSP contribution. This means instead of getting a tax refund once a year, you get one every pay period.

- Your after-tax income is greater, which means you have more money to afford the monthly RRSP contributions. If effect, your own rebated tax dollars are being used to fund your retirement assets.

- Not only will this plump your after-tax cash flow, but your monthly contributions greatly increase your ability to compound gains within your RRSP. Just make sure the cash is not put into some dead-end, low-interest GIC, but rather in growth assets.

If such things are possible, why are they legal?

That may be a better question than you realize. While Canadians are way behind the curve when it comes to retirement savings, and while the Boomers represent a retirement crisis in painful slow motion, nonetheless we're in a new game now. Ottawa's looking at every possible way to cut spending and raise revenues, so obviously doing some of the things I've been writing about here represent ways you can save serious money, while the feds seriously need it.

In fact, RRSPs cost the federal government billions a year in lost revenue. If we all took full advantage of the good stuff this tax shelter has to offer, jammed our mortgages in them, split income, borrowed to fill unused contribution room and dumped assets we already own into our plans for a refund, that number would explode higher. But, it's high enough to attract major interest in the big white building in Ottawa that houses the Department of Finance.

So, we should all be aware that over the next five years of increasing red ink and a mounting debt-deficit crisis, this most generous, flexible and creative of tax shelters could take a big hit. After all, if (as is the case) wealthier Canadians are making out like bandits using it while most middle-income people are not, how politically unpopular could it be to start turning off the tap?

Having been an MP in Ottawa, I can vouch for the fact that a tax-the-rich mentality is alive and kicking, and that short-term political expediency rules the caucus rooms. If a retirement crisis materializes in 2020 in part because RRSPs were nailed in 2013 well, that's some other government's problem. It's a hell of an attitude, but it just underscores for me the urgency of getting your finances in order, of taking every legal break there is and leaving as little to chance as humanly possible.

So, what might Ottawa do in a desperate anti-deficit tax system overhaul?

- The big, fat RRSP tax deduction could be turned into a tax credit. The existing system means simply the more money you make, the more you can shove into an RRSP and the greater the tax reward for doing so.

  For example, someone in the top marginal tax bracket can get back more than 50 cents of every dollar they contribute, while the guy making $30,000 a year gets back half that amount. This is because a deduction is taken from total taxable income—and the higher the income, the higher the tax bracket, the bigger the refund. If the deduction became a credit against actual tax paid, lower-income folks would be treated about the same while higher income-earners would see their windfall tumble by close to half.

- The ability to carry forward unused contributions could be ended. After all, if most people were in their right minds today, they would borrow scads of money at rock-bottom rates, stick it into growth assets inside their RRSPs, then use the tax refund to repay a good piece of the loan. That, as I explained earlier, is what is called a positive carry trade—an almost riskless strategy for building wealth. If Ottawa closes this door now, it would be a major opportunity lost. Forever.

- Also possible, but less likely, is a reduction in annual RRSP contribution limits, a modest tax applied to all existing RRSP assets (on the theory that only 'rich' people actually look after their finances) or a change (again) to when RRSPs have to be rolled over into RRIFs (registered retirement income funds). Back in 1996 the age at which you can no longer contribute to an RRSP was dropped from 71 to 69, but then a decade later (in the 2007 budget) that was reversed.

Now, this brings us to what happens when you retire, and what a pain it can be to get money out of your retirement plan without paying a lot of tax. Fortunately, I have good news here, too.

Does life begin again at 71?

Well, not exactly. But if you like being creative about avoiding taxes, having disposable income when you no longer need to pour it into your kids or your mortgage and turning the finance minister's crank, I have good news. There are some options for keeping the RRSP-type tax shelter going long after you are supposed to cash it in.

As I've explained, all the growth or earned income that assets inside an RRSP generate do so without attracting tax. The point of this is to allow all the new wealth to compound and grow a lot faster than it would out in the cruel taxable real world. Then, when you retire and are presumably in a lower tax bracket than during the working years, you can withdraw this money and have more of it to spend. So the official benefits of an RRSP are threefold: (1) to encourage tax-free compounding of your savings, (2) to give you a tax deduction while you're working to encourage this savings and (3) to let you remove the wealth later at a reduced tax rate.

Fine. And for some people this works wonderfully. But for others, an RRSP can be a big disappointment. They are the ones who retire with enough cash flow—from a corporate pension, non-registered investments, CPP and OAS or other sources—to put them in a high tax bracket. Then they discover half the money taken out of an RRSP is sucked away in income taxes, and they're little better off than when they were working (except the RRSP money has grown faster).

Also a disadvantage is the fact that everything coming out of an RRSP is taxed as if it were regular income, not capital gains or dividends. So if you made a killing on Google stock inside your plan, then withdrew proceeds, it would be 100% subject to tax at your marginal rate, rather than 50% tax exempt.

Some of these folks make this discovery when they turn 71. That's when everyone is compelled to close down all RRSPs, and are prevented from making any more contributions (except into a spousal plan for a wife or hubs who is still a junior senior). By the way, the RRSP must end during the calendar year that you turn 71 rather than on your birthday—so you have until December 31 to do one of four things.

- Cash in your RRSPs and take a cheque. This is a very bad idea (full tax is applied).
- Set up a life annuity with an insurance company, which will pay you an income until you check out. Also a bad idea in an environment of very low interest rates, since you are locked in forever at this rate of return.
- Buy a fixed-term annuity, for example to age 90, from a financial institution like a bank (also not advisable when rates are so low).
- Convert the RRSP into a RRIF—registered retirement income fund. Best option by far.

A RRIF is a good thing in that it works just like an RRSP, can hold exactly the same assets as the retirement savings plan did, and shelters any increase from taxes. It can be self-directed, like an RRSP, and can hold everything from a mortgage to stocks to bonds. The bad news is that you're now required to take an annual income from the plan (that's why it's called an income fund), which starts modestly and increases every year as you age. This income, as I said, is taxed 100% at a person's marginal rate. So if there is other income, plus the public pension money coming in, it doesn't take too much to push a lot of people into a high bracket—and an elevated state of frustration, especially when they are forced to take income they don't actually need or want.

This is why everyone should be aware of the meltdown strategy.

How to melt away retirement income taxes

A meltdown is designed to do two cool things—shift wealth from inside a tax-sheltered RRSP or RRIF into a non-registered account where it can be accessed freely, and do that without triggering any tax. Like everything else, it does not work for all taxpayers, and you should not be doing this unless you're confident and well-versed. An advisor will happily set this up for you, and a fee-based one won't be looking for any commissions during the process.

The meltdown strategy uses borrowed money to achieve this goal, which is still incredibly cheap by historic standards. Here's how to pull it off.

- Set up an investment loan—at the bank, from your advisor's contacts or anywhere else that will provide you with an annual statement of the interest paid, like an existing bank line of credit.

- That loan will typically require monthly payments, which you can arrange to be interest only. Therefore all the money you pay is 100% deductible from taxable income so long as the loan proceeds are invested in income-generating assets (or ones with the potential to pay capital gains, such as common stock or mutual funds).

- Use the money to set up or enhance the balanced, sane investment portfolio previously outlined here—some fixed-income, some stocks and this time a whole mess of dividend-paying high-quality equities.

- Now remove cash from your RRSP or RRIF (where a minimum amount must be taken into income, anyway). Use this money to make the payments on the investment loan.

- When you file your income tax form, you'll be required to record the income from your retirement plan as part of your taxable income, with tax payable at your marginal rate. However, at the same time, 100% of the interest on the loan payments (which are probably interest-only) can be deducted from the same taxable income. The best outcome would be to have zero tax payable between the two.

This means you are steadily transferring money out of the RRSP or the RRIF, the tax on which is being nullified by the deductible interest on the investment loan. Therefore this constitutes an ongoing shift in wealth from inside the tax shelter to the non-registered portfolio with no cost to you.

It also means all those dividend-paying stocks held outside your retirement plan can churn out income in the most tax-advantaged way, whereas inside your shelter that benefit would have been lost.

In an ideal world, the RRSP or RRIF income taken would perfectly match the interest payments on the investment loan. But in a low-rate environment, this might only be possible with a large borrowing. For example, $150,000 borrowed at 3% would require only $4,500 a year to service. If you were in the 50% tax bracket, that means $4,500 would be deductible from your taxable income—enough to offset $4,500 in retirement plan withdrawals. So, if you wished to melt down $10,000 in RRSP or RRIF withdrawals, the investment loan at 3% would need to be about $330,000.

That might be more leverage than a lot of retired people can stomach. The good news, though, is if you invested $200,000 of that in dividend-producing stocks with a yield of 6% (a typical return on bank preferred shares as I write this), your annual income would be $12,000. In other words, you'd remove $10,000 a year from your RRIF or RRSP, pay no tax on that withdrawal, have $300,000 in a new non-registered portfolio earning you at least $12,000 annually and have no cash flow requirements for the loan payments.

Not a bad deal. But because it involves the use of other people's money you have to be a borrower and investor with confidence, have a well-executed and dependable portfolio and the stomach to ride out the inevitable ups and downs of modern markets.

Or, you can worry about it all and pay a lot of tax. Some choice.

The account that eats taxes

In early 2006 I found myself sitting in the House of Commons again—obsessed, as I always am, about how to make the tax system fairer and encourage people to save and prosper. I set three goals to accomplish as an MP:

1. achieve changes that would let retired couples split income between them instead of having one pay big taxes on a pension while the other earned nothing,
2. convince the gnarly finance minister to eventually allow income-splitting between all married couples, so stay-at-home parents would no longer be penalized compared to two-income families and
3. bring to Canada the idea of a tax-free savings account—a version of an RRSP that would have more flexibility and broader appeal.

Two of my three crusades actually made it into legislation.

Today retired couples can indeed split pension income received, substantially chopping the taxes payable for hundreds of thousands of them. And, we got the TFSA. Not exactly as I had proposed (which was solely as a retirement savings vehicle to complement the RRSP), but close enough. And with the advent of this, Canadians have a whole new way of keeping more of what they earn.

You should have a TFSA. Everybody should. I'm actually not convinced Ottawa has any idea how many billions of dollars these things will save Canadians in unpaid (not just deferred) taxes, or how much more costly they will be than RRSPs. That also raises a concern about how long they can last in their present form, and underscores the fact you should get as much money into TFSAs as fast as you can.

Here are the basic rules, then we'll discuss how to make them sing.

- The maximum annual contribution is $5,000 per taxpayer, or $10,000 for a couple.
- All unused contribution room can be carried forward forever, as with RRSPs.

- Unlike RRSPs, though, there's no ability to deduct the money you put into a TFSA from your general taxable income, to net a refund.
- But, also unlike an RRSP, you can take money out of a TFSA at any time without generating a tax bill.
- And any money withdrawn from a TFSA can be replaced, without affecting your ability to add another $5,000 every year.
- Most importantly, everything you stick in a TSFA (as with an RRSP) grows free of any tax. That means interest or capital gains accrue and compound with the proceeds available to withdraw or replace without being diminished.
- The best TFSA is a self-directed one, in which you can place a vast range of securities from stocks to derivatives to savings accounts.

When the new accounts came into being at the beginning of 2009 they were quickly recognized as a gold mine by sophisticated investors—the kind of people who can spot a loophole when it's swinging in front of them. Within a few months, some TFSAs were teeming with hundreds of thousands of dollars put into high-octane speculative securities. Although there was a penalty in place for over-contributing, that paled in comparison with the ability to turn thousands into millions and have it all sheltered from tax. So, as you might imagine, the rules were changed in an embarrassed panic. But there are still a lot of things we can all do to use these accounts in the noble pursuit of avoiding taxation. Check out the Traffic Signal for some creative ideas.

CREATIVE USES FOR TAX-FREE SAVINGS ACCOUNTS (THAT DON'T INVOLVE SAVING)

1. Outside of an RRSP, get as many of your assets as you can inside a TFSA. Stocks, bonds, strips, T-bills, options—everything qualifies for a self-directed account opened with an advisor or a brokerage company.

2. Make the maximum annual contribution, and if you don't have the money then you can simply transfer in assets you already own in the form of a contribution in kind. This could include GICs, equities or a futures contract. Remember to get things in first that are subject to the highest rate of tax, such as interest-bearing investments or foreign securities that pay dividend income. (Also remember a capital gain could be triggered if you transfer securities on which you've made unrealized profits.)

3. Use the TFSA to do some serious income splitting. If you give your wife $5,000 as a gift, for example, then she can open a TFSA and contribute the maximum amount, investing this money in growth securities. None of that income will be attributed back to you. And unlike a spousal RRSP, she can take money out at any time and use it for any purpose—even the day after your gift—and there will be no tax consequences.

4. In fact, you could put money in your TFSA, make a big profit on high-growth stocks, withdraw the profits tax free, give them to your son or daughter or mother, and they could then use that money to establish their own TFSA—a great way to recycle tax-free capital gains.

5. You can also take tax-free capital gains out of a TFSA and use them to make an RRSP contribution, which will in turn get a sizeable tax refund because of the deductible nature of the retirement plan payment. This tax refund can then be used to replace some of the money you took from the TFSA, which allows it to grow further without triggering any tax consequences.

   In other words, you have used a tax shelter to create an untaxed capital gain, then withdrawn that profit, tax free, in order to contribute to another tax shelter. By doing so, you receive a very large tax deduction, which reduces your taxable income, with a refund that can be reinvested in the first tax shelter. How can you afford not to do this?

6. If you're retired and worried that your investments could grow in value and throw off income putting you in a higher tax bracket, or cause some government benefits to be clawed back, then simply shelter them inside the TFSA. There they can then grow wildly in value, and you can withdraw cash whenever you want, without tax and without even having to report it as a part of your overall income.

7. The TFSA can help with tax-loss selling. For example, if you dump a stock that's lost value in order to claim a year-end capital loss against other capital gains, do it outside the TFSA. Then put the money inside your tax-free plan where it can be used to buy back the security and any future gains will be sheltered, while you circumvent the superficial loss rule.

8. In retirement, having a fat TFSA solves some of the problems you might need an RRSP melt down strategy to solve. That's because all withdrawals from a TFSA are

free of withholding tax (unlike dipping into an RRSP),
and do not add to your taxable income. So, it makes
perfect sense to draw the TFSA down before you start
cashing in that RRSP.

Use it before we lose it—open one now

No wonder it's estimated that, unless modified or restricted,
TFSAs will eclipse RRSPs within a few years—even though retirement savings plans have been with us since 1957. One forecaster
says Canadians could have an astonishing $160 billion in tax-
free savings accounts within a decade, while total RRSPs are
worth less than $40 billion. And why not? With this new shelter
now available, why on earth would you have a mutual fund or
a few stocks or even a boring GIC out in the open where it can
be taxed?

Just one reason: Not paying attention.

In fact, the TFSA is emerging as such a powerful weapon in
the battle to keep your money it's hard to imagine Ottawa will
maintain its current flexibility. Without tagging it for just retirement savings purposes (as I had originally suggested), the tax-free
savings account is now a wide-open, tax-free *investment* account.
With each passing year—and the ability to carry-forward unused
contributions from January 1, 2009, it becomes a place every investor can dump securities, reap a profit, then take that money into
income without consequence. For example, a taxpayer who is 18
years old in 2009 has the ability to carry-forward $5,000 a year
in potential TFSA contributions endlessly. By age 39 he has
$100,000 worth of 'room' accumulated and can dump his whole
non-registered investment portfolio into a TFSA, where it will

grow completely tax free for the next 25 years. That will provide a retirement nest egg that can then be removed and taken into income without the withholding tax an RRSP attracts.

So, one action is obvious: every Canadian over the age of 18 should immediately open a TFSA and make at least the minimum deposit (that varies from $500 to $1,000 depending on where you get it). In case rules are modified again, that'll establish the starting point for your carry-forward of contributions, which means even after years of inactivity you can still show up with a bag full of money (or contributions in kind) and give it a nice tax-free home.

Final note: as I have tried to emphasize, don't waste a beautiful thing like a TFSA on saving money. That includes assets like high-yield savings accounts or Canada Savings Bonds, which have been paying an absurdly low rate of interest. In the tax-free environment of a TFSA you want to get as much growth as possible because there's unlimited potential for gain and absolutely no consequences when you take income out.

This was my bright idea when I gave it to the finance minister years ago. Don't let me down.

How to profit from your children

Okay, so not exactly. But this is the third key leg on the tax-free stool the government has given you. It's called the RESP, or registered education savings plan. This was set up about the time the cost of university went through the roof and governments decided that students and their families, as opposed to all taxpaying families, should shoulder the brunt of the costs.

If you have kids, you know the time bomb that awaits when they graduate from high school. Back in the Palaeolithic period when I went to university, tuition for everyone was a flat $550 a year, plus books and board and booze. These days tuition runs about $5,000 a year, with a four-year arts degree easily costing $50,000 by the time accommodation is factored in. The situation has become so bad that in 2009, student debt surpassed $13 billion in Canada.

An RESP works similarly to the tax-free savings account in that money can be contributed into a plan where it grows tax free, and yet there is no deduction from your taxable income for the payments you make into the plan. But there is one important addition: the feds will kick money in every year to plump up the RESP total. Another key benefit is this allows for income-splitting within a family.

Here are the basic points.

- There's no limit to the amount you can contribute in a year.
- The lifetime total, however, is $50,000 per child.
- Contributions can be made for 21 years, and the plan must be collapsed within 25 years.
- An RESP can be self-directed, like an RRSP or TSFA, or you can sign on to a 'pooled' plan run by any number of companies. (I'd take the self-directed one every time.)
- You can set up an RESP for one child, or several, naming them as beneficiaries. If one kid drops out and becomes a hip-hop star, then the money can be used for those who fail and become lawyers.
- The feds give you up to 20% of the first $2,500 contributed each year, per child, which is not deducted from your contribution limit. This is worth between $500 and $600 depending on family income (the full benefit is for families making under $38,000). The maximum total grant possible over the life of a plan is $7,200.

If you have children, then you need an RESP. One decent idea is to open an RRSP, make the maximum annual contribution, then use the refund to feed your RESP. The reason is simple: if the government is willing to give you $7,200, then you should take it. That is the equivalent of $15,000 in pre-tax earnings for a lot of middle-class families. Plus if you are smart enough to put the government money into long-term growth assets, it can double, triple or quadruple by the time the plan is collapsed. Check out the Traffic Signal to make RESPs the most profitable.

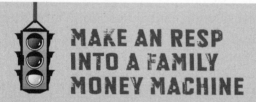

MAKE AN RESP INTO A FAMILY MONEY MACHINE

Here are a few key strategies on making the most of the registered education savings plan.

■ This is a great way to get income in the hands of your children, without it being attributed to you. When your kid gets to college, he or she can start to withdraw the money and only that portion which was not original investment capital (the money you put in) is taxable to them. Presumably they pay little or nothing in tax, so this turns out to be a guaranteed way to income split.

■ If things don't work out, and all of your kids end up becoming uneducated multi-millionaire recording artists with chateaus in Europe, you can roll a bunch of the money accumulated into your own RRSP.

■ In that case, the original capital you contributed is returned to you—tax free. The grant money (maximum of $7,200) gets repaid to the government. And up to $50,000 of the earnings within the plan can slide into your own RRSP, provided you have the unused contribution room

and that the RESP is at least ten years old. If you don't
have the room, or are older than 71, then the earnings
are taxable, plus a 20% penalty.

■ Now, where to put the RESP money inside the plan? Since
this cash is going to be working for 15 or 20 years, there
is no doubt it needs to go into growth assets—and not
interest-bearing GICs or bonds paying next to nothing.

■ A good long-term choice would be index funds or ETFs
(exchange-trade funds) that will mirror the TSX or the S&P,
along with key sectors like energy or precious metals
destined to do well in a world of peak oil and peak debt.

How to make your mortgage tax-deductible

I've written a lot already about real estate. Wise Canadians will
be working hard over the next few years to diversify, making
sure they don't have too much of their net worth in an asset that
we've allowed to become dangerously overvalued, and can turn
cold and illiquid in a bad market. Also remember how millions
of aging and house-heavy Boomers are likely to affect the real
estate market, especially in the decade following 2015. Best to
get ready now.

One way of doing this is to remove equity through a HELOC,
or home equity line of credit. These loans are available from
virtually any financial institution and, because they're secured
by your real estate, usually cheap—available at the prime rate.
Even better, if you use the proceeds to help build a non-registered
investment portfolio, all of the interest is deductible from your
taxable income. A HELOC lets you access up to 80% of your equity
or, of course, one can be used instead of a mortgage, with the

advantage of making interest-only payments or of whacking down the loan principal as quickly as you want.

Here's another option to turn a mortgage into a giant tax deduction, for people who have both a home loan outstanding and a sizeable investment portfolio.

- First, liquidate your investment assets.

- Then pay off your residential mortgage.

- There may be costs associated with this if your mortgage is not open—a three-month penalty or an interest rate differential (the difference between your mortgage rate and market rates). However, this can be reduced or eliminated with your commitment to do the following:

- Negotiate a new mortgage for the same amount, but this time take out a long-term fixed-rate home loan with a higher rate.

- Use the mortgage proceeds to repurchase the same assets for your investment portfolio.

- Now you have a totally tax-deductible mortgage.

For example, a $200,000 mortgage can be paid off with the proceeds of a $200,000 investment account. Then after you arrange a new home loan, use the money to recreate the account. You end up with the same financial situation—a house with a mortgage and a non-registered portfolio, but now all of the interest on your mortgage (which is virtually the entire monthly payment in the early years) is deductible from your taxable income.

What could this mean? Well, a $200,000 mortgage locked in for a five-year term at 6% would give you $183,852 in deductible interest over a 25-year term, or more than $1,000 a month for the first few years. That is a huge tax savings—all for making a mortgage payment that you had to make anyway. Of course, this additional amount of cash flow can be used for better purposes than plumping bank profits. It can go into buying more assets for your own portfolio or, even more dynamically, totally fund a TFSA for you and your spouse.

Isn't this a great country?

MORE TOLL-BUSTING USES FOR YOUR SPOUSE

If you ever doubt the value of marriage, just remember income-splitting. You can do it with a spousal RRSP. You can also do it simply by transferring money to a spouse who makes less than you do without triggering the attribution rules. A loan is one way (but actual interest must be paid each year—no big deal when rates are at historic lows), but simply adjusting household expenses is another.

- It's a good idea to have the spouse making the greatest amount of money pay for all the family expenses— groceries, clothes, utilities, gasoline etc.—which would leave all the after-tax income of the person making less to invest. The benefit is that all investment returns would flow into the family through the hands of the person in the lower tax bracket.

- If you do loan money to your less-taxed spouse while interest rates are still low, have him or her get it into investments with a stable yield or the potential for capital gains. For example, loaning $50,000 to your wife at 3% would cost $1,500 in interest, but if that were invested in blue-chip preferreds with a 6.25% dividend yield, the income would be $3,125 a year, of which almost $3,000 would be after-tax income in the 22% federal tax bracket. That is double the amount of interest required to service the loan, or a 100% return.

- Retired couples can split income in one of two ways. There's the ability to split regular pension income, as I mentioned at the beginning of this chapter. Fill out Form T1032 and up to 50% of your pension income can be registered in the name of your spouse. If he or she is in a lower tax bracket, then you may substantially lessen the overall tax burden.

- Plus, couples collecting CPP and OAS can also elect to split the income. This can happen from age 60 on, and even if just one of you is a pensioner.

- And don't forget the inherent pleasures of marrying somebody younger. At the top of the list, of course, is the fact you can make spousal RRSP contributions every year until your spouse turns 71, despite how ancient you may be. This can be a significant tax break for someone who's had to convert their own RRSP to a RRIF and needs the tax break to offset taxable income from the retirement fund.

So, there are a few dozen ways to avoid taxes, not evade them. All are legal and, for most people, all of them work. They make use of the generous and flexible tools you have been given—the RRSP, the TSFA and the RESP—plus the ability to earn serious income in tax-advantaged ways like dividends and capital gains. Remember that those people who will be the most heavily taxed, with the least amount of disposable income and the most dangerous futures are the ones who work hard for salaries and shun risk with interest-bearing investments. Ironically, most believe they are being steady and safe.

Given what lies down the road, they're anything but.

ROAD MAP

Here's where it gets interesting

The financial advisory company's chief executive officer looked up from his sea bass and pilaf rice with amused disbelief. The restaurant was noisy and packed. It would lead to a fleeting moment or two of embarrassment twenty minutes later when he tried to pay with an expired gift card.

My question seemed straightforward, yet even the company's vice president of compliance, sitting beside his CEO, smirked a little. Where, I asked, do you guys stand on investor education? How much emphasis do you put on assisting your clients?

We met as I was writing this book. In fact, over the course of a few months I sat in corporate corner offices, airport lounges, bars and panelled board rooms with a bunch of guys who, in one way or another, control 90% of the financial planning business in Canada. But they no longer call it that. Now it's 'wealth management' with 'integrated investment management solutions.'

Without a doubt, the business of managing money is a big one. In recent years it's become intensely regulated, with a regimen of courses, exams, training and accreditation. Advisors can have an alphabet soup of letters behind their names, as my CEO luncheon host did, and it's not uncommon for one to have a 'book' of twenty-five or fifty or a hundred million dollars in clients' assets under management. Successful wealth management types are always looking for new prospects, because the vast majority of them earn their living from commissions, usually paid by the companies whose products they recommend.

My meetings were research on the state of the industry I'd been around for decades, as a lecturer, book author, columnist, media analyst and financial commentator. As I expanded my own focus to hands-on financial planning, guiding folks through the quagmire of our times, it was important to know how industry leaders saw their business. After all, I knew what Canadians thought. Financial advisors compete with used car lot operators and insurance salesguys for the bottom of the list of professionals. The very people we need to trust the most, since we give them our life savings, are dissed mercilessly. Is it unfair?

'Eat what you kill'

Laying down his fork, the CEO made it clear in a few words.

"The people who work for us," he said, "eat what they kill."

As blunt as that was, the point was driven home within days as I sat in the lavishly opulent office of another industry executive a hundred kilometres distant. His words were an echo. "We're an entrepreneurial company," he explained when I asked about the organization and its clients. "Our clients are the advisors. And if they don't kill, they don't eat."

I drove off with my head full of images of *CSI Miami's* unit boss, Horatio, slowly removing his shades and crouching to look at the eviscerated, bloodied remains of a family that had been murdered and dismembered in their own garage, wildly covered with mutual fund certificates. And I was reminded again why so many people fail financially, when all it takes to succeed is some knowledge, some determination and a road map that's true.

Eat what you kill. What does that mean?

Unfortunately, it defines a large and growing swath of the financial business. New companies have sprung up in recent years that spend virtually nothing on educating Canadians in the things this book describes, but scads on marketing. Being 'entrepreneurial' means they hire professional financial advisors, and yet don't pay them. As a result, these people—many of them highly trained, extremely competent and worthy of a salary—are left to make their way in the world by selling products to investors from companies that pay them commissions for doing so. The potential for a conflict of interest is self-evident. Front-end loads, deferred sales charges or trailer fees, reward advisors for directing client funds into lucrative products.

As I said, a plethora of rules based on 'know your client' and professionalism are in place. And the vast majority of the people in the wealth management business truly have the best interests of their clients at heart. But in a model where advisors, even those with the fancy logos of big-name companies on their business cards, are compensated only by the money they rustle up, problems will occur.

While that doesn't mean many mutual funds, for example, aren't excellent assets that do an exceptional job in building and maintaining wealth, this business structure has been crafted for the benefit of the executives and the corporations, not the clients. The good news is that, increasingly, more fee-based planners are emerging who make their money not from commissions, but from either selling their time and expertise to form a plan—like a lawyer or accountant would do—or taking a small cut of assets under management. In that way, they benefit more when a client's wealth increases.

Two of the dangers you face

I mention this because you should know it. Signing on with an advisor who's strongly motivated by his company to sell you products is one danger. Not signing on is another.

In fact, the risks faced daily by do-it-yourself investors are staggering. Online trading accounts and grocery stores that sell mutual funds are commonplace. Web sites teeming with stock tips and condo sales offices beckoning no-money-down deals are tempting for lots of people who have desire, but little experience or not enough money to recover if a deal goes south. The number of investors who are consistently successful managing their own portfolios is a small fraction of those who try. And while there are a lot of strategies in this book you can accomplish on your own, many critical ones take financial training and experience.

In finding and selecting a person to help you, word of mouth means a lot, since personal recommendations count. If that's not an option, use Google or the phone book or a web site like <advocis.ca>. Select three or four (or more) who specialize in the areas you're interested in, then go and interview them. Ask these questions.

- What's your experience as an advisor?
- What kind of services can you provide?
- How do you work with your clients?
- How do you get paid?
- How often do you buy and sell investments?
- How will you decide what's best for me?

Also do this: (1) request personal references of clients you can call and speak with; (2) ask for an analysis of your own existing investments and plans and (3) get specific recommendations on what this advisor would do if you signed on as a client. You should be given at least 30 minutes of their time, and hopefully an hour, to complete this process. You should leave that office with a list of concrete ideas that will benefit you whether you sign up or not. And you should not feel pressured, pushed or intimidated into signing up or writing a cheque.

Go home and think about things. Take the list of ideas to the next guy and get a second opinion. Determine who seems not only to be the smartest advisor, but the one you'll feel comfortable calling on a Friday night at 10 after the market drops 450 points. In other words, you are looking for a relationship, not a salesman.

If you've found this book useful, perhaps you'll add me to the list of people you interview. My site is <*www.garth.ca*>, and my personal email is <*garth@garth.ca*>.

I promise not to eat you.

■ ■ ■

It's not too late to act now

The road ahead will surely be uneven. You can see it coming. Tens of thousands of people are heading out of university into a future in which they have to deal with peak oil, climate change or the repudiation of capitalism. Middle-aged parents wonder how anyone can get ahead in a country where just affording a house takes half or two-thirds of family income. As taxes, interest rates and inflation bubble higher, Boomers wonder how they're supposed to finance 25 years of not working. Corporate pension plans are fading, governments everywhere are cash-strapped and increasingly it seems like economic hope is on the other side of the world, in the gleaming towers of Asia.

That's why I said in the opening pages of this book, when you hear about these things on the six o'clock television news or obsessed over in a blog, it's probably too late to react.

But it's not too late now.

The days have passed when Canadians can be slipshod or dismissive of investing, tax planning and saving. By 2015 eight people in ten will have no company pension, while public pensions will be stagnant or actually available to fewer people if we follow the US model and raise the retirement age to 67. No longer can two-thirds of us afford to ignore tax shelters like RRSPs or TFSAs, or finish working with enough money saved to last just a couple of years.

The second decade of this century will bring us nose-to-nose with a retirement crisis, as millions of people run out of money, largely due to their own inaction. The resentment among GenXers and GenYers will be immense. Rightly so. Seems a whole generation of Boomers thought real estate would rise in value eternally, and there'd be enough greater fools around to bail them all out. Instead, we're setting ourselves up for an equity bath as the supply of houses overwhelms demand and property values correct.

The good news is we know these things now.

We know the problems indebted governments face and the only two ways out—cutting services and raising taxes. We know interest rates will rise, since they couldn't get any lower than the emergency levels after the crash. We know the economy will be slow as consumers struggle with higher mortgage and loan costs and stiffer taxes. We know what that'll do to real estate values. We know the population's aging and the costs that will bring.

So what will you do about it?

Make sure you don't miss the opportunities

Plenty, I hope. For there's as much to look forward to as worry about. The needs of an aging population will bring big opportunities in health care and housing. The end of the oil age spells the dawn of renewable and alternative technologies. The retreat of real estate from investment to shelter will unleash trillions into equity and bond markets. Shifting global wealth and developing markets will open up new investment options as powerful as ever existed here. And hopefully a budding awareness by millions of the need to learn and do more to control their own lives will have them avoiding taxes, diversifying, shunning the risks and building wealth.

It's up to you. None of the strategies in this book are theoretical or untested. The basics of analysis, portfolio theory, asset allocation and risk management have been proven to work over and over and over again. Aggressive tax avoidance is wholly legal and practiced every day by those who have no intention of paying more than their fair share. Investing in the economy, not some silver bullet asset, is what'll guide you on the road to security and financial peace.

Over the years I've followed this path. Being a contrarian and an independent has served me well, but also put me at odds with conventional wisdom. Not everything I've done has worked out, but on balance this approach has been the right one. Experience has shown most people make mostly the wrong choices most of the time.

If there's anything you can be sure about, this is it.

Watch closely. Act boldly.

INDEX

Garth Turner is a financial counsellor, author, lecturer, former Member of Canada's Parliament, federal cabinet minister, broadcaster and entrepreneur.

He has written 14 best-selling financial books, run Canada's tax system, educated audiences from coast to coast and continues to be the country's leading independent voice on economic, real estate and financial issues.

He writes Canada's premier daily economic blog and is a sought after analyst on the residential real estate market, fiscal, monetary and taxation policy.

To contact Garth Turner:

By email
garth@garth.ca

Web site
www.garth.ca

Blog
www.GreaterFool.ca

Phone
416-346-0086